REPORTER SERVICES AND THEIR USE

How Reporter Services Can Help You In Law School and Beyond

- **Excel in Law School**, by giving you quick access to relevant information for your courses and projects (including information that other students and professors may not have);

- **Do Well as a Summer Associate or Clerk**, by allowing you to complete assignments quickly, thoroughly, and with the latest information;

- **Learn Real-World Research Techniques**, by using legal research tools used by law firms and lawyers, who must pay for access to electronic databases;

- **Pass the Bar Exam**, by familiarizing you with fact situations and current issues frequently found on bar exams;

- **Become an Informed Lawyer**, by giving you fast, easy, well-organized, well-indexed access to significant developments and cutting-edge legal theories, strategies, and trends.

The Bureau of National Affairs, Inc., is a leading publisher of print and electronic news and information services reporting on developments in legal, business, tax, environment and safety, government, and other areas. BNA's materials also provide comprehensive, objective, and accurate information about the courts and the federal and state governments. BNA products are used by attorneys, law students, judges, legislators, business executives, government officials, and other professionals.

REPORTER SERVICES AND THEIR USE

Third Edition

How Reporter Services Can Help You
In Law School and Beyond

The Bureau of National Affairs, Inc.
Washington, DC 20037

The Bureau of National Affairs, Inc.
1231 25th Street, N.W.
Washington, D.C. 20037

Library of Congress Cataloging-in-Publication Data

Reporter services and their use: how reporter services
can help you in law school and beyond.—3rd ed.
p. cm.

1. Legal research—United States. 2. Law reports,
digests, etc.—United States. I. Bureau of National
Affairs (Washington, D.C.)
KF240.R47 1992 340'072073—dc20 92-40703
ISBN 1-55871-287-9 CIP

International Standard Book Number 1-55871-287-9
Printed in the United States of America

CONTENTS

I. Introduction . . . 1

1. What Is a Reporter Service? . . . 1
2. How Reporter Services Help Students . . . 2
3. How Reporter Services Help Lawyers . . . 4
4. Advantages of Reporter Services . . . 6
   a. Speed . . . 6
   b. Unity . . . 6
   c. Comprehensiveness . . . 7
   d. Indexing . . . 7
5. Organization and Content . . . 8
   a. Traditional . . . 9
   b. Notification . . . 9
   c. Portfolio . . . 10
   d. Decisional . . . 10
6. Indexes and Other Finding Aids . . . 11
7. Citation of Reporter Services . . . 12
8. Availability of Reporter Services . . . 13
9. Electronic Access . . . 14
10. Practical Advantages for Law Students . . . 17
11. Reporter Services by Law School Courses . . . 18

II. Particular BNA Services of Interest to Students . . . 21

1. The United States Law Week . . . 22
2. The Criminal Law Reporter . . . 26
3. The Family Law Reporter . . . 30
4. ABA/BNA Lawyers' Manual on Professional Conduct . . . 34
5. BNA Civil Trial Manual . . . 38
6. BNA Criminal Practice Manual . . . 42
7. Toxics Law Reporter . . . 46
8. Product Safety & Liability Reporter . . . 50
9. Labor Relations Reporter . . . 52
10. Media Law Reporter . . . 56
11. United States Patents Quarterly . . . 60
12. BNA's Patent, Trademark & Copyright Journal . . . 62
13. World Intellectual Property Report . . . 66
14. Employee Benefits Cases . . . 68
15. BNA Pension Reporter . . . 70

16. BNA's Americans With Disabilities Act Manual . . . 72
17. Environment Reporter . . . 74
18. Occupational Safety & Health Reporter . . . 78
19. International Trade Reporter . . . 80
20. Antitrust & Trade Regulation Report . . . 82
21. Securities Regulation & Law Report . . . 86
22. BNA's Bankruptcy Law Reporter . . . 90
23. BNA's Health Law Reporter . . . 92
24. BNA's Banking Report . . . 94
25. Federal Contracts Report . . . 96
26. Tax Management . . . 98
27. Corporate Practice Series . . . 102
28. Other BNA Services . . . 104

III. Methods of Research . . . 109
1. Example: Traditional and Decisional—Labor Relations Reporter . . . 110
2. Example: Notification—The United States Law Week . . . 115

What Is a Reporter Service?

Reporter services are valuable sources of information for law students and lawyers. These services, which are available in most law school libraries, can help you do well in law school and beyond. This book will show you how.

A reporter service is any print or electronic product that provides timely information on specific or general areas of law, business, or government. Law students and professors use such services on specialized fields of law—such as criminal law, products liability, or labor law—and in services on general topics, such as civil litigation.

"Reporter services" and "information services" are interchangeable terms used by publishers, lawyers, and researchers to describe several formats used to supply and update information on legal developments. These services also come in the form of decisional, looseleaf, newsletter, notification, portfolio, reference—and even electronic—services. Most services are published on a weekly basis, but some are published daily, biweekly, or monthly.

BNA reporter services are easy to use, quick to scan, well-organized, and well-indexed. They are designed for ready access to timely information on significant developments in particular subject areas. A BNA print service can include information that is not readily available in other sources, including electronic databases. Legal-oriented services typically report on pretrial maneuverings, case law, settlements, verdicts, and other legal developments, as well as relevant information on legislative, regulatory, administrative, industry, and public interest issues.

How Reporter Services Can Help Students

Let's imagine you are registered for a product liability course. Let's also imagine you are the only student in the course who has decided to review BNA's Product Safety & Liability Reporter – a typical reporter service – on a regular basis.

This could apply to almost any area of law. BNA has a service for almost every course you take in law school. See the list on pages 18-19.

Each week, while you're in the library, you pull the binder containing the publication's weekly "Current Reports." Sometimes, you simply scan the highlights page (which takes about 30 seconds) or read the highlights page (one minute). Other times, you read the highlights page and several stories of particular interest (10 minutes). Any way you use the reporter, you are kept up to date on significant, cutting-edge legal, legislative, regulatory, and industry developments.

One week, your professor is discussing the "duty-to-warn" doctrine. The professor doesn't know that the Texas Supreme Court has just issued a major ruling on warnings on alcohol products—but you do. The professor is duly impressed when you brief the case assigned, and then inform the class that the doctrine enunciated in the assigned case has now been called into question by a new, important ruling.

Later in the semester, you are asked to write a brief on a case involving warnings on appliances. Before you conduct your online search for case law, you consult the index and finding aids in the BNA reporter service. You quickly learn about a recent case, a new regulatory safety standard, and a new voluntary standard adopted by the appliance industry.

You read the account of the case, prepared by an attorney-journalist on the BNA staff. The account includes a detailed discussion of the briefs in the case and the pertinent case law. This one short article saves you lots of time and research, and raises four issues that you had not yet considered. Your brief is the only one to raise those issues, cite the recent case, and mention the new regulatory and industry standards. You get an "A" on the brief and the course, and the professor writes you a glowing letter of recommendation.

You use the same strategy—consulting the relevant reporter service—before your moot court competition on labor law. Once again, you know what others don't.

Several months later, you contact the law firm that handled the appliance case about a job. Before the job interview, you review the latest issues of BNA's reporter service, and find out the firm has just won a major automobile case. You ask the interviewer: "What was the key to your firm's victory in last month's automobile case?" The interviewer, impressed with you and your knowledge, offers you a job.

Before you take the job, you pass the bar, in part because one of the essay questions discussed a fact situation and legal issue that you had read about in BNA.

Sound far fetched? Not really, except that it's highly unlikely you'll be the only student who decides to consult a BNA reporter service, and your professor probably reviews the relevant service as well. Still, as in the practice of law, you're far better off being among those who use and take advantage of the myriad benefits of reporter services.

How Reporter Services Can Help Lawyers

In addition to law students, practicing attorneys derive considerable benefits and advantages by prudent use of reporter services.

Take the case of *Love v. Kwitney,* 20 USPQ2d 1037 (DC SNY 1991). The *Love* case involved copyright infringement. The plaintiff's attorney cited and quoted from a case published in BNA's *United States Patents Quarterly.* Apparently, the defense attorneys had done an online search, but had not reviewed the BNA publication. Hence, they were caught off guard and uninformed. As the court explained:

> Defendant's response is rather less helpful than it might have been, apparently because defendant confined its search . . . to (an online database) . . . , which includes only a summary order. Had defense counsel consulted the book plaintiff cites, published by the Bureau of National Affairs, rather than relying on the electronic data base compiled by that publisher's competitor, they would have found the quotation . . . and perhaps been in a position to point out that the licensor recipient . . . was not a party.

The lesson? The only way you can be sure your legal research and knowledge is complete and up-to-date: review the relevant BNA reporter services.

THE
UNITED STATES
LAW WEEK
B
N
A
SUPREME COURT
SECTIONS
THE
UNITED STATES
LAW WEEK
B
N
A
GENERAL LAW
SECTIONS
ABA
BNA
Lawyers'
Manual
On
Professional
Conduct
Manual
BNA
ABA
BNA
Lawyers'
Manual
On
Professional
Conduct
Current
Reports
BNA

ADVANTAGES OF REPORTER SERVICES

Reporter services blend together several elements often missing from other forms of legal source materials – speed, unity, comprehensiveness, and indexing.

Speed

There are several ways to publish the latest available developments in any field of the law: recompiled and revised editions of books; new editions; pocket parts; and looseleaf publication intended either for interpagination or for cumulation. The last—the method used by reporter services—is by far the fastest method of dissemination of current information. Most reporter services are issued weekly or biweekly, although some reporters, such as BNA's *Daily Tax Report* and its *Daily Labor Report,* are printed daily. Some weekly services, such as *The United States Law Week,* publish special items as soon as they are available. Every U.S. Supreme Court opinion is prepared for publication on the date it is issued and then is mailed to *Law Week* subscribers.

Unity

The second major advantage of reporter services is their unity—each service is devoted to a particular subject matter and consists of as many volumes or binders as are needed to cover the subject. Some services, such as BNA's *Labor Relations Reporter* and *Environment Reporter,* can fill a whole library shelf, or even several shelves, with a variety of binders and bound volumes containing full text of relevant laws and court decisions, reference manuals, and current notification reports. Other services—*The Family Law Reporter,* for instance—pull together their information into two binders—a reference manual and a binder housing the weekly or biweekly current notification reports. Still others manage to get everything into one current binder, such as the *Media Law Reporter's* full-text cases or *The Criminal Law Reporter's* current reports of court decisions and other news. Even services in this last category cumulate into annual or semi-annual volumes that can be saved for years to come.

Comprehensiveness

Each specialized field of law covered by a reporter service is treated comprehensively. All types of legal authority are collected and coordinated with appropriate editorial comment, analyses, and finding aids. Many reporter services pull together into one source all relevant primary sources, such as legislation, administrative regulations, executive orders, agency rulings, and judicial decisions affecting the particular legal topic. Reporter services continue their comprehensiveness beyond primary source materials into areas not touched upon by other research tools. For each specialized field, reporter services closely follow and report important new court decisions, proposed and enacted legislation, and other government regulations and actions. They include the latest news coverage of both legal and nonlegal developments. They report the activities and actions of the leading professional groups, and of significant conferences, seminars, and other meetings. Finally, analyses and reference manuals interpret primary materials, forecast trends, and note corresponding areas of interest.

Indexing

The last major advantage offered by reporter services lies in their indexing. Since such services are limited to specialized fields, their indexing is inherently more specialized and thorough, and thus more usable, than the indexes of more general compilations. Like the substantive matter covered, the indexes are kept current through regular updates and compilations. Each service usually contains at least a topical index and a table of cases, as well as more specialized finding aids.

Organization and Content

The organization and formats of reporter services vary as the subject matter of each publication dictates. Nonetheless, most reporter services fall into one of several broad categories, which are described below, and all services share certain common features.

Binders

Each service is housed in a binder, or series of binders, of either the ring or the post variety, and each binder is divided into subparts by tabs.

There are several methods of dividing a service's specialized subject matter into cohesive subparts of binders and tabs. The approach taken by many BNA services is a topical one. BNA's *Labor Relations Reporter,* as an example, is organized into six parts (some with a number of binders) that parallel basic labor law subject areas: labor-management relations, labor arbitration, wages and hours, fair employment practices, individual employment rights, and disabled workers. BNA's tax service, *Tax Management,* is also organized topically into series covering the broad areas of U.S. income; estates, gifts, and trusts; and foreign income. Within each series are individual portfolios in which experienced tax specialists address specific tax problems.

Another type of division is by type of source material. BNA's *Environment Reporter,* for instance, is organized initially into current developments, decisions, and reference file binders. The reference file binders are further divided into federal laws, federal regulations, and specific types of state laws and regulations. *The United States Law Week* also is organized by type of material: one binder houses the General Law portion of this service, which includes weekly digests of state and federal court decisions of general significance; the second binder includes all material relevant to the U.S. Supreme Court, including extensive coverage of its docket activity and full text of all Supreme Court decisions.

Tabs

The individual binders for most services are further divided by a series of tabs. Again, the scheme for this division usually corresponds to topic, statute section, or type of source material.

Despite their diversity, reporter services usually fall into one of four general categories in terms of their organization and content:

Traditional

Probably the most common type of reporter service is founded upon one or several pre-eminent statutes or regulations, and serves as an ongoing repository of information about that area of law. Services that fall into this category often begin with a full-text reproduction of the governing law. For instance, BNA's *Labor Relations Reporter* devotes part of one binder to the text of the statutes that serve as the major foundations for the federal law of labor-management relations, namely, the Taft-Hartley Act and the Landrum-Griffin Act. Other binders contain full text of court and administrative decisions in labor law, and still others contain editorial explanations of various aspects of the field.

Another example, the *ABA/BNA Lawyers' Manual on Professional Conduct,* begins with the full text of the American Bar Association's Model Rules of Professional Conduct and Model Code of Professional Responsibility, which serve as the basis for most states' legal ethics rules. Following this are a number of tabbed sections each containing an editorial analysis of a particular area of professional concern that is raised either by the ethics rules or by other law—topics such as conflicts of interest, client confidentiality, fees, and legal malpractice.

In both these looseleaf services, as in others like them, all material is constantly kept up-to-date by regular publication of interpaginations (i.e., subscribers are sent new, updated pages to replace dated ones). In addition, both services, like almost all reporter services, contain a notification element. *Labor Relations Reporter* issues a weekly report called Analysis/News and Background Information, which contains a summary of recent developments and an in-depth analysis of a recent court decision. The notification prong of the *Lawyers' Manual* is a biweekly report summarizing recent court decisions, ethics opinions, and other events affecting the way lawyers practice their profession. The most important items mentioned in these current reports soon find their way into the interpaginations for the looseleaf manuals. However, the current reports also serve a reference function, and are indexed for re search purposes just as the manuals are.

Both these services, which are being used only as examples of traditional reporter services, also contain other elements as part of their thorough coverage of their topics. The *Labor Relations* Reporter publishes court and agency decisions involving labor-management relations, wages and hours, labor arbitration, employment discrimination, and individual employment rights.

Notification

Many reporter services cover areas of the law that are not so tied up in specific sets of statutes or rules. These less traditional services, such as BNA's *The Criminal Law Reporter,* serve primarily a notification function, but as with almost all reporter services, they can be retained in storage binders for years on end and serve as a ready and cohesive source for research purposes. Moreover, they often contain other elements that complement their coverage of their chosen fields. *The Family Law Reporter,* for instance, has a Reference File that houses relevant federal statutes, uniform and model acts, summaries of state divorce laws, and a tax guide. *The United States Law Week* and *The Criminal Law Reporter* provide full-text coverage of U.S. Supreme Court decisions. Many other notification-type services report selected court decisions, legislation, and regulations in full text.

Portfolio

Two BNA services illustrate yet a third approach. *Tax Management* and the *Corporate Practice Series* utilize a portfolio format, consisting of series of individual spiral-bound pamphlets or papers, each addressing a specific area of tax or corporate law. The three *Tax Management* portfolio series—the *U.S. Income Series,* the *Estates, Gifts, and Trusts Series,* and the *Foreign Income Series*—and the one *Corporate Practice Series* are constantly expanded and regularly updated by hundreds of practicing specialists. Each of the hundreds of portfolios deals with one deliberately narrow area of the law. Every portfolio is kept up-to-date by Changes and Additions sheets, which are designed to be inserted in the front of the portfolio. Periodically, portfolios are completely revised and reissued. New portfolios are added to the series as the need arises.

Besides the portfolios, both these services have incorporated aspects of other types of reporter services. *Tax Management* has Reference Files on several diverse subjects, including Estates, Gifts, and Trusts, and Financial Planning. It also provides, in its Primary Sources binders, a continuing legislative history of the Internal Revenue Code. The service has several notification elements as well: a weekly report of new tax developments, a biweekly memorandum on specific tax issues, and monthly or bimonthly journals covering several different areas of tax law. The *Corporate Practice Series,* too, serves a notification function, through its weekly newsletter: *BNA's Corporate Counsel Weekly.*

Decisional

A final, often utilized format for reporter services—the decisional or full-text case reporter—shares many characteristics of the official state and regional case reporters with which law students are probably most familiar. They publish court decisions in full text and precede them with headnotes, written by lawyer-editors, that pinpoint the legal issues decided in the opinions. However, they differ from the official reporters in two important respects. First, each decisional reporter service covers one distinct area of the law exclusively. Second, they usually publish decisions weekly or biweekly and thus are more current than official reporters.

A good example of the decisional service is BNA's *Media Law Reporter.* Cases are issued to subscribers on a weekly basis and, with rare exceptions, are reported in full text. The weekly issues are stored in a binder where they cumulate until they are republished in a bound volume. Each reported case is preceded by one or more headnotes summarizing the legal points decided in the case. Each headnote is assigned a number or numbers showing where it fits into the service's indexing system, which is called Cumulative Digest and Index, or CDI for short.

Indexes and Other Finding Aids

Reporter services are replete with indexes, tables, and finding lists designed to provide the researcher with the greatest number of alternative entries into the services.

Every service has a master, usually topical, index that serves as the focal point for reference and research. This index can be general, covering all binders of a multi-volume service, or specific, covering one of several major subdivisions of the subject matter.

Some services use a numerical system for indexing purposes. BNA's *Labor Relations Reporter* and *Media Law Reporter* use "Classification Guide Numbers" that are assigned to each case headnote in order to key a user into their Cumulative Digest and Index (CDI) systems. The CDI is based on an Outline of Classifications that classifies the field of law by topic and subtopic and assigns classification numbers to each topic and subtopic. By reference to the classification number alone, the researcher can locate digests of all decisions related to a particular point of law. At the end of each digest is a citation that leads to the text of the decision.

Other services use a descriptive or key-word approach to indexing. For example, users of *The Criminal Law Reporter* interested in court decisions on police inventory searches of impounded automobiles would turn in the service's index to the major heading "Search and Seizure." Under that heading, they would find the entry "Automobiles and other vehicles" and under that the more specific entry "Inventory and impoundment," where they would find brief summaries of the relevant cases reported in the service with their page numbers.

Entry into a service is also possible by case name through a service's Table of Cases. Some services provide more information than just the case name and the page on which it can be located. For example, *The United States Law Week's* U.S. Supreme Court Table of Cases and its related Docket Number Table will reveal whether Supreme Court review has been sought in a recently rendered federal or state court decision. If so, the tables will give the case's current status in the Supreme Court: whether review has been granted or denied; if granted, whether oral argument has been scheduled or heard; and whether the court has actually handed down a decision.

Reporter services often contain other finding aids that are specifically relevant to the individual area of law each service covers.

Whatever indexing method is used, and regardless of the number of finding aids involved, reporter services make as much effort to keep their indexes current as they do to report current substantive information. Indexes are republished several times a year to keep them current. Services usually have a set schedule, such as monthly, bimonthly, or semiannually, for updating their indexes. At times, therefore, some of the material included in the service will not yet be indexed and other finding aids for the issues not yet covered will have to be consulted. When using an index, it is essential that the dates of its coverage be noted.

CITATION OF REPORTER SERVICES

Reporter services are the best citation for relevant case law until official reports are published.

The time lag between a reporter service's publication of a case and an official publication makes the former often the best cite. In some cases, such as memorandum decisions never officially reported, the reporter service becomes the only "official" cite. Non-decisional materials available only in reporter services may also need to be referred to by a reporter service citation.

A Uniform System of Citation, the "blue book," says to cite *The United States Law Week* for U.S. Supreme Court decisions that have not yet appeared in either the official reporter (U.S.) or the Supreme Court Reporter (S.Ct.).

The "blue book" also describes how to cite other reporter services. They should be cited by volume, name, publisher, subdivision, and date. In citing a section of a service that will eventually be bound, the name of the bound form is added in parentheses unless it is identical to name of the looseleaf form.

A Uniform System of Citation lists the most commonly used reporter services with their abbreviations.

AVAILABILITY OF REPORTER SERVICES

BNA's services are readily available in virtually every law school library.

The American Bar Association, which accredits law schools, stated in its 1987 Standards of Approval for Law Schools that a law school library should include "generally recognized texts, treatises, and looseleaf services appropriate to the program of the law school." The average law school library will contain a variety of reporter services, including many of those described throughout the rest of this book, and students are urged to consult their libraries' catalogues early in their law school careers.

BNA also offers students substantially discounted subscription rates. For more information, see page 122 at the back of this book or contact BNA Customer Relations by telephone toll-free at 1-800-372-1033, or by fax toll-free at 1-800-253-0332.

ELECTRONIC ACCESS

As legal research has moved into the world of computers, reporter services have moved right along with it. BNA offers many of its existing services in electronic formats. Some new services are designed exclusively for access on electronic media.

Many of the BNA services described in this book are available on several online networks, including WESTLAW, LEXIS, and NEXIS. A particular issue of any of these publications, often going back to 1982, can be accessed and read much like it would be in print. The primary use, however, is research and retrieval of information through key-word searches. These searches reveal every instance the searched-for words appeared throughout a series of issues of that publication. Such searches could involve topics, case names, bill numbers, statutes or regulations, or any other "search strategy."

Other *BNA Online* services are designed for and are available only online. Among these are *Law Week Daily Edition,* which is updated every day, and *BNA Tax Updates,* which is updated twice a day.

Another computer-assisted technology, CD-ROM, allows huge databases to be stored on a small compact disc and used on any personal computer equipped with a CD-ROM player. *Tax Management* is the first BNA service to be made available on CD-ROM.

The availability of reporter services through computer-assisted or electronic technologies is increasing at a rapid pace. For the latest information on what BNA services are available and on how to access or obtain them, call *BNA Online* toll-free 1-800-862-4636, except in Washington, D.C., where the number is 202-452-4132.

The chart on the next two pages shows the BNA services that currently are online on LEXIS, NEXIS, or WESTLAW.

BNA SERVICE	LEXIS	NEXIS	WESTLAW
BNA Antitrust & Trade Regulation Daily* ++	BNAATD		BNA-ATD
Antitrust & Trade Regulation Report	TRADRG	TRADRG	BNA-ATRR
BNA Banking Daily* ++	BNABD	BNABD	BNA-BBD
BNA's Banking Report	BNABNK	BNABNK	BNA-BNK
BNA Bankruptcy Law Daily* ++	BNABLD		BNA-BLD
Benefits Today	BENDAY		BNA-BENE
BNA California Environment Daily* ++	BNACED		BNA-CED
BNA Chemical Regulation Daily* ++	BNACRD		BNA-CRD
Chemical Regulation Reporter	CHEMRG		BNA-CHEM
Daily Labor Report	DLABRT	DLABRT	BNA-DLR
Daily Report for Executives+		DREXEC	BNA-DER
Daily Tax Report+	BNADTR		BNA-DTR
Environment Reporter	ENVREP		BNA-ER
BNA Federal Contracts Daily* ++	BNAFCD		BNA-FCD
Federal Contracts Report	FDCONT	FDCONT	BNA-FCR
Government Employee Relations Report	GOVEMP	GOVEMP	BNA-GERR
BNA Health Care Daily* ++	BNAHCD		BNA-HCD
BNA International Business & Finance Daily* ++	BNAIBD	BNAIBD	BNA-IBD
BNA International Environment Daily* ++	BNAIED	BNAIED	BNA-IED
BNA International Trade Daily* ++	BNAITD	BNAITD	BNA-BTD
International Trade Reporter	INTRAD	INTRAD	BNA-ITR
BNA LRR Fair Employment Practice Cases	LRRFEP		FLB-SCT FLB-CTA FLB-DCT
BNA LRR Individual Employment Rights Cases	LRRIER		"
BNA LRR Individual Employment Rights Newsletter	IERNEW		LRR-IERN
BNA Labor Arbitrators' Biographies	ARBBIO	ARBBIO	LRR-DIR
BNA LRR Labor Arbitration Reports	LRRLA		LRR-LA
BNA LRR Labor Arbitration Unpublished Decisions			*coming*

* indicates an electronic-only publication
++ available on DIALOG
+ available on BT Tymnet DIALCOM

BNA SERVICE	LEXIS	NEXIS	WESTLAW
BNA Labor Relations Reference Manual	LRRM		FLB-SCT FLB-CTA FLB-DCT
BNA LRR Analysis/News & Background Information	LRRNEW		LRR-NEWS
BNA LRR Wages & Hours Cases	LRRWH		FLB-SCT FLB-CTA FLB-DCT
BNA Management Briefing* ++	BNAMB		BNA-MB
BNA National Environment Daily* ++	BNANED		BNA-NED
BNA Occupational Safety & Health Daily* ++	BNAOHD		BNA-OSHD
Occupational Safety & Health Reporter	OSHR		
BNA Patent, Trademark & Copyright Law Daily* ++	BNAPTD		BNA-PTD
BNA's Patent, Trademark & Copyright Journal	PTCJNL		BNA-PTCJ
BNA Pensions & Benefits Daily* ++	BNAPEN	BNAPEN	BNA-PBD
BNA Pension Reporter	PENSN	PENSN	BNA-PEN
BNA Product Liability Daily* ++	BNAPLD		BNA-PLD
BNA Securities Law Daily* ++	BNASLD		BNA-SLD
Securities Regulation & Law Report	SECREG	SECREG	BNA-SRLR
BNA State Environment Daily	BNASED		BNA-SED
Tax Management Journals	TMJNL		TM-ALLJNL
Tax Management Portfolios	TMPORT		TM-ALLPORT
BNA Tax Updates* ++	BNABTU		BNA-BTU
BNA Toxics Law Daily* ++	BNA-TLD		BNA-TLD
Toxics Law Reporter	TOXICS		
United States Law Week	USLW	USLW	BNA-USLW
U.S. Law Week - Daily Edition*	USLWD	USLWD	BNA-USLWD
United States Patents Quarterly			USPQ
BNA Washington Insider* ++	BNAWI	BNAWI	BNA-BWI

* indicates an electronic-only publication
++ available on DIALOG
+ available on BT Tymnet DIALCOM

PRACTICAL ADVANTAGES FOR LAW STUDENTS

As you can see by the preceding examples, reporter services can help you save time, gain valuable knowledge and excel – in law school and beyond.

Why? Because they provide timely information on significant developments in the law, including information that is not available from any other source. Since these services include exclusive, important information, lawyers and future lawyers must read these services if they want to excel.

In summary, these services can help you:

- accomplish thorough, **up-to-date legal research**;
- develop research **skills** actually used in the practice of law (including skills that can save money, time—and help win cases);
- **learn** which lawyers, law firms, companies, and professional groups are involved in significant cases and related activities (leading to excellent job-search, networking, and research opportunities);
- **find out** about significant developments that are not available in electronic databases or other sources
- **refine** and complement **on-line searches**;
- **learn** about trends, hot legal issues, and cutting-edge strategies;
- **learn** how the law is applied in real-life situations; and
- **become familiar** with tools used by lawyers to stay abreast of developments in specialized fields.

And as a result of these benefits, reporter services can help you excel in law school; do well as a summer associate or clerk; learn real-world research techniques; pass the bar exam; and become an informed lawyer.

This book will help you realize the benefits of using BNA reporter services.

Reporter Services by Law School Course

This list identifies reporter services that will interest law students enrolled in specific law school courses. They are published by BNA or by its Pike & Fischer (P&F) subsidiary.

1. Administrative Law
   -*Administrative Law, Third Series* (P&F)
2. Admiralty
   -*Shipping Regulation Reports* (P&F)
3. Antitrust and Trade Regulation
   -*Antitrust & Trade Regulation Report*
4. Banking Law
   -*BNA's Banking Report*
5. Bankruptcy
   -*BNA's Bankruptcy Law Reporter*
6. Civil Procedure and Practice
   -*BNA Civil Trial Manual*
   -*Civil Litigation Reporter*
7. Civil Rights Law
   -*Labor Relations Reporter: Fair Employment Practices*
   -*United States Law Week*
8. Communications Law
   -*Broadcast Rules Service* (P&F)
   -*Cable TV Rules Service* (P&F)
   -*Common Carrier Rules Service* (P&F)
   -*Equipment Rules Service* (P&F)
   -*Media Law Reporter*
   -*Private Radio Rules Service* (P&F)
   -*Radio Common Carrier Rules Service* (P&F)
   -*Radio Regulation, Second Series* (P&F)
9. Constitutional Law
   -*United States Law Week*
10. Copyright Law
    -*BNA's Patent, Trademark & Copyright Journal*
    -*United States Patents Quarterly*
    -*World Intellectual Property Report*
11. Corporations
    -*BNA/ACCA Compliance Manual: Prevention of Corporate Liability*
    -*BNA's Corporate Counsel Weekly*
    -*Corporate Practice Series*
12. Criminal Law, Practice, and Procedure
    -*BNA Criminal Practice Manual*
    -*The Criminal Law Reporter*
13. Environmental Law
    -*Air & Water Pollution Control*
    -*BNA's Environmental Due Diligence Guide*
    -*Chemical Regulation Reporter*
    -*Daily Environment Report*
    -*Environment Reporter*
    -*International Environment Reporter*
    -*Toxics Law Reporter*
14. Estate Planning
    -*Tax Management: Estates, Gifts, and Trusts*
15. Evidence
    -*BNA Civil Trial Manual*
    -*BNA Criminal Practice Manual*
16. Family Law
    -*Family Law Reporter*

17. Government Contracts
   - *Federal Contracts Reports*
18. Health Law
   - *BNA's Health Law Reporter*
   - *BNA's Medicare Report*
19. International Law
   - *BNA's Eastern Europe Reporter*
   - *International Environment Reporter*
   - *International Trade Reporter*
   - *Tax Management: International Forum*
   - *Tax Management: International Journal*
   - *World Intellectual Property Report*
20. Labor and Employment Relations Law
   - *BNA's Americans With Disabilities Act Manual*
   - *BNA's Employee Relations Weekly*
   - *BNA Pension Reporter*
   - *Collective Bargaining Negotiations and Contracts*
   - *Daily Labor Report*
   - *Employee Benefits Cases*
   - *Labor Relations Reporter*
   - *Occupational Safety & Health Reporter*
21. Patent and Trademark Law
   - *BNA's Patent, Trademark & Copyright Journal*
   - *United States Patents Quarterly*
   - *World Intellectual Property Report*
22. Products Liability
   - *Product Safety & Liability Reporter*
23. Professional Responsibility
   - *ABA/BNA Lawyers' Manual on Professional Conduct*
24. Securities Regulation
   - *Securities Regulation & Law Report*
25. Tax
   - *Daily Tax Report*
   - *Tax Management*
26. Torts
   - *BNA Civil Trial Manual*
   - *Product Safety & Liability Reporter*
   - *Toxics Law Reporter*
27. Trial Advocacy
   - *BNA Civil Trial Manual*
   - *BNA Criminal Practice Manual*
28. Workers' Compensation
   - *BNA's Workers' Compensation Report*

Particular BNA Services of Interest to Students

The United States Law Week

The United States Law Week is a reporter service that cuts across the entire spectrum of the legal profession—across all subject-matter lines—and offers something for every lawyer and every law student. It is primarily a notification service, designed to be used weekly to keep abreast of significant legal developments in all fields. As with all notification services, however, *U.S. Law Week* has an important secondary value as a reference tool.

U.S. Law Week is probably best known within the legal profession for its coverage of the U.S. Supreme Court. The full text of every Supreme Court opinion is mailed to subscribers on the same day the court issues it. The holding of each case is spelled out, or headnoted, by the publication's editors. Moreover, the publication keeps track of every Appellate Docket case filed in the Supreme Court. Indeed, *A Uniform System of Citation*, the "blue book," dictates that *U.S. Law Week* (U.S.L.W) be cited for every Supreme Court opinion or action that has yet to be reported in either the *United States Reports* or West's *Supreme Court Reporter*.

This service also covers much more than the Supreme Court. The *U.S. Law Week* editors examine thousands of court decisions a year from all across the country—from state trial courts to federal circuits, and every kind of court in between—and they select the most significant to headnote and summarize for each week's issue.

A weekly issue consists of three or four separate sections. Section 1, Summary and Analysis, reviews and analyzes the eight or so most significant court decisions or other events reported in the issue's other sections. This section also contains a Topical Summary listing the entire contents of the rest of the issue.

Section 2 is the heart of the publication's non-Supreme Court coverage. Here the user finds accounts of the most significant recent decisions of state courts and of federal district courts and courts of appeals. The section is organized under broad subject-matter headings such as antitrust, attorneys, civil rights, corporations, courts and procedure, constitutional law, criminal law and procedure, environment and conservation, family law, labor, schools and colleges, securities and exchanges, taxation, and torts.

The essence of each decision—the law as applied to the facts involved—is contained in a boldface lead paragraph. The court's reasoning, which is digested from the case itself, follows. Significant federal agency rulings and regulations are given similar treatment, and the section also contains periodic reports of important professional conferences and seminars.

The United States LAW WEEK®

A NATIONAL SURVEY OF CURRENT LAW

February 28, 1989 • THE BUREAU OF NATIONAL AFFAIRS, INC., WASHINGTON, D.C. • Volume 57, No. 33

SUMMARY AND ANALYSIS

Social Services Agency Has No Duty To Protect Kids Known To Be In Peril

States and their subdivisions have no constitutional obligation to protect children known to be at risk for child abuse, a 6-3 U.S. Supreme Court held Feb. 22, rejecting a 42 USC 1983 claim alleging a violation of the Fourteenth Amendment's Due Process Clause based on a county's failure to protect a child. (*DeShaney v. Winnebago County Department of Social Services*, US SupCt, No. 87-154, 2/22/89)

Complaints of a young boy's abuse at the hands of his father were investigated by a county child protection agency, which briefly removed the child on one occasion. The child was returned, however, when the agency determined that abuse charges could not be proven. Although a social worker continued to visit the home, she took no action, despite continued reports and her own suspicions of abuse. The child was later beaten so severely that he suffered brain damage. The mother brought this Section 1983 action.

In an opinion by Chief Justice Rehnquist, the court noted that the state has no general duty to protect against harm by private persons. It declined to recognize the existence of a "special relationship," arising from the state's statutory commitment to protect the child and its awareness of the child's situation, that would impose upon the state an affirmative duty to protect. Only when a state takes an individual into custody does it acquire an affirmative obligation to look after that person's safety, Rehnquist made clear.

In the first of two sharply worded dissents, Justice Brennan, joined by Justices Marshall and Blackmun, disagreed with the majority's depiction of the state's inaction as somehow more benign than action would have been. Justice Blackmun, dissenting separately, stated that a broader reading of the court's precedents would allow the lawsuit to go forward, and would recognize that "compassion need not be exiled from the province of judging." (Page 4218)

FCC's Fade-Out Of Fairness Doctrine Upheld By D.C. Circuit

The Federal Communications Commission's decision to scrap the "fairness doctrine" as no longer in the public interest was reasonable, the U.S. Court of Appeals for the District of Columbia Circuit held Feb. 10. (*Syracuse Peace Council v. FCC*, CA DC, No. 87-1516, 2/10/89)

Under the doctrine, the FCC has required broadcast licensees to provide coverage of controversial issues of interest in the communities they serve, and to provide a reasonable opportunity for presentation of contrasting viewpoints on such issues. Here, a licensee was alleged to have breached the second prong of the doctrine by failing to offer conflicting views after it ran ads endorsing a nuclear power plant. Relying heavily on its own 1985 study, the FCC agreed with the licensee that the doctrine violates the First Amendment and disserves the public interest.

Although the FCC said the two bases for its decision were "inextricably intertwined," the D.C. Circuit, which had ordered the agency to address the constitutional issue in a prior appeal, this time invoked the canon that a court should not pass on a constitutional issue if it may otherwise dispose of a case. Observing that the FCC's 1985 report had concluded that the doctrine disserved the public interest without addressing the constitutional issue, the court held that the order here was also sustainable on policy grounds alone.

The court said the FCC made a permissible finding that the doctrine has "very substantial deterrent effects"—dissuading broadcasters from any treatment of controversial issues. Making the "normative judgment" that "governmentally-coerced speech" is in any event abhorrent, the FCC rejected the doctrine as a matter of policy. The court said that judgment was not arbitrary, but quite similar to the U.S. Supreme Court's findings in print media cases. (Page 2488)

Use Of SAT Scores To Award Scholarships Discriminates Against Female Students

New York's sole reliance upon Scholastic Aptitude Test scores to award state-sponsored merit scholarships will likely be shown to have a discriminatory impact on women in violation of Title IX of the 1972 Education Amendments, the U.S. District Court for the Southern District of New York declared Feb. 3 in issuing a preliminary injunction. The case is apparently the first to mount a disparate impact challenge

Section 1 — 57 LW 1129

0148-8139/89/$0+.50

Law Week's Section 1, "Summary and Analysis," is a four-page report briefly summarizing the week's most important court decisions. On the back page is a more complete list of the decisions reported in that week's issue.

In Section 2 are digests of recent federal and state court decisions and of significant federal agency actions. Each court decision begins with a boldface headnote setting forth the court's holding. The decision is then summarized with special focus on the court's reasoning.

2-28-89 — *The United States* LAW WEEK — 57 LW 2491

plan participant encompass a former employee who has become an employer and, nevertheless, is permitted to purchase plan coverage in his status as employer?

An employer cannot ordinarily be an employee or participant under ERISA. It is a fundamental requirement of ERISA that "the assets of a plan shall never inure to the benefit of any employer ...." 29 USC 1103(c)(1). *Peckham v. Board of Trustees*, 653 F2d 424 (CA 10 1981), held that this statutory mandate precluded sole proprietors from having the dual status of employer-employee for ERISA purposes.

Jones, however, contends that it has been held that an employer may have "dual status" standing as a fiduciary to sue under ERISA, recognizing a general principle of multiple roles for employers that permits an employer to have standing whenever he also has the status of a plan participant.

However, that an employer may have standing as a fiduciary does absolutely nothing to advance the argument that an employer may similarly have standing as a participant. When an employer files suit as a fiduciary, he acts for the benefit of plan participants and beneficiaries; he does not act in his own interest and thus does not risk running afoul of the requirement that the assets of a plan may not inure to the benefit of an employer.

Jones next argues that, as an employer, he has an implied cause of action under ERISA because he was injured by the trustees' actions and that those injuries fall within the zone of interests protected by ERISA. He cites *Fentron Industries v. National Shopmen Pension Fund*, 674 F2d 1300 (CA 9 1982), which held that ERISA does not prohibit employers from suing to enforce its provisions.

The *Fentron* approach has generally been rejected by most other courts on the ground that it improperly assumes a grant of subject matter jurisdiction. These cases demonstrate that the key question is whether the grant of jurisdiction in ERISA is limited to the list of parties enumerated in Section 1132(e)(1). If so, then the district courts lack subject matter jurisdiction to engage in an analysis whether standing is to be implied.

Courts should not imply an additional private right of action when a statute already has an elaborate enforcement mechanism. In *Franchise Tax Bd. v. Laborers Vacation Trust*, 463 U.S. 1 (1982), the court stated: "The express grant of federal jurisdiction in ERISA is limited to suits brought by certain parties ... as to whom Congress presumably determined that a right to enter federal court was necessary to further the statute's purposes." Further, in *Massachusetts Mutual Life Insurance Co. v. Russell*, 473 U.S. 134, 53 LW 4938 (1984), the court elaborated on congressional intent in ERISA: "The six carefully integrated civil enforcement provisions found in §502(a) ... provide strong evidence that Congress did *not* intend to authorize other remedies that it simply forgot to incorporate expressly. The assumption of inadvertent omission is rendered especially suspect upon close consideration of ERISA's interlocking, interrelated, and interdependent remedial scheme ...." Although the court considered whether a court may imply a cause of action for extra-contractual damages, as opposed to the precise issue here, it nevertheless made it clear that the statutory scheme of ERISA does not lend itself to judicial expansion of available remedies. We hold that the grant of subject matter jurisdiction in Section 1132(e)(1) is exclusive and may not be expanded to imply a cause of action for non-enumerated parties.—Gordon, J.

Concurrence. Jones, as participant, may seek to recover even if Jones, as employer, may not. However, the counterclaim had to be dismissed for failure to allege fraud with particularity.—Easterbrook, J.

Schools and Colleges

DISCRIMINATION—

Likelihood that female students will prevail on claim that state's sole reliance upon Scholastic Aptitude Test scores to award state-sponsored merit scholarships constitutes sex discrimination prohibited by Title IX of 1972 Education Amendments and Equal Protection Clause warrants preliminary injunction against such use of test scores.

(*Sharif v. New York State Education Department*, DC SNY, No. 88 Civ. 8435 (JMW), 2/3/89)

Female high school students sued the state education department alleging that New York's exclusive reliance on the SAT test to award scholarships discriminates against female students in violation of the Fourteenth Amendment's Equal Protection Clause, Title IX of the 1972 Education Amendments, and Title IX regulations. They contend that the state's reliance upon the SAT disproportionately impacts female students without advancing the legislature's purpose of recognizing and awarding superior high school achievement.

The Educational Testing Service developed the SAT in order to predict academic performance in college. The ability of the SAT to serve this purpose has been statistically "validated." It is undisputed, however, that the SAT predicts the success of students differently for males and females. While the SAT will predict college success as well for males within the universe of males as for females within the universe of females, when predictions are within the combined universe of males and females, the SAT underpredicts academic performance of females in their freshmen year of college and overpredicts such academic performance for males. The SAT has never been validated as a measure of past high school performance.

Males have outscored females on the verbal portion of the SAT since 1972, with an average score differential of at least 10 points since 1981. Males have also consistently outscored females on the mathematics portion, with an average differential of at least 40 points since 1967. In 1988, for example, girls scored 56 points lower than boys on the test.

The students invoke Title IX, which prohibits sex discrimination in federally funded educational programs. They do not claim that the state has intentionally discriminated against them based on their sex, but, rather, that the state's practice of sole reliance upon SAT scores to award the scholarships disparately impacts female students. This is the first disparate impact case challenging educational testing practices under Title IX.

Neither the U.S. Supreme Court nor any court in the Second Circuit has determined whether intent must be shown in Title IX cases. However, recognizing that Title IX was patterned after Title VI of the 1964 Civil Rights Act, courts examining Title IX questions have looked to the substantial body of law developed under Title VI, which prohibits race discrimination in federally funded programs, and Title VII, which prohibits employment discrimination.

In *Guardians Association v. Civil Service Commission*, 463 U.S. 582 (1983), the Supreme Court held that a violation of Title VI itself requires proof of discriminatory intent. However, a majority also agreed that proof of discriminatory effect suffices to establish liability when a suit is brought to enforce the regulations promulgated under Title VI, rather than the statute itself.

The students' complaint explicitly alleges both violations of Title IX and its implementing regulations. This court finds that Title IX regulations, like the Title VI regulations at issue in *Guardians*, prohibit testing practices with a discriminatory effect on one sex. Consequently, the students need not prove intentional discrimination.

In Title VII testing cases, the Supreme Court has developed a three-pronged formulation to analyze disparate impact claims. Under this scheme, plaintiffs first must show that a facially neutral practice has a disproportionate effect. After such a showing, the burden shifts to defendant to prove a "business necessity" for its practice. The plaintiffs then may ultimately prevail by offering either an equally effective alternative practice that has a less discriminatory impact, or proof that the legitimate practices are a pretext for discrimination. In educational testing cases under Title VI, instead of requiring defendants to demonstrate a "business necessity," courts have required defendants to show an "educational necessity."

0148-8139/89/$0+.50

The service's coverage of the U.S. Supreme Court begins with Section 3, which provides the user with a running history of the court's caseload. Cases on the court's Appellate Docket (everything but the indigent cases) are listed as they are filed. The questions each case presents for the court's review are summarized, as is the decision of the court below. Then, when the court acts on the case either to grant or to deny review, this fact is noted. If review is granted, the case is followed through oral argument and final decision or other disposition. If the court issues an opinion on a case without hearing argument on it, the full text of the decision is reported in this section.

Section 4 reproduces in full text every Supreme Court opinion handed down after oral argument. This section may not be published every week, but is issued whenever the Supreme Court releases an opinion, even on days that *U.S. Law Week* normally does not publish.

A year's worth of issues are filed and stored in two binders—Sections 1 and 2 in the General Law binder and Sections 3 and 4 in the Supreme Court binder. Each binder is fully indexed with regular updates.

Law Week *headnotes and publishes Supreme Court opinions the same day the court issues them. The service also follows the court's docket in detail, including:*

- *Cases Docketed*
- *Summary of Orders*
- *Hearings Scheduled*
- *Arguments Heard*
- *Opinions Announced*

A complete description of how to do research in Law Week *appears later in the book in the chapter Methods of Research.*

57 LW 3612 — *The United States* LAW WEEK — 3–21–89

they would be subject to review under an abuse of discretion standard. Additionally, he said, lawyers may demonstrate that they are not competent to handle particular matters, that they have exceptionally large case loads, or that they have conflicts of interest.

O'Connor turned the court's attention to ethics of the situation. Would state ethics rules require lawyers to take indigent cases regardless of what the statute said? she asked. Allen said Iowa's rules encourage lawyers to take pro bono matters. However, as Justice Byron R. White pointed out, those same rules state that a lawyer who is not competent to accept a matter should decline representation.

REAL PROPERTY

88-1013 DE LEO v. ANTHONY A. NUNES INC.

Ruling below (RI SupCt, 546 A2d 1344):

Ample evidence supports trial court's finding that defendant in slander-of-title action maliciously made false statements about plaintiff's ownership of real estate that interfered with plaintiff's development plans and resulted in pecuniary loss to plaintiff. (**Appeal dismissed; certiorari denied**)

Summary Of Orders

At its March 20, 1989, session, the Supreme Court granted review in three cases on the Appellate Docket and summarily disposed of two others. By other orders, the Court denied review in 86 Appellate Docket cases. Review was also denied in 110 cases in the 5000 series, which is sometimes called the in forma pauperis docket. The Court acted summarily in two 5000-series cases.

Grant of review, as used in the following summary of orders, is evidenced in appeal cases by the Court's action noting probable jurisdiction or postponing the question of jurisdiction to the hearing on the merits; in certiorari cases, by the granting of certiorari. In all cases where review is granted, oral argument will ordinarily follow.

Disposal by summary action is evidenced in appeal cases by a per curiam order affirming, reversing, or vacating the judgment below or dismissing the appeal; in certiorari cases, by a per curiam order granting the petition for certiorari and simultaneously affirming, reversing, or vacating the judgment below.

Denial of review relates principally to certiorari cases and is normally evidenced by denial of certiorari.

The summary below lists the cases on the Appellate Docket in which the Court granted review, took summary action, or denied review. For each case, there is given (1) its number and title; (2) a citation to the lower court's opinion or order; (3) the ruling of the court below; and (4) the principal questions presented if the case has been granted review.

Other orders appear only in the journal of proceedings elsewhere in this issue of Law Week.

Review Granted

CRIMINAL LAW AND PROCEDURE

88-1213 EMPLOYMENT DIVISION, OREGON DEPT. OF HUMAN RESOURCES v. SMITH

Ruling below (Ore SupCt, 307 Ore 68, 763 P2d 146):

On remand from U.S. Supreme Court, 56 LW 4357 (US SupCt 1988), for determination of whether ingestion of peyote in religious ceremony violates state's criminal laws, it is held that state controlled substance statute makes no exception for sacramental use of peyote but that First Amendment would forbid state from using its criminal law to punish good-faith religious use of peyote by adult members of Native American Church; accordingly, prior holding that First Amendment entitles employees who have been discharged for ingesting peyote in Native American Church ceremonies to unemployment compensation is reaffirmed.

Question presented: Does First Amendment's Free Exercise Clause protect person's religiously motivated use of peyote from reach of state's general criminal law prohibition?

EMPLOYMENT DISCRIMINATION

88-1203 HOFFMAN-LA ROCHE INC. v. SPERLING

Ruling below (CA 3, 862 F2d 439):

Federal district courts have authority in Age Discrimination in Employment Act cases, which are subject to Fair Labor Standards Act's requirement that class members must opt-in, to approve issuance of notice of pending ADEA suit to putative class members who have not yet filed consents to join action.

Questions presented: In case brought pursuant to Age Discrimination in Employment Act, where joinder in action of persons other than named plaintiffs is governed by 29 USC 216(b), does district court possess authority to authorize and facilitate notice of action to said persons who have not yet filed consents to join action?

ENVIRONMENT AND CONSERVATION

88-42 HALLSTROM v. TILLAMOOK COUNTY

Ruling below (CA 9, 844 F2d 598, 26 ERC 1809):

Citizens' failure to comply with requirement of Resource Conservation and Recovery Act that citizens give 60 days notice to state and federal officials prior to suit against alleged violators deprives federal district court of jurisdiction over suit.

Question presented: Is 60 day notice provision of RCRA procedural, requiring stay for 60 days after notice, or jurisdictional, requiring dismissal and subsequent refiling?

Summary Action

MASS MEDIA

88-844 CHRISMAN v. TIMES MIRROR CO.

Ruling below (Calif CtApp 4thDist, 5/9/88, unpublished):

Although Navy responded to newspaper article concerning grounding of Navy vessel by reopening investigation and subsequently commencing court martial proceedings against vessel's captain, in which captain was charged with but acquitted of being intoxicated at time of grounding, Navy was legal cause of court martial, not newspaper, and thus newspaper cannot be held liable in captain's libel action for articles published prior to court martial; newspaper articles recounting court martial proceedings, while omitting certain testimony as was within newspaper's discretion, reported prosecution version of facts, defense version of facts, and decision, and thus were true and fair reports protected by privilege of Calif. Civil Code 47(4). (**Appeal dismissed; certiorari denied**)

Review Denied

ANTITRUST

88-1068 NANAVATI v. BURDETTE TOMLIN MEMORIAL HOSPITAL

Ruling below (CA 3, 857 F2d 96):

Neither individual physicians nor executive committee of physicians has interest in competition with hospital, and plaintiff physician presented no evidence linking alleged boycott of referrals to him to hospital's involvement in executive committee's decision to revoke his staff privileges, and thus evidence of emergency room physicians' alleged conspiratorial acts, even if related to revocation decision, did not support jury's finding that hospital was conspirator within meaning of Section 1 of Sherman Act; physician did not allege that physicians' executive committee took any group action, and thus it did not constitute combination as matter of law; district court correctly determined that evidence did not support verdict against hospital or executive committee based on alleged boycott of referrals; physician did not prove any damages resulting from five day period during which revocation of staff privileges was in effect, and thus judgment n.o.v. for hospital and executive committee on Section 1 claims was proper.

88-1247 CENTRAL MILK PRODUCERS COOPERATIVE v. NATIONAL FARMERS ORGANIZATION

Ruling below (*National Farmers Organization v. Associated Milk Producers Inc.*, CA 8, 850 F2d 1286, 57 LW 2055):

Dairy farmers' cooperatives engaged in broad conspiracy of acts to monopolize marketing of milk, including discriminatory pricing, actual or threatened supply cutoffs, litigation, and similar harassment and such conspiracy resulted in substantial injury to farmers' organization; lesser standard of proof applies to assessment of damages in antitrust action, requiring that antitrust plaintiff need only present evidence from which fact-finder can make just and reasonable estimate of damage that is not based on speculation; "test market theory" of damages, by which antitrust plaintiff uses its performance in identifiable portion relevant market as yardstick to measure performance in remainder of market provides just and reasonable estimate of overall damages.

88-1248 ASSOCIATED MILK PRODUCERS INC. v. NATIONAL FARMERS' ORGANIZATION INC.

Ruling below (CA 8, 850 F2d 1286, 57 LW 2055):

Lesser standard of proof applies to assessment of damages in antitrust action, requiring that antitrust plaintiff need only present evidence from which fact-finder can make just and reasonable estimate of damage that is not based on speculation; "test market theory" of damages, by which antitrust plaintiff uses its performance in identifiable portion relevant market as yardstick to measure performance in remainder of market

0148-8139/89/$0+.50

Law Week's Section 3 keeps track of virtually everything that happens in the U.S. Supreme Court—filings, decisions to grant or deny review, and oral arguments. One regular feature is a summary of the court's previous day's orders.

The full text of Supreme Court opinions appear in Section 4. This front-page example of Section 4 shows the headnotes for all the opinions released that day. Inside is the full text of each opinion. *Law Week* releases Extra Editions like this one whenever opinions are issued on days *Law Week* does not normally publish.

EXTRA EDITION NO. 1

BNA *The United States* **LAW WEEK**

Supreme Court Opinions

February 21, 1989 • THE BUREAU OF NATIONAL AFFAIRS, INC., WASHINGTON, D.C. • Volume 57, No. 32

Opinions Announced February 22, 1989

The Supreme Court decided:

BANKRUPTCY—Interest

Section 506(b) of Bankruptcy Code, which allows holders of over-secured claims to recover, in addition to pre-petition amount of claim, "interest on such claim, and any reasonable fees, costs, or charges provided for under the agreement under which such claim arose," entitles holders of non-consensual over-secured claims to unqualified recovery of post-petition interest. (*U.S. v. Ron Pair Enterprises Inc.*, No. 87-1043) Page 4256

CITIES AND COUNTIES—Civil Rights Liability

Fourteenth Amendment's Due Process Clause does not impose affirmative duty on state to protect individuals who are not in state custody from harm by private actors, and thus county social services agency that failed to protect child from severe beatings by father, despite knowledge of abuse allegations and continuing agency contact with family, did not violate child's due process rights. (*DeShaney v. Winnebago County Department of Social Services*, No. 87-154) .... Page 4218

CRIMINAL LAW AND PROCEDURE—Habeas Corpus

"Plain statement" rule of *Michigan v. Long*, 463 U.S. 1042 (1983), that U.S. Supreme Court may reach federal question earlier raised in state court proceeding if it appears that state court below rested its decision primarily on federal law unless state court plainly stated that its decision rested upon adequate and independent state grounds, applies not only to cases on direct review but also to cases on federal habeas review; therefore, procedural default in state proceedings does not bar consideration of federal claim on habeas review unless last state court rendering judgment in case clearly stated that its judgment rested on state procedural bar. (*Harris v. Reed*, No. 87-5677) .... Page 4224

CRIMINAL LAW AND PROCEDURE—Habeas Corpus

Requirement that claim raised on federal habeas corpus previously have been "fairly presented" to state courts is not satisfied by first-time presentation of claim to state appellate court under procedure that, by state rule, permits discretionary review "only when there are special and important reasons therefor." (*Castille v. Peoples*, No. 87-1602) .... Page 4249

CRIMINAL LAW AND PROCEDURE—Jury Selection

Claim that Sixth Amendment's fair cross-section requirement forbids exercise of peremptory jury challenges on racial grounds will not be considered on review of collateral attack upon final conviction; decision in *Batson v. Kentucky*, 476 U.S. 79, 54 LW 4425 (1986), which lessened evidentiary showing required under *Swain v. Alabama*, 380 U.S. 702 (1965), for establishing prima facie case of racial discrimination in exercise of peremptory jury challenges, cannot be invoked on collateral attack by habeas petitioner whose conviction, though not final at time when *Swain*'s continued vitality was questioned in opinions concurring in and dissenting from denial of certiorari, became final before *Batson* was decided; procedural default, no excuse for which has been shown, precludes consideration of habeas petitioner's argument that *Swain*'s evidentiary hurdle can be ignored if prosecution volunteers reasons for its exercise of peremptory challenges. (*Teague v. Lane*, No. 87-5259) .... Page 4233

ELECTIONS—Political Parties

California statutes that prohibit official governing bodies of political parties from endorsing or opposing candidates in primary elections burden parties' freedoms of speech and association while serving no compelling governmental interest and thus violate First Amendment; California statutes that regulate size, composition, and selection of political parties' official governing bodies burden freedom of association of parties and their members, but are not demonstrably necessary to achieve state's compelling interest in preserving integrity of election process, and therefore violate First Amendment. (*Eu v. San Francisco County Democratic Central Committee*, No. 87-1269) .... Page 4251

NOTICE: These opinions are subject to formal revision before publication in the preliminary print of the United States Reports. Readers are requested to notify the Reporter of Decisions, Supreme Court of the United States, Washington, D.C. 20543, of any typographical or other formal errors, in order that corrections may be made before the preliminary print goes to press.

NOTE: Where it is deemed desirable, a syllabus (headnote) will be released * * * at the time the opinion is issued. The syllabus constitutes no part of the opinion of the Court but has been prepared by the Reporter of Decisions for the convenience of the reader. See *United States v. Detroit Lumber Co.*, 200 U.S. 321, 337.

Section 4 — Copyright © 1989 by The Bureau of National Affairs, Inc. 0148-8139/89/$0+.50 — 57 LW 4217

The Criminal Law Reporter

The Criminal Law Reporter is a weekly notification service providing comprehensive coverage of significant developments in the field of criminal law and procedure. Very similar in format to *U.S. Law Week,* this service contains digests of the most important criminal law cases from across the county—from state, local, and federal courts. All U.S. Supreme Court decisions affecting the criminal law are reported in full text, and each issue contains information on Supreme Court activities, including cases filed in the court and oral arguments heard by the court. *The Criminal Law Reporter* also covers significant federal legislation, the activities of important professional organizations involved in the field of criminal law, and other events and reports.

Each issue of *The Criminal Law Reporter* consists of two or three separate sections, all housed in a single binder with an index. The service's second section is not printed when the Supreme Court fails to issue any criminal law opinions. For research purposes, back issues are kept and stored in volumes in six-month increments.

The first of this service's three separate sections, Courts and Legislatures, begins with a one-column highlights box noting the major items reported in the issue. Each entry directs the reader to another page for a more complete account of the court decision or other event. The bulk of this Section 1 consists of digests of state and federal court opinions on criminal law and procedure. The digests summarize the opinions and quote key language directly from the text of the opinions. Each digest is preceded by an editorial report of the opinion's holding and rationale. Less significant opinions in each issue are given more abbreviated treatment.

Section 1 also contains reports on federal legislative action and on other events affecting criminal law. On the back page of the section are a Table of Cases, which lists each court decision reported in the issue, and a Topical Summary, which organizes the issue's contents by subject matter and provides short descriptions of the developments reported in the issue.

In the second, Text section, the entire text of Supreme Court opinions, significant federal legislation, and selected documents produced by agencies such as the U.S. Sentencing Commission is reported. For each Supreme Court opinion, there is a headnote prepared by the editors that sets forth the holding or holdings of the case, followed by an editorial report and analysis.

Decisions of state and federal courts on criminal law and practice are reported in Section 1. The box on the left side of the page highlights the cases and other developments reported in this section and elsewhere in the issue. The case discussion that begins in the right column is a typical example of how *The Criminal Law Reporter* and some other BNA services report cases. The material in the larger type is an editorial explanation of the court's holding and rationale; the smaller type is a digest of the decision itself, with significant portions quoted in full text.

The CRIMINAL LAW REPORTER

Court Decisions
Legislative Action
Reports and Proposals

A Weekly Review of Developments in Criminal Law

September 16, 1992 THE BUREAU OF NATIONAL AFFAIRS, INC. **Volume 51, No. 23**

IN THE COURTS

HIGHLIGHTS

An unfulfilled request for an attorney in an aborted state prosecution may bar federal authorities from interrogating the defendant in connection with a federal prosecution for the same conduct, the Ninth Circuit concluded. Although the Sixth Amendment right to counsel is offense specific, not conduct specific, collusion between the sovereigns can blur this distinction. (Page 1505)

DNA evidence is admissible in the Ohio courts, the Ohio Supreme Court ruled. Recent cases from some other jurisdictions have found problems with the statistical assumptions commonly used in describing the significance of a match. But under the relevancy test, which Ohio follows in preference to the *Frye* standard, these matters go only to the weight of the evidence, the court said. (Page 1497)

A thermal imaging device may be used to detect heat coming off of a suspected pot growing operation without complying with the Fourth Amendment, a federal district court in Pennsylvania held. People do not have a protected privacy interest in lost heat, the court said. (Page 1499)

Racially motivated assaults are not expressions of opinion protected by the First Amendment and its state counterpart, the Oregon Supreme Court decided as it upheld the state's "intimidation law." The use of a defendant's speech to prove that he believed the victim belonged to a protected group does not punish speech, the court said. (Page 1507)

Oregon's exclusionary rule applies in probation revocation proceedings, the Oregon Supreme Court declared. The court reasoned that such proceedings can lead to a loss of liberty and thus the remedy of suppression of illegally seized evidence should be available. (Page 1500)

Conduct leading up to an arrest is not governed by the Fourth Amendment, the Seventh Circuit held. The Fourth Amendment is not triggered until a "seizure" actually occurs; thus the reasonableness or unreasonableness of a plan by police to lure an arrest target to a lonely spot and surprise him is not a Fourth Amendment concern. (Page 1503)

In this issue: Sections 1 (Courts and Legislatures), and 3 (Supreme Court Proceedings).

OHIO APPROVES ADMISSION OF DNA EVIDENCE UNDER GENERAL RELEVANCY APPROACH

Court rebuffs objections going to lack of uniform standard for identifying matches, assumptions underlying statistical evidence.

Expert testimony asserting that a defendant's DNA matches DNA from tissue left in the aftermath of a crime and expressing, in statistical terms, the likelihood that someone other than the defendant could have the same DNA can be relevant and therefore admissible in the courts of Ohio, the Ohio Supreme Court held September 2. The special test for scientific evidence set out in *Frye v. U.S.*, 293 F 1013 (CA DC 1923), has not been adopted in Ohio; instead, expert testimony is admissible if it is relevant, not barred by the Constitution or other rule, is not too prejudicial as compared to its probative value, and can assist the trier of fact. DNA evidence can meet that standard, the court said. The doubts that have led some courts to declare DNA evidence inadmissible, such as questions about the assumptions underlying the so-called "product rule" used in determining the statistical likelihood of a mistaken match, are merely matters that go to the weight of the evidence rather than its admissibility, the court said. No pretrial hearing into the reliability of such evidence is necessary; however, the factfinder may reject it as unreliable or misleading. (State (Ohio) v. Pierce, **Ohio SupCt**, No. 90-1898, 9/2/92)

Digest of Opinion: DNA evidence based on tests performed by Cellmark Diagnostics was introduced at the trial of defendant Louis Pierce Jr. for rape and other offenses. He had moved to suppress the DNA evidence, but the trial judge concluded that the jury should determine the weight and reliability of the evidence.

As of 1990, DNA evidence had been admitted or used to obtain a plea in 183 cases in 38 states. However, jurisdictions differ on what standard should be applied. Pierce urges us to adopt the test of *Frye v. U.S.*, 293 F 1013 (CA DC 1923), which requires that the scientific principle underlying new scientific evidence be "sufficiently established to have gained general acceptance in the particular field in which it belongs." In so arguing, he asks us to reject the relevancy standard we recognized in *State v. Williams*, 466 NE2d 444 (1983). Under that standard, the admission of scientific evidence is governed by Rules 402, 403, and 702 of the Ohio Rules of Evidence. Under those rules, all relevant evidence is admissible unless it is excluded by the Constitution or other authority (Rule 402), or if its probative value is outweighed by danger of unfair prejudice, confusion of the issues, or misleading the jury, (Rule 403); qualified expert witnesses may testify to scientific or other specialized knowledge if that knowledge will assist the

Section 1 Copyright © 1992 by The Bureau of National Affairs, Inc. 0011-1341/92/$00.50 **51 CrL 1497**

U.S. Supreme Court proceedings in criminal cases are faithfully recorded in Section 3, including the actions taken by the court to grant or deny review.

The CRIMINAL LAW REPORTER

Supreme Court Proceedings
Arguments, Actions and
Filings

May 27, 1992 THE BUREAU OF NATIONAL AFFAIRS, INC. **Volume 51, No. 9**

ACTIONS TAKEN

At its session on May 26, 1992, the U.S. Supreme Court granted review in one case on the Appellate Docket case and denied review in eight Appellate Docket cases.

The summaries below are of the criminal cases on the Appellate Docket in which the Supreme Court granted or denied review. The excerpts from the Supreme Court Journal of Proceedings which follow the summaries include the actions taken in 5000 Series as well as Appellate Docket cases.

REVIEW GRANTED

The court granted certiorari in the following case:

91-1300 U.S. v. DUNNIGAN

Sentencing — Federal guidelines — Sentence enhancement based on perjury.

Ruling below (CA 4, 944 F2d 178, 49 CrL 1505, 60 LW 2179 (1991)):

Provision of federal Sentencing Guidelines that enhances sentence if defendant is found to have obstructed justice in course of his prosecution, §3C1.1, unconstitutionally burdens defendant's constitutional right to testify in his own defense as applied to defendant's trial testimony that adverse jury verdict implies is false.

Question presented: Does Constitution prohibit court from enhancing defendant's sentence under Sentencing Guidelines §3C1.1 if court finds that defendant committed perjury while testifying at trial?

REVIEW DENIED

The court denied certiorari in the following cases:

91-1233 ZARZECKI v. U.S.

Securities violations — Fraud — Trader's hope to affect price of securities.

Ruling below (*U.S. v. Regan*, CA 2, 937 F2d 823, as amended by 946 F2d 188 (1991)):

Defendant, head trader at investment firm, violated §10(b) of 1934 Securities Exchange Act and SEC Rule 10b-5, which bar use of scheme to defraud or any manipulative or deceptive device, by participating in arrangement with underwriter of convertible bond offering by which his firm made short sale of sizable block of convertible bond issuer's stock in order to counter efforts by issuer to levitate price of its stock for purposes related to bond offering, without revealing that firm was seller or that moving party was underwriter of bond offering; liability for market manipulation does not depend upon existence of fiduciary relationship, but may be based on failure to disclose that market prices are being artificially depressed.

91-1404 AMEJI v. COWAN

Habeas corpus — Due process attack on state conviction — Weight of evidence.

Ruling below (CA 6, 9/13/91, unpublished):

Habeas petitioner's state court convictions of bribing and intimidating witness are supported by sufficient, albeit circumstantial, evidence; petitioner's claim that testimony was improperly admitted at trial is question of state law that does not raise constitutional issue.

91-1417 SINGLETARY v. BLANCO

Capital punishment — Habeas corpus — Evidentiary hearing in federal court.

Ruling below (CA 11, 943 F2d 1477 (1991)):

District court did not abuse discretion it enjoys under 28 USC 2254(d) and *Townsend v. Sain*, 372 U.S. 293 (1963), by holding evidentiary hearing on habeas corpus petitioner's claims that his attorneys at his capital trial were constitutionally ineffective for failing to subpoena certain witnesses, for failing to ensure presence of interpreter throughout trial proceedings, and for failing to determine whether defendant was competent to stand trial; trial counsel rendered ineffective assistance at sentencing phase, in violation of Sixth Amendment, by revealing confidential, damaging information to trial judge concerning reasons why defense would present no witnesses in mitigation; counsel was also ineffective in failing to conduct adequate investigation into availability of mitigating evidence, failing to present such evidence, and failing to present evidence of petitioner's mental health problems; counsel's improper revelations to judge prejudiced petitioner in view of finding that trial court considered what petitioner and counsel said as aggravating evidence for purposes of capital sentencing.

91-1597 PENNSYLVANIA v. CHAMBERS

Capital punishment — Biblical references by prosecutor — Establishment of religion.

Ruling below (Pa SupCt, 599 A2d 630, 50 CrL 1176 (1991)):

Prosecutor in capital proceeding overstepped bounds of permissible advocacy when he quoted passage in Bible that "the murderer shall be put to death"; prosecutor's assertion that Bible dogmatically commands that murderer be put to death injected religious law into proceedings as additional factor not arising from evidence; argument was deliberate attempt to destroy objectivity and impartiality of jury and requires new sentencing hearing.

PER CURIAM OPINION

Capital punishment — Coleman v. Thompson, Warden 3064

For full text of U.S. Supreme Court opinions in criminal cases, see Section 2.

51 CrL 3061 0011-1341/92/$00.50 **5-27-92**

With Section 3, Supreme Court Proceedings, the user can keep abreast of every Appellate Docket case in the Supreme Court that relates to criminal law and procedure, from the initial filing of the case to the court's decision either to grant or deny review. This section also contains summaries of oral arguments in particularly significant cases.

The holding of the court below in each case is briefly summarized, as are the questions being presented to the Supreme Court. This section also contains previews of the cases to be argued before the court and summaries of many actual oral arguments, with emphasis on the justices' questions and the lawyers' answers. Every summer, the court's criminal law decisions during the previous term are reviewed.

For research purposes, *The Criminal Law Reporter* is fully indexed by subject matter and by case name. A researcher finds the appropriate subject entry in the "Topical Index" and then proceeds to the appropriate citation in the body of the *Reporter*. Research can be done similarly by using the separate "Tables of Cases" for Supreme Court and for state and federal decisions. Pages numbered 1001-1999 refer to Section 1, 2001-2999 to Section 2, and 3001-3999 to Section 3.

The service does for criminal law what Law Week *does for constitutional law in general. It follows criminal law cases in the Supreme Court from the time they are filed to the time the court disposes of them. Supreme Court decisions in the criminal law field are reported in full text as soon as they are issued.*

By concentrating on a specific field of law, moreover, The Criminal Law Reporter *also collects and summarizes the most important criminal law decisions from all over the country.*

The Criminal Law Reporter's Section 2 is devoted to the opinions of the U.S. Supreme Court. The holding or holdings of each criminal law opinion the court issues is spelled out in a boldface headnote, followed by an editorial analysis of the decision.

The CRIMINAL LAW REPORTER

EXTRA EDITION NO. 1
Text No. 11

June 24, 1992 THE BUREAU OF NATIONAL AFFAIRS, INC. Volume 51, No. 13

OPINION OF THE U.S. SUPREME COURT

SUMMARY

SPEEDY TRIAL — **Presumptive prejudice to a defendant's ability to defend against criminal charges, arising from a delay of eight and one-half years between indictment and arrest, requires, when considered together with the facts that the delay was extraordinarily long, that it was due to the government's negligence in locating the defendant, and that the defendant asserted the right to speedy trial promptly after learning of the charges, dismissal of the indictment under the Sixth Amendment right to speedy trial.** (Doggett v. U.S., No. 90-857, 6/24/92) 2244

A lengthy delay between a defendant's indictment and arrest can violate the Sixth Amendment's Speedy Trial Clause even if the only possible prejudice to the defendant was impairment of his ability to respond to the charges, and even if no actual prejudice of this sort was shown, a majority of the U.S. Supreme Court ruled June 24. After considering presumptive prejudice along with the other factors set out in *Barker v. Wingo*, 407 U.S. 514 (1972), the majority concluded that a delay period of eight and one-half years, during which the defendant was neither incarcerated nor even aware of the indictment, violated his constitutional right to a speedy trial.

The defendant was indicted on drug charges in 1980, but not arrested until 1988. He left the country in 1980 but returned in 1982; however, authorities spent most of the ensuing period under the mistaken assumption that the defendant was still abroad, and they made little effort to find him.

His motion to dismiss on speedy trial grounds was denied by the lower courts under the four-factor balancing test announced in *Barker*. That test weighs the length of the delay, the reason for the delay, the defendant's assertion of his right, and prejudice resulting from the delay. The court of appeals in this case said that the government's negligence caused the delay, and that because the defendant was not aware of the pending indictment during most of the period, his assertion of his right soon after the arrest was timely. However, the court ultimately rejected the defendant's speedy trial claim for lack of prejudice caused by the delay, 906 F2d 573 (CA 4 1990).

Justice Souter, writing for a 5–4 majority, accepted the court's findings on the cause and assertion-of-right prongs of *Barker*, as well as the lower court's further finding that the length of the delay weighed against the government. The main issue, as Souter saw it, was whether the defendant was prejudiced by the delay, and what role any such prejudice should play in the *Barker* balancing analysis.

Barker identified three sorts of harm caused by unreasonable delay between accusation and trial: oppressive pretrial incarceration, anxiety and concern on the part of the accused, and "the possibility that the [accused's] defense will be impaired" by dimming memories and loss of exculpatory evidence. The government, citing cases decided both before and after *Barker*, argued that the last variety of prejudice is not really a concern of the Speedy Trial Clause but is, rather, a due process issue. But Souter rejected this view, stating that "the speedy trial enquiry must weigh the effect of delay on the accused's defense just as it has to weigh any other form of prejudice that *Barker* recognized."

The government's second line of defense was its claim that the defendant had failed to demonstrate how in fact he was prejudiced by the delay. Souter acknowledged that the defendant "did indeed come up short in this respect," but he parried the government's thrust by asserting that "affirmative proof of particularized prejudice is not essential to every speedy trial claim." Souter declared that excessive delay presumptively compromises the reliability of a trial in ways that cannot, and therefore need not, be proved.

A delay of this magnitude, caused by "inexcusable oversights" on the government's part, "far exceeds the threshold needed to state a speedy trial claim," Souter said. "When the Government's negligence thus causes delay six times as long as that generally sufficient to trigger judicial review . . ., and when the presumption of prejudice, albeit unspecified, is neither extenuated, as by the defendant's acquiescence . . . nor persuasively rebutted, the defendant is entitled to relief."

Justice O'Connor, in a brief dissent, contended that any harm to the defendant was "speculative."

Justice Thomas, dissenting and joined by Chief Justice Rehnquist and Justice Scalia, maintained that the prejudice identified by the majority is not protected by the Speedy Trial Clause. Language in *Barker* identifying this sort of prejudice as a speedy trial concern cannot be reconciled with the court's other cases, Thomas argued. Addressing an additional question that the majority left undecided, Thomas said that the Speedy Trial Clause does not protect "a right to repose, free from secret or unknown indictments."

Section 2

51 CrL 2243

Next comes the full text of the Supreme Court's opinion, exactly as the court issued it.

FULL TEXT OF OPINION

No. 90–857

MARC GILBERT DOGGETT, PETITIONER *v.* UNITED STATES

ON WRIT OF CERTIORARI TO THE UNITED STATES COURT OF APPEALS FOR THE ELEVENTH CIRCUIT

Syllabus

No. 90–857. Argued October 9, 1991—Reargued February 24, 1992—Decided June 24, 1992

In February 1980, petitioner Doggett was indicted on federal drug charges, but he left the country before the Drug Enforcement Agency could secure his arrest. The DEA knew that he was later imprisoned in Panama, but after requesting that he be expelled back to the United States, never followed up on his status. Once the DEA discovered that he had left Panama for Colombia, it made no further attempt to locate him. Thus, it was unaware that he reentered this country in 1982 and subsequently married, earned a college degree, found steady employment, lived openly under his own name, and stayed within the law. The Marshal's Service eventually located him during a simple credit check on individuals with outstanding warrants. He was arrested in September 1988, 8½ years after his indictment. He moved to dismiss the indictment on the ground that the Government's failure to prosecute him earlier violated his Sixth Amendment right to a speedy trial, but the District Court denied the motion, and he entered a conditional guilty plea. The Court of Appeals affirmed.

Held: The delay between Doggett's indictment and arrest violated his right to a speedy trial. His claim meets the *Barker* v. *Wingo*, 407 U. S. 514, 530, criteria for evaluating speedy trial claims. First, the extraordinary 8½ year lag between his indictment and arrest clearly suffices to trigger the speedy trial enquiry. Second, the Government was to blame for the delay. The District Court's finding that the Government was negligent in pursuing Doggett should be viewed with considerable deference, and neither the Government nor the record provides any reason to reject that finding. Third, Doggett asserted in due course his right to a speedy trial. The courts below found that he did not know of his indictment before his arrest, and, in the factual basis supporting his guilty plea, the Government essentially conceded this point. Finally, the negligent delay between Doggett's indictment and arrest presumptively prejudiced his ability to prepare an adequate defense. The Government errs in arguing that the Speedy Trial Clause does not significantly protect a defendant's interest in fair adjudication. *United States* v. *Marion*, 404 U. S. 307, 320–323; *United States* v. *MacDonald*, 456 U. S. 1, 8; *United States* v. *Loud Hawk*, 474 U. S. 302, 312, distinguished. Nor does Doggett's failure to cite any specifically demonstrable prejudice doom his claim, since excessive delay can compromise a trial's reliability in unidentifiable ways. Presumptive prejudice is part of the mix of relevant *Barker* factors and increases in importance with the length of the delay. Here, the Government's egregious persistence in failing to prosecute Doggett is sufficient to warrant granting relief. The negligence caused delay six times as long as that generally deemed sufficient to trigger judicial review, and the presumption of prejudice is neither extenuated, as by Doggett's acquiescence, nor persuasively rebutted.

906 F. 2d 573, reversed and remanded.

SOUTER, J., delivered the opinion of the Court, in which WHITE, BLACKMUN, STEVENS, and KENNEDY, JJ., joined. O'CONNOR, J., filed a dissenting opinion. THOMAS, J., filed a dissenting opinion, in which REHNQUIST, C. J., and SCALIA, J., joined.

JUSTICE SOUTER delivered the opinion of the Court.

In this case we consider whether the delay of 8½ years between petitioner's indictment and arrest violated his Sixth Amendment right to a speedy trial. We hold that it did.

I

On February 22, 1980, petitioner Marc Doggett was indicted for conspiring with several others to import and distribute cocaine. See 84 Stat. 1265, 1291, as amended, 21 U. S. C. §§846, 963. Douglas Driver, the Drug Enforcement Administration's principal agent investigating the conspiracy, told the United States Marshal's Service that the DEA would oversee the apprehension of Doggett and his confederates. On March 18, 1980, two police officers set out under Driver's orders to arrest Doggett at his parents' house in Raleigh, North Carolina, only to find that he was not there. His mother told the officers that he had left for Colombia four days earlier.

To catch Doggett on his return to the United States, Driver sent word of his outstanding arrest warrant to all United States Customs stations and to a number of law enforcement organizations. He also placed Doggett's name in the Treasury Enforcement Communication System (TECS), a computer network that helps Customs agents screen people entering the country, and in the National Crime Information Center computer system, which serves similar ends. The TECS entry expired that September, however, and Doggett's name vanished from the system.

In September 1981, Driver found out that Doggett was under arrest on drug charges in Panama and, thinking that a formal extradition request would be futile, simply asked Panama to "expel" Doggett to the United States. Although the Panamanian authorities promised to comply when their own proceedings had run their course, they freed Doggett the following July and let him go to Colombia, where he stayed with an aunt for several months. On September 25, 1982, he passed unhindered through Customs in New York City and settled down in Virginia. Since his return to the United States, he has married, earned a college degree, found a steady job as a computer operations manager, lived openly under his own name, and stayed within the law.

Doggett's travels abroad had not wholly escaped the Government's notice, however. In 1982, the American Embassy in Panama told the State Department of his departure to Colombia, but that information, for whatever reason, eluded the DEA, and Agent Driver assumed for several years that his quarry was still serving time in a Panamanian prison. Driver never asked DEA officials in Panama to check into Doggett's status, and only after his own fortuitous assignment to that country in 1985 did he discover Doggett's departure for Colombia. Driver then simply assumed Doggett had settled there, and he made no effort to find out for sure or to track Doggett down, either abroad or in the United States. Thus Doggett remained lost to the American criminal justice system until September 1988, when the Marshal's Service ran a simple credit check on several thousand people subject to outstanding arrest warrants and, within minutes, found out where Doggett lived and worked. On September 5, 1988, nearly 6 years

The Criminal Law Reporter (ISSN 0011-1341) is published weekly each Wednesday except the second Wednesday in July, Labor Day Week, and the Wednesday following Christmas at a subscription rate of $570.00 for the first year and $540.00 per year thereafter, by The Bureau of National Affairs, Inc., 1231 25th Street, N.W., Washington, D.C. 20037. Second-class postage paid at Washington, D.C., and additional mailing offices. POSTMASTER: Send address changes to The Criminal Law Reporter, The Bureau of National Affairs, Inc., P.O. Box 40949, Washington, D.C. 20016–0949.

51 CrL 2244 6–24–92

The Family Law Reporter

The Family Law Reporter is a weekly notification and reference service on all aspects of family law. The term "family law"—as defined by the service's coverage—is a broad one, encompassing the traditional areas of divorce, alimony, property distribution, and child custody and support, as well as such topics as adoption and foster care, paternity, marital and premarital planning, surrogate parenthood, and tax planning.

The service consists of two binders. New developments in the field of family law are reported weekly in "Current Developments" and are stored in a binder by that name. Material with a more permanent reference value is included in the "Reference File and Tax Guide" binder.

The weekly Current Developments report the most recent significant occurrences in family law, including court decisions, legislative actions, Internal Revenue Service rulings, and other news.

The Reference File and Tax Guide's five sections cover federal laws pertaining to family law, uniform and model acts, state divorce laws, guidance on divorce taxation, and practice aids.

Issues of this service's Current Developments consist of anywhere from one to three sections. The front page of the first section points the reader to the most important highlights of each issue, while the second page categorizes and briefly summarizes every item in the issue and lists the name of every court decision.

Section 1, primarily covering recent judicial and legislative developments, is issued every week and is the core of the service. It includes digests of important new court decisions, with textual excerpts of particularly siginificant language, and reports on congressional and state legislative actions. Also covered are IRS private letter rulings and other actions, summaries of attorneys general opinions, and reports of professional conferences, such as those of the American Bar Association's Family Law Section.

Section 2, the full-text section, is issued whenever the U.S. Supreme Court releases an opinion affecting family law. Also given full-text treatment are selected state and federal court decisions, federal laws and regulations, and other materials deemed by the editors to be of particular importance.

Several times a year, monographs by family law practitioners and other experts in the field are published in Section 3. These monongraphs are detailed treatments of timely, practice related issues. Past monographs have dealt with such subjects as the gift and tax aspects of divorce and separation, the status of state laws on access to adoption records, and the practical side to pensions and qualified domestic relations orders.

THE FAMILY LAW REPORTER

August 25, 1992 | THE BUREAU OF NATIONAL AFFAIRS, INC. | Volume 18, No. 40

HIGHLIGHTS

"CUSTODY PROCEEDINGS" under the Uniform Child Custody Jurisdiction Act encompass adoption and termination of parental rights proceedings, the Wisconsin Court of Appeals, Second District, has decided. The court recently held that the paternal grandparents of an out-of-wedlock child who had been granted visitation with the child by an Illinois court should have been informed of Wisconsin proceedings in which the child's mother sought termination of the parental rights of the child's biological father and her husband petitioned to adopt the child. The court noted that a majority of other jurisdictions hold that the act covers termination and adoption proceedings. (Page 1479)

THE AUTOMATIC STAY in a debtor's Chapter 11 proceeding has been lifted by the U.S. Bankruptcy Court for the Western District of Tennessee to allow his divorce action, commenced after his bankruptcy filing, to proceed. The bankruptcy court granted relief from the stay to permit a state court to decide the issues of dissolution, custody, visitation, and support. It also deferred to the state court regarding distribution of the parties' marital assets, but ordered that the stay remain in effect to preclude enforcement of any property division to the extent that it involves the bankruptcy estate. The court added, however, that the wife may have an unsecured claim for the value of the bankruptcy estate property awarded to her. (Page 1480)

A **"RETENTION OF JURISDICTION"** clause included in the custody terms of a Wyoming divorce decree did not constitute a valid forum selection clause, the Wyoming Supreme Court ruled August 7. Although the court noted that Wyoming retained exclusive custody modification jurisdiction under the Parental Kidnapping Prevention Act because the divorced wife continued to live in the state, it decided that the clause at issue did not impose upon her ex-husband a duty not to attempt to modify custody in another state. It thus held that the lower court erred in finding that the former husband's commencement of a modification action in Texas, where he resided with the parties' child, constituted criminal contempt. (Page 1482)

THE MARITAL EXEMPTION in Illinois' criminal sexual offense statutes, which bars prosecution of a spouse for forcible sexual conduct without penetration, is invalid, the Illinois Appellate Court, Second District, has ruled. The court rejected a man's claim that his conviction for the aggravated criminal assault of his wife was unconstitutional because the statutory spousal exemption should equally apply to assault offenses involving penetration (such as his conduct); instead, it took the opposite view—that the exemption itself is unconstitutional in any type of sexual offense. The court agreed with the reasoning of courts in Alabama and New York that the justifications for the marital exemption do not withstand equal protection and due process challenges. (Page 1481)

ALIMONY PAYMENTS may not be deducted from a man's income for purposes of determining his modified support obligation for the child of that marriage, the Illinois Appellate Court, Fourth District, ruled July 30. The court rejected the man's argument that the payments to his ex-wife are a "prior" maintenance obligation that, under state law, is to be deducted before determining his net income. It explained that the prior obligation cannot arise in the same action as the support duty. It further held that the trial court properly considered the man's present wife's financial resources in the support proceeding. (Page 1484)

BANKRUPTCY COURTS must always consider the intent of divorced parties as a factor in determining the dischargeability of a marital obligation, the U.S. District Court for the District of Colorado ruled July 24. The court said that even if the agreement at issue is unambiguous, a bankruptcy judge's initial inquiry should be to determine the parties' intent in entering into the agreement. It went on to hold that an apparently unambiguous agreement under which a man agreed to pay his ex-wife $275,000 in monthly payments over 96 months was in fact a non-dischargeable support agreement. It pointed out that the ex-wife was in need of support and both parties had treated the payments as alimony for tax purposes. (Page 1485)

Section 1 18 FLR 1477

The weekly issues, like those of many BNA notification services, begin with a Highlights page summarizing the most significant contents of the issue.

Inside are full reports of recent court decisions and other developments in the family law field. The court decisions are reported in the same style as that used in *The Criminal Law Reporter*.

BNA

Court Opinions
Legislative Activities
Reports and Proposals
U.S. Supreme Court Proceedings

IN THE COURTS

CA 8 TAKES MAJORITY POSITION ON INTERSPOUSAL WIRETAPPING

Court rejects claim that federal wiretap act, which provides for civil liability, was not intended to cover interspousal eavesdropping.

A federal district court erred in dismissing a woman's action for damages against her husband under the federal wiretap statute, 18 USC 2510 et seq., the U.S. Court of Appeals for the Eighth Circuit ruled February 21. The court found no indication in the statute or its legislative history to support the view that it was not intended to apply to secret surveillance by one spouse of the other's telephone conversations. Noting that the lower court based its decision on a Fifth Circuit case upholding the concept of a domestic relations exception to the statute, the court pointed out that that case has been criticized by courts in several other circuits; the court went on to adopt the majority position that an eavesdropping spouse is not insulated from liability under the federal law. (Kempf v. Kempf, 2/21/89)

Digest of Opinion: While Jillian and Karl Kempf were living together as husband and wife, Karl suspected that Jillian was having extramarital affairs. To confirm his suspicions, Karl intercepted and recorded her telephone conversations between June 4, 1985, and August 9, 1985, by connecting a cassette tape recorder to the receiver of an extension phone in plain view in the basement of their home. These recorded conversations confirmed Karl's suspicions, and he filed for a dissolution of their marriage. In that proceeding, the tapes of the conversations were admitted into evidence over Jillian's objection. In May 1987, the Missouri trial court entered judgment dissolving the marriage.

In June 1987 Jillian filed the present action against Karl, seeking damages for violation of Title III of the Omnibus Crime Control and Safe Streets Act of 1968, 18 USC 2510 et seq., and invasion of her privacy. The district court, however, granted Karl's motion for summary judgment, finding that Title III's wiretapping prohibition does not apply to interspousal wiretapping committed within the marital home, and that state courts rather than federal courts are better facilitated to handle domestic conflicts of this nature. *Kempf v. Kempf*, 677 FSupp 618, 14 FLR 1147 (DC EMo 1988). The district court specifically relied on the Fifth Circuit's reasoning in *Simpson v. Simpson*, 490 F2d 803, cert. denied 419 U.S. 897 (1974), in which the court held that Title III was not intended to apply to a husband's wiretapping of his wife's phone conversations while the couple were living together as husband and wife.

18 USC 2511 provides in part:

> (1) Except as otherwise specifically provided in this chapter any person who—
>
> (a) intentionally intercepts, endeavors to intercept, or procures any other person to intercept or endeavor to intercept, any wire, oral or electronic communication;
>
> (b) intentionally uses, endeavors to use, or procures any other person to use or endeavor to use any electronic, mechanical, or other device to intercept any oral communication when—
>
> (1) such device is affixed to, or otherwise transmits a signal through, a wire, cable, or other like connection used in wire communication;
>
> . . .
>
> (c) intentionally discloses, or endeavors to disclose, to any other person the contents of any wire, oral, or electronic communication, knowing or having reason to know that the information was obtained through the interception of a wife, oral, or electronic communication in violation of this subsection; or
>
> (d) intentionally uses, or endeavors to use, the contents of any wire, oral, or electronic communication, knowing or having reason to know that the information was obtained through the interception of a wife, oral or electronic communication in violation of this subsection;
>
> shall be punished as provided in subsection (4) or shall be subject to suit as provided in subsection (5).

The Supreme Court has stated, "[t]he purpose of the legislation . . . was effectively to prohibit . . . all interceptions of oral and wire communications, except those specifically provided for in the Act." *U.S. v. Giordano*, 416 U.S. 505, 514 (1974). No exception to the proscriptions of § 2511(1)(a) is relevant to this case.

Section 2520(a), as amended, further provides in relevant part that "[a]ny person whose wire, oral, or electronic communication is intercepted, disclosed, or intentionally used in violation of this chapter may in a civil action recover from the person or entity which engaged in that violation such relief as may be appropriate."

The remedy clearly applies to any "person," defined as "any individual." See 18 USC 2510(6).

Simpson, although relied upon by the district court, has been widely criticized. *See Pritchard v. Pritchard*, 732 F2d 372, 10 FLR 1387 (CA 4 1984); *U.S. v. Jones*, 542 F2d 661, 3 FLR 2010 (CA 6 1976); *Nations v. Nations*, 670 FSupp 1432, 14 FLR 1009 (DC WArk 1987); *Flynn v. Flynn*, 560 FSupp 922 (DC NOhio 1983); *Heyman v. Heyman*, 548 FSupp 1041, 9 FLR 2011 (DC NIll 1982); *Gill v. Willer*, 482 FSupp 776 (DC WNY 1980); *Kratz v. Kratz*, 477 FSupp 463, 5 FLR 2871 (DC EPa 1979); Blakely, *Interspousal Electronic Surveillance Immunity*, 7 U. Tol. L. Rev. 185 (1975).

As indicated, we find no exceptions in § 2511 that apply to Karl. We note that Congress was aware that electronic surveillance is used in domestic relations, as evidenced by Senator Long's comments at the Hearings on Invasions of Privacy: "the three major areas in which private electronic surveillance was widespread were '(1) industrial, (2) divorce cases, and (3) politics.'" *Kratz*, supra, 477 FSupp at 471.

We agree with the Fourth Circuit's conclusion in *Pritchard v. Pritchard*, supra, 732 F2d at 372:

> Title III prohibits all wiretapping activities unless specifically excepted. There is no express exception for instances of willful, unconsented to electronic surveillance between spouses. Nor is there any indication in the statutory language or in the legislative history that Congress intended to

3-21-89 15 FLR 1235

Current Developments are fully indexed, with new cumulative indexes released every two months. Issues of Current Developments cumulate into yearly volumes, which usually are stored in separate binders with a final index.

The Reference File and Tax Guide is continually kept current by the removal of old and the addition of new pages. It is divided by tabs into five parts. Behind the first tab, Federal Laws, is a comprehensive, codified compilation of federal laws affecting domestic relations. The second section, Uniform and Model Acts, contains the full text of several widely adopted uniform acts, such as the Uniform Child Custody Jurisdiction Act and the Uniform Premarital Agreement Act.

The Tax Guide, the third section in the binder, is written in cooperation with BNA's *Tax Management* and is designed to be a comprehensive guide to tax matters confronting practitioners in domestic relations law. Contents include detailed analyses, planning guides, forms, and legislative materials.

State divorce laws are summarized behind the next tab in the binder, and the final section contains various practice aids, a collection of prototypes available for adaptation by the reader.

Like The Criminal Law Reporter, The Family Law Reporter *takes the format of* U.S. Law Week *and uses it to fully report on a specific area of the law. Every weekly issue reports the latest court decisions and other events affecting family law.*

Like many of the services described later in this book, The Family Law Reporter *also complements its notification coverage with a reference file of textual materials and practice guides.*

S-118
340:061

PREMARITAL PLANNING

PRACTICE GUIDE

Couples entering a marriage should plan for the following:

- Forms of ownership of property acquired before and during marriage: should the property be held separately or in some form of co-ownership?
- The need for life insurance.
- Writing wills.
- Revising beneficiary designations on life insurance policies and company benefit plans.
- Advisability and content of a premarital agreement.

An attorney should help a client understand the primary goals of a premarital agreement: to help prevent future disputes, assure that the couple's property arrangements are understood and agreed to by each, and to provide a mechanism to resolve disputes if they occur. Parties to a valid separation agreement must enter into it freely and voluntarily, with a full understanding of its consequences. To this end, the attorney should avoid joint representation in preparation of the agreement. Trusts are useful for holding transfers made to spouses as part of a premarital agreement.

1. In General

Financial planning is not often a part of a couple's premarital planning, at least where both spouses are entering their first marriages. In some respects, premarital financial planning anticipates the eventual termination of the marital relationship, either by the death of one spouse or by separation. This is because financial planning concentrates on such matters as control of assets, wills, and agreements to avoid disputes over ownership of property.

Brides and bridegrooms are often reluctant to enter a marriage with visions of termination clouding otherwise sunlit futures. However, this reluctance to plan is often overcome if either spouse has been previously married (especially if the previous marriage ended in a bitter divorce), or if either enters the marriage with substantial assets. An attorney might overcome a couple's reluctance to plan by pointing out that decisions regarding money matters are much easier to make when both parties are alive and on friendly terms than at any other time. In addition, not all premarital planning concerns the eventual breakup of the marriage.

Premarital planning should involve looking at the following issues:

(1) Form of ownership of property acquired prior to and during marriage
(2) The advisability of a premarital agreement as well as the contents of that agreement
(3) The need for life insurance or additional life insurance for the primary income earner or, more frequently in this modern world, the lives of both income earners
(4) The advisability of writing wills
(5) Revision of beneficiary designations on life insurance policies, employer benefit programs, and other beneficiary designation questions.

2. Forms Of Ownership Of Property

Spouses may enter a marriage owning property individually. Consideration should be given to whether that property will continue to be held as separate property, or should be held in some form of co-ownership.[1] Some thought might also be given to the form of holding property that will be acquired after the marriage.

3. Insurance

The marital commitment of a couple will likely include the commitment to provide financial security to

[1] See discussion of the legal and tax implications of various forms of ownership of property, pp. 320:041 et seq.

7-19-88

17

The Family Law Reporter also has a reference file: a binder containing material, such as statutes and model acts, with a permanent reference value. The binder is continually kept up-to-date through the removal of dated and the insertion of new looseleaf pages. This is a sample page from the binder's Tax Guide.

S-119
441:001

The FAMILY LAW REPORTER®

SOUTH CAROLINA
Divorce Laws

SOUTH CAROLINA

SUMMARY

References are to Code of Laws of South Carolina, 1976.

Residence: One year (either party); three months (plaintiff) if both parties reside in state. § 20-3-30.

Divorce Grounds: No fault: Upon application of either party after continuously living separate and apart for one year.

Other grounds: Adultery, desertion for one year, physical cruelty, and habitual drunkenness (defined as including that caused by use of a narcotic drug). § 20-3-10.

Alimony: "In every judgment of divorce from the bonds of matrimony the court shall make such orders touching the maintenance, alimony and suit money of either party or any allowance to be made to him or her and, if any, the security to be given as from the circumstances of the parties and the nature of the case may be just. No alimony shall be granted an adulterous spouse. In any award of permanent alimony the court shall have jurisdiction to order periodic payments or payment in lump sum." § 20-3-130.

Property: "During the marriage, a spouse shall acquire, based upon the factors set out in § 20-7-472, a vested special equity and ownership right in the marital property as defined in § 20-7-473, which equity and ownership right [is] subject to apportionment between the spouses by the family courts of this State at the time marital litigation is filed or commenced as provided in § 20-7-472." § 20-7-471.

"In a proceeding for divorce a vinculo matrimonii or separate support and maintenance, or in a proceeding for disposition of property following a prior decree of dissolution of marriage by a court which lacked personal jurisdiction over an absent spouse or which lacked jurisdiction to dispose of the property, and in other marital litigation between the parties, the court shall make a final equitable apportionment between the parties of the parties' marital property upon request by either party in the pleadings.

"In making apportionment, the court must give weight in such proportion as it finds appropriate to all of the following factors": (1) the duration of the marriage; (2) marital misconduct or fault, whether or not used as basis of divorce, that affects or has affected the parties' economic circumstances or contributed to the breakup of the marriage (no evidence of personal shall be considered if it took place after: entry of a pendente lite order, signing of written property or marital settlement agreement, or entry of a permanent order of separate maintenance and support or approving a property or marital settlement agreement between the parties); (3) the value of the marital property, and each spouse's contributions to the acquisition, preservation, depreciation, or appreciation in value of the marital property, including homemaker contributions; (4) the income and earning capacity of each spouse and the opportunity for future acquisition of capital assets; (5) the health of each spouse; (6) the need of each or either spouse for additional training or education to achieve his or

11-8-88

11

Another feature of the reference file is a summary of each state's divorce laws.

ABA/BNA Lawyers' Manual on Professional Conduct

The *ABA/BNA Lawyers' Manual on Professional Conduct* is a practical guide to the broad range of professional and ethical concerns facing lawyers. Combining the reference and notification functions of reporter services, the *Lawyers' Manual* is a particularly useful service for law students, almost all of whom are required to take a legal ethics course during their law school careers.

The service is divided into two parts—the reference "Manual" and the "Current Reports"—each with its own binder.

The Manual binder is designed to provide quick and current guidance on the various ethical and professional problems that regularly crop up in the practice of law. Organized by subject matter, fully indexed, and continually updated, the Manual is the place to start any research into a professional or ethical question.

Current Reports—the service's notification component—is a biweekly summary and review of the latest developments in professional conduct.

This service's reference Manual begins with full text of the ABA Model Rules of Professional Conduct and of the ABA Model Code of Professional Responsibility, as well as descriptions of the important differences between these models and the ethics rules actually in force in the various states.

The bulk of the Manual is devoted to topical examinations of the issues and dilemmas raised both by the ethics codes and by related professional concerns of practicing lawyers. Among the many subjects covered in the Manual are conflicts of interest, the duty of confidentiality, advertising and solicitation, attorney's fees, lawyer malpractice, and professional discipline.

The Manual is divided into tabs, with each tab covering a broad subject such as conflicts of interest. Immediately behind each tab is a table of contents listing the several chapters on more specific topics that make up the contents of the tab.

Each chapter is divided into separate sections. A chapter's Practice Guide gives a brief overview of the topic covered in the chapter and provides the user with a quick answer to the ethical dilemmas at issue. The next section, the Background, provides more detailed information, such as the text of the relevant ethics rules and an analysis, with full case citations, of the state of the law on the topic. The Background is divided by subheads so that the user can go quickly to the specific areas in which he or she is interested. Finally, the Application section shows how courts and ethics committees have applied the law in specific factual situations. Bibliographies also are provided for many topics.

No. 45 51:301

CONFLICTS OF INTEREST

Multiple Representation

PRACTICE GUIDE

A lawyer may represent more than one client in a particular matter only if the lawyer reasonably believes that he or she can adequately represent the interest of each client and all the clients consent to the representation after full disclosure of the implications of the multiple representation.

Client consent notwithstanding, a lawyer may not represent opposing parties in litigation, nor may the lawyer, outside of the litigation context, represent multiple parties to the same transaction whose interests or positions are fundamentally antagonistic. But it is ethically permissible for a lawyer to represent multiple parties whose interests are generally aligned, such as the parties to the formation of a corporation. However, should it become evident during the multiple representation that the lawyer cannot adequately represent the interests of each party, or should any party revoke consent, the lawyer must withdraw and may not thereafter represent one party against another on the same matter.

Multiple representation of criminal codefendants implicates not only the lawyer's ethical obligations but also the defendants' constitutional right to effective assistance of counsel. In multiple-defendant cases, a trial court may not appoint a lawyer to represent more than one of the defendants over the objection of a defendant or of the lawyer, without inquiring into whether the defendants may have conflicting interests.

If no timely objection to multiple representation by appointed or retained counsel is made, a defendant seeking to overturn his conviction on conflict-of-interest grounds must prove that there was an actual conflict of interest that affected his lawyer's performance, but he need not show any further prejudice. A defendant may waive his right to representation by a lawyer who has a conflict of interest, but the waiver must be voluntary and intelligent.

BACKGROUND

Model Rules

Model Rule 1.7 provides:

"(a) A lawyer shall not represent a client if the representation of that client will be directly adverse to another client, unless:

"(1) the lawyer reasonably believes the representation will not adversely affect the relationship with the other client; and

"(2) each client consents after consultation.

"(b) A lawyer shall not represent a client if the representation of that client may be materially limited by the lawyer's responsibilities to another client or

04-15-87 Copyright © 1987 American Bar Association/The Bureau of National Affairs, Inc. 7
0740-4050/87/$0+.50

The *Lawyers' Manual* is divided by tabs into major ethical topics, such as Conflicts of Interest, and then more specifically into chapters, such as Multiple Representation. Each chapter begins with a summary or Practice Guide, which is followed by the Background section's fuller explanation of the problem, with citations to court decisions and the text of the applicable ethics rules.

No. 45 MULTIPLE REPRESENTATION 51:311

Permissible Multiple Representations

Adequate Representation

The Model Code permits a lawyer to represent multiple clients so long as the lawyer believes that he can "adequately" represent each clients' interest and the clients consent after full disclosure. This "adequacy" standard has been criticized because "courts and commentators cannot agree how to define 'adequacy' in individual or even categories of cases." Moore, *Simultaneous Representation of Multiple Clients: A Proposed Solution to the Current Confusion and Controversy,* 61 Tex. L. Rev. 211, 220 (1982). Under the Model Rules, a lawyer may, with consent, represent multiple clients if the lawyer "reasonably believes the representation will not adversely affect the relationship with the other client...."

Client Consent

Counsel has an affirmative duty to disclose to clients any potential conflicts of interest. *Woodruff v. Tomlin,* 616 F2d 924, 936 (CA6 1980); *Klemm v. Superior Court,* 142 CalRptr 509, 514 (CtApp 1977). "Full disclosure requires the attorney to explain to the client in detail the risks and the foreseeable pitfalls that may arise in the course of the transaction so that the client can understand the reasons why it may be desirable for him or her to have independent counsel." *Acheson v. White,* 487 A2d 197, 199 n.5 (Conn 1985). While courts accord great deference to an individual's choice of counsel, there is a paramount public interest "in maintaining the highest standards of professional conduct and the scrupulous administration of justice." *Baglini v. Pulman, Inc.,* 412 FSupp 1060, 1066 (EDPa), *aff'd mem sub nom. Fraboni v. Pullman, Inc.,* 547 F2d 1160 (CA3 1976).

Obviously, a lawyer, even with client consent, would not be able to represent in litigation parties with conflicting interests. *Klemm v. Superior Court,* 142 CalRptr 509, 514 (CtApp 1977). "As a matter of law a purported consent to dual representation of litigants with adverse interests at a contested hearing would be neither intelligent nor informed.... However, if the conflict is merely potential, there being no existing dispute or contest between the parties represented as to any point in litigation, then with full disclosure to and informed consent of both clients there may be dual representation at a hearing or trial." *Id* at 514. *See Greene v. Greene,* 391 NE2d 1355, 418 NYS2d 379, 381 (CtApp 1979) (dual representation is so fraught with potential for irreconcilable conflict, it will rarely be sanctioned even with full disclosure and consent). The Model Code's EC 5-15 takes a similar view: "there would be few situations in which [a lawyer] would be justified in representing in litigation multiple clients with potentially differing interests."

"In contrast," as one commentator has stated, "an inquiry limited to the validity of consent seems more justifiable in the nonlitigation context, in which the risks are fewer." *Developments in the Law — Conflicts of Interest,* 94 Harv. L. Rev. 1244, 1309 (1981). *See also* EC 5-15: "there are many instances in which a lawyer may properly serve multiple clients having potentially differing interests in matters not involving litigation."

APPLICATION

Insurance Cases

Lawyers who are employed by insurance companies to represent insured defendants often are confronted with conflicting obligations that may require disclosure to the insured if not withdrawal from representation of both the insured and the insurer.

In *Rogers v. Robson, Masters, Ryan, Brummond & Belom,* 81 Ill2d 201, 407

04-15-87 Copyright © 1987 American Bar Association/The Bureau of National Affairs, Inc. 17
0740-4050/87/$0+.50

The Application section in each chapter provides real-life examples of how lawyers and courts have dealt with the problem under discussion.

The Manual contains full text of ethics opinions issued by the American Bar Association and digests or synopses of virtually every ethics opinion issued by state and local bar associations all across the country. Ethics opinions, which usually are the product of bar committees made up of lawyers and local experts on legal ethics, answer specific professional and ethical questions put to the committees by practicing lawyers.

The Manual contains two indexes—one for the ethics opinions and one for the rest of the binder.

The biweekly Current Reports provide ongoing coverage of the professional and ethical issues facing lawyers, through reports on recent court decisions, ethics opinions, disciplinary actions, and news events. It is fully indexed and cumulates in yearly volumes.

To research an ethical question in the Lawyers' Manual*:*

▶ *Look up the subject matter in question in the Manual's main Topical Index behind Tab 799, and read the pages to which the index directs you.*

▶ *Or go directly to the relevant chapters by using the Manual's system of tabs and tables of contents.*

▶ *Next, obtain additional information on the question by referring to the Ethics Opinions Index and reading the ethics opinions to which you are directed.*

▶ *Finally, look for even more information in recent Current Reports, using the Current Reports index and/or the topical summaries on the second page of each issue.*

The *Lawyers' Manual* also contains digests of ethics opinions issued by state and local bar associations, as well as the full text of American Bar Association ethics opinions.

No. 68 901:2501

ETHICS OPINIONS

Florida

THE FLORIDA BAR

Opinions are issued by the Professional Ethics Committee of The Florida Bar. Proposed opinions are published in *The Florida Bar News* before they become final. The bar may be contacted at The Florida Bar Center, 650 Apalachee Parkway, Tallahassee, FL 32399-2300, (904) 222-5286.

Opinion 86-1 (4/1/86) **Name of firm.** A law firm may use the term "associates" in its law firm name, provided the employing lawyer is included in the firm name and that lawyer does in fact employ other lawyers to assist him in his practice. The committee withdraws opinions 66-34, 66-34 Supp., 76-10, 76-17, 76-22 and 81-4.

Opinion 86-2 (4/15/86) **Costs and expenses of litigation; Interest.** An attorney may charge a lawful rate of interest on liquidated fees and on advancements of costs, either as provided in advance by written agreement, or in the absence of a written agreement, upon reasonable notice. Sixty days constitutes reasonable notice. Opinion 71-26.

Opinion 86-3 (12/15/86) **Confidentiality; Disclosure.** A lawyer who learns from his client, or through independent investigation during the course of representation, that his client has a criminal record of prior convictions may not disclose this information to the court at a sentencing hearing even though the court is basing its sentence on inaccurate or incomplete information as to the client's criminal record. The lawyer or his client may not affirmatively misrepresent to the court that the client has no prior record. The information acquired by the lawyer during the course of representation concerning his client's criminal record constitutes a confidence or secret, the disclosure of which would be detrimental to the client. The lawyer therefore may not reveal the information unless the client consents. If the lawyer is asked directly by the court as to whether his client has any prior convictions, the lawyer must assert the attorney-client privilege. The lawyer or his client may not falsely assert that the client has no prior record. If the client falsely testifies that he does not have a prior criminal record, the lawyer must request that the client rectify the fraud, and if the client refuses, the lawyer may disclose the fraud. Opinion 75-19; DR 4-101(A)(C)(2), 7-101(A), 7-102(A)(3)(4)(5), 7-102(B); EC 4-4; Canon 7.

Opinion 86-4 (8/1/86) **Letterhead; Business cards; Employees of lawyers.** A law firm may include on its letterhead the names and titles of its nonlawyer employees, specifically paralegals and legal assistants. Further, nonlawyer employees may be issued business cards imprinted with their name, title and firm name, address and telephone number. The nonlawyer's title indicating nonlawyer status must appear beneath his name on both the cards and the letterhead. Opinions 71-39, 71-43, 77-14; DRs 2-102, 3-104(E); Rule 4-7.5; EC 3-6.

Opinion 86-5 (8/1/86) **Conflicts of interest; Confidentiality; Employees of lawyers.** A lawyer or law firm whose nonlawyer employee has accepted a position with an opposing lawyer or law firm must admonish the employee that he has an ethical and moral obligation not to reveal to the hiring lawyer or firm any client confidences and secrets acquired during the employment. Similarly, the hiring lawyer or law firm must not request or permit the employee's disclosure

9-28-88 45

0740-4050/88/$0+50

ABA/BNA LAWYERS' MANUAL ON PROFESSIONAL CONDUCT

Vol. 5 No. 2 February 15, 1989

CURRENT REPORTS

RULE ON "SPECIALIST" CLAIMS PASSES CONSTITUTIONAL MUSTER

A lawyer who noted on his letterhead that he is "certified" as a "civil trial specialist" by a well known private organization is censured by the Illinois Supreme Court. The state's disciplinary rule that prohibits claims of specialization by most lawyers (everyone but admiralty, patent, and trademark attorneys) is constitutional, the court concludes. Such claims constitute misleading advertising, which may be banned entirely, the court says. (Page 19)

DATING OPPONENT'S EMPLOYEE DOESN'T DISQUALIFY LAWYER

A lawyer who had social contacts with a secretary in an opponent's law firm acted unprofessionally, but his poor judgment does not require his disqualification from the underlying case, the California Court of Appeal, First District, rules. Absent some evidence that confidential information was likely disclosed, the court finds disqualification unwarranted. Nevertheless, further discovery in the case is permitted so that issues regarding the nature of the relationship and the matters discussed may be developed. (Page 20)

CLIENT'S SUICIDE IS NOT BASIS FOR LEGAL MALPRACTICE LAWSUIT

The family of a man who jumped to his death through a courtroom window after hearing the jury pronounce him guilty of rape cannot win a malpractice suit against the deceased's lawyer, the Pennsylvania Superior Court decides in a case of first impression in that state. Whether or not the lawyer botched the client's defense, the court explains, his client's suicide was unforeseeable and thus not proximately caused by the lawyer's conduct. (Page 23)

ABA AMENDS RULE 7.3 AT ITS MIDYEAR MEETING

The ABA House of Delegates, gathering in Denver for the association's midyear meeting, drops the prohibition against targeted direct mail advertising from the ABA Model Rules, but adds provisions regulating its use. Recorded contacts with prospective clients also are specifically permitted subject to regulation. The midyear meeting included sessions on professional stress and lawyer discipline. (Page 31)

TRIAL COURTS MUST MONITOR MULTIPLE REPRESENTATION CASES

Although it finds no deprivation of constitutional rights as a result of one lawyer's acting both as lead counsel for a criminal defendant and as local counsel for a codefendant, the U.S. Court of Appeals for the First Circuit nevertheless advises federal district courts to avoid such situations in the future. Multiple representation is rife with the potential for conflicts of interest, the court observes, and in the ordinary case a defendant's right to counsel of choice is outweighed by the need to uphold ethical standards and maintain the fairness of trials. (Page 21)

IN THE MANUAL

Supplement No. 74, which is being mailed with this issue, contains a new chapter entitled "Avoiding Malpractice." The chapter identifies the most common reasons lawyers are sued for malpractice and provides guidance on how to avoid these pitfalls. The supplement also contains a bibliography on legal malpractice.

0740-4050/89/$0+50

The biweekly Current Reports notify readers of recent developments in the field. Supplements to the looseleaf Manual are mailed with the Current Reports and keep the Manual up-to-date.

BNA Civil Trial Manual

The litigation process, from initial client interview through trial, is the subject of the *BNA Civil Trial Manual*—a reporter service that should particularly interest law students in clinical programs and those considering careers in civil litigation. With a two-binder reference-and-notification format virtually identical to that of the *ABA/BNA Lawyers' Manual on Professional Conduct*, the *BNA Civil Trial Manual* joins another similar service, the *BNA Criminal Practice Manual*, in making up the *BNA Trial Practice Series*.

Written and continually updated by experienced litigators, the publication's reference "Manual" is divided into 11 major subject areas, each detailing legal guidelines, strategies, tactics, and litigation techniques. Practical aids such as sample forms, question-and-answer approaches, and checklists also are included.

The biweekly notification part of the service – the *Civil Litigation Reporter* – provides timely notification of decisions on civil procedure and evidence, recent verdicts and settlements in civil litigation, and new procedures and practice techniques.

This service is designed both to acquaint the novice litigator with every step in the litigation process and to provide experienced trial lawyers with a quick reference to emerging and innovative techniques and strategies.

The Manual binder divides the litigation process, by tabs, into its major chronological parts, from investigation to jury deliberations and verdict, and everything in between, including discovery, motions, negotiation and settlement, trial preparation, exhibits, and examination of witnesses.

Each tab is further divided into chapters that describe in detail specific subject areas. For example, the Negotiation and Settlement tab contains chapters on a variety of subjects, from the basic ones essential to an understanding of the general area, such as valuating the case, negotiation strategies and techniques, and settlement agreements and releases, to the more innovative and esoteric subjects of Mary Carter agreements, structured settlements, partial settlements, and summary jury trials.

A chapter begins with an Overview of the subject covered in the chapter. The Overview outlines the scope of the chapter and the major areas of concern. The lengthier Commentary section that follows provides more detailed analysis of the topic, with citations to court decisions, statutes, and rules. After the legal framework has been established, strategic options usually are explored. Most chapters also contain a Practice Aid, such as a sample form or motion or testimony excerpted from an actual trial, that helps explain the application of the law discussed in the rest of the chapter. Chapters end with bibliographies listing annotations, treatises, and law review articles that also cover the topic.

No. 51 51:641

NEGOTIATION AND SETTLEMENT

Mary Carter Agreements

OVERVIEW

Never very popular, Mary Carter contracts are perhaps one of most mysterious forms of settlement. Concealed from nonsettling parties and masking the true interests of settling parties, the secret Mary Carter agreement easily confounds trial participants not privy to her terms. The jury puzzles over why a particular defendant seems so helpful to the plaintiff, while counsel for nonsettling parties finds himself snared between the collusive tactics of agreeing parties.

Nevertheless, such agreements were popularized by the decision in *Booth v. Mary Carter Paint Co.*, 202 So2d 8 (Fla App 1967). They enjoyed a slight surge in popularity in the 1970's, despite their prohibition on public policy grounds in a few states. California, however, recently breathed new life into its version of Mary Carter settlements by refusing to find such an agreement a "bad faith" settlement where the settlement amount falls within the reasonable range of the settling defendant's proportional share of comparative liability.

On balance, it looks as though Mary Carter agreements are here to stay, even if in a somewhat diluted form.

This chapter examines the Mary Carter settlement as it would evolve in a typical case. First, it briefly reviews the familiar debate on the pros and cons of a Mary Carter contract. The discussion then turns to the drafting process, exploring the many options that counsel has in writing a Mary Carter agreement, and examining some of extra-contractual factors that counsel must consider, such as the effect of contribution rules and, of course, any ethical strictures surrounding the settlement.

Next, the chapter looks at the Mary Carter settlement in the trial phases of cases. Discovery issues, problems of admissibility, and alternative approaches to conducting a case are some of the topics discussed.

The Practice Aids section includes three distinct Mary Carter agreements and two sample memorandums challenging a proposed Mary Carter-like settlement.

COMMENTARY

Preliminary Considerations

What makes Mary Carter agreements so attractive? For plaintiffs, the agreement offers several advantages over traditional settlement devices. First, a Mary Carter settlement ensures a minimum recovery without, in most cases, reducing the potential liability of nonsettling defendants. Mary Carter agreements also increase the chances of a significant verdict against nonsettling defendants, freeing plaintiffs from the burden of litigat-

2-10-88

0-87179-486-1/88/$0+.50

Each chapter in the *BNA Civil Trial Manual* begins with an Overview outlining the scope of the chapter and the major areas of concern. The Commentary section, which follows, explains the subject in greater detail, with full case, rule, and statutory citations.

No. 51 MARY CARTER AGREEMENTS 51:657

570 P2d 782 (Ariz App 1977). See also Bodine, *The Case Against Guaranteed Verdict Agreements*, 29 Def LJ 233, 246 (1980) (characterizing Arizona approach as one that assigns trial judges "monitor duty" over attorneys' conduct).

The Future of Mary Carter

To date, only three states have expressly disapproved of Mary Carter agreements or similar guaranteed verdict devices. *Schick v. Rodenburg*, 397 NW2d 464 (SD 1986) (Pierringer agreement); *Lum v. Stinnet*, 488 P2d 354 (Okla 1978) (Mary Carter agreement); *Trampe v. Wisconsin Telephone Co.*, 252 NW 675 (Wis 1934) (Mary Carter-type agreement). Yet condemnation is widespread and severe. See, e.g., *Scurlock Oil Co. v. Smithwick*, 724 SW2d 1, 8 (Tex 1986) (Spears, J., concurring) ("I am ready to hold Mary Carter agreements void as against public policy.").

Recently, however, the California Supreme Court gave its seal of approval to sliding scale agreements (the California equivalent of a Mary Carter contract) in *Abbott Ford, Inc. v. Superior Court of Los Angeles County*, 3 BNA CivTrMan 388 (Cal Sup Ct 9/3/87). The most significant aspect of *Abbott Ford* is the California court's treatment of the guaranteed recovery clause. The nonsettling defendants argued that such clauses turn sliding scale agreements into "bad faith" transactions because sliding scale agreements, by their nature, conflict with the twin statutory goals of apportioning loss fairly and encouraging settlements.

As to apportioning loss, the nonsettling defendants observed that should plaintiffs recover more than the guaranteed amount, the settling defendant — the party who, by all appearances, is the most culpable tortfeasor — escapes any ultimate out-of-pocket expenses.

The court acknowledged that while this scenario seems "difficult to reconcile" with the fair apportionment objective, "[i]f a court finds that a settling defendant ... has realistically paid a consideration' that is within [the] ballpark and if the nonsettling defendants obtain a reduction in the plaintiff's claims against them in an amount equal to that consideration, the statutory fair apportionment objective should be satisfied."

The court then examined the practical problem of how the agreement should be valued. Actuarial or other methods should be avoided; instead, a joint valuation by the plaintiff and settling defendant should govern.

Accordingly, once the parties to the agreement have declared its value, the nonsettling defendant can either (1) accept that value and attempt to show that the settlement is not in good faith because the assigned value is not within the reasonable range of the settling tortfeasor's proportional share of liability, or (2) prove that the assigned value is too low and therefore warrants a greater reduction in plaintiff's claims against the nonsettling defendants.

This precedent-setting procedure may well determine the future of Mary Carter in California and other jurisdictions.

PRACTICE AID

Typical Mary Carter Agreement

The Mary Carter agreement contained in the following letter incorporates typical provisions for this kind of settlement. It is executed between the plaintiff and the settling defendant directly, it places a ceiling on the settling defendant's liability, and it requires the plaintiff to wait until the conclusion of trial before receiving any funds. This particular agreement was used in General Motors Corp. v. Lahocki, 410 A2d 1039 (MdCtApp 1980). It was in the form of a letter from counsel for Contee [the

2-10-88

0-87179-486-1/88/$0+.50

Practice Aids provide sample motions, Q & A examinations, checklists, letters, and agreements.

The Manual binder also contains full text of the Federal Rules of Civil Procedure and its Appendix of Forms, of the Federal Rules of Evidence, and of the Federal Multidistrict Litigation Rules.

Because of its looseleaf format, the Manual can be updated whenever necessary, with outdated pages discarded and replaced with new pages reflecting changes in the law. The binder is fully indexed to aid users in finding the subjects they want. Users also can turn directly to a subject by using the tabs and the table of contents that follows each tab.

The Manual's companion binder houses the biweekly *Civil Litigation Reporter*, which keeps subscribers abreast of recent developments affecting civil litigation. These reports summarize court decisions, analyze recent verdicts and settlements, provide notification of news events, and contain analysis and perspective pieces. Fully indexed, these reports should also be referred to whenever research is being done in *BNA Civil Trial Manual.*

This service puts civil procedure into practice, taking the litigator through every step in the process. The tabbed sections in the reference or practice manual cover:

- *Investigation and Pleadings*
- *Discovery and Motions*
- *Negotiation and Settlement*
- *Trial Preparation*
- *Jury Selection and Arguments*
- *Exhibits and Witnesses*
- *Verdict*

TRIAL PRACTICE SERIES

BNA CIVIL TRIAL MANUAL

Vol. 8 No. 19 Current Reports October 14, 1992

CIVIL LITIGATION REPORTER

AMENDMENTS TO FED.R.CIV.P. ARE APPROVED BY CONFERENCE

The U.S. Judicial Conference approves amendments to 30 Federal Rules of Civil Procedure and three Federal Rules of Evidence. Most notable among the proposed changes are an amendment making sanctions under Fed.R.Civ.P. 11 discretionary and a rewrite of Fed.R.Civ.P. 26 requiring parties to disclose certain key information prior to formal discovery. Next, the proposed amendments will be sent to the U.S. Supreme Court, which must forward any amendments it approves to Congress by May 1, 1993. The amendments that survive both court and congressional review go into effect Dec. 1, 1993.

Descriptions of all the proposed amendments begin on page 431.

COURTS DEFINE PARAMETERS OF PATIENT-DUMPING SUITS

The federal Emergency Medical Treatment and Active Labor Act has engendered a discrete body of lawsuits since its enactment in 1986. Under the act's enforcement provisions, people in need of emergency medical care who are "dumped"—i.e., refused treatment because of their inability to pay—may sue the offending hospital for civil damages. Some of the issues that have arisen in these cases—including whether a state's cap on medical malpractice damages applies—are examined in this issue's Analysis section. (Page 437)

In one such lawsuit, a federal jury awards $5 million to a woman for whom a local hospital failed to provide a screening test when she went to the emergency room. The district judge held that damages were not limited by Virginia's cap on medical malpractice damages. The attorneys on both sides agree that EMTALA is not a federal medical malpractice act. (Page 430)

FTCA MALPRACTICE CLAIM SUBJECT TO STATE CAP

When the United States is sued under the Federal Tort Claims Act for medical malpractice in Nebraska, it enjoys the protection of the state's $1 million cap on medical malpractice awards for qualified private health care providers, the U.S. Court of Appeals for the Eighth Circuit rules. This is so despite the fact that the federal government has failed to comply with the Nebraska statute's eligibility requirements for participating private health care providers. (Page 426)

CA 5 VACATES PENDENT CLAIMS AFTER FEDERAL CLAIM DISMISSED

Federal courts must assess factors of economy, convenience, fairness, and comity in their justification for retaining pendent jurisdiction over state claims, the U.S. Court of Appeals for the Fifth Circuit holds. The court vacates a jury's award of $185 million and finds that the district court abused its discretion in retaining jurisdiction over state claims after it dismissed the plaintiff's only federal claim. (Page 420)

NO AUTOMATIC DISCOVERY FOR SURVEILLANCE MATERIALS

The Missouri Court of Appeals holds that post-accident surveillance evidence is not subject to discovery under a state discovery rule that requires the production of statements made by the parties. The appeals court reverses a lower court's holding that the evidence was automatically discoverable, but leaves open the possibility that the plaintiffs may acquire the surveillance evidence if they can show a substantial need for the materials and that they are unable, without undue hardship, to obtain the substantial equivalent of the materials by other means. (Page 425)

0-87179-486-1/92/$0+.50

The biweekly *Civil Litigation Reporter*, the notification partner of the *BNA Civil Trial Manual*, keeps the reader informed about major cases, trials, and legislation involving procedural and evidentiary issues.

The final article in most issues of the *Civil Litigation Reporter* is a Perspective, Analysis, Practice Guide, or Technique providing an in-depth discussion of an evidentiary or procedural issue.

BNA Civil Trial Manual 69

PERSPECTIVE

"ULTIMATE SANCTION" CASES RAISE TROUBLING R. 11 ISSUES

It's finally happened. A district court judge, citing Rule 11, has imposed a whopping $1,034,381.36 sanction on a small, public interest law firm. The sanction is nearly four times the net assets of the firm, threatening to throw its lawyers out on the streets and leave clients scrambling to find substitute counsel (*Avirgan v. Hull*, USDC SFla, 86-1146-CIV-King, King, CJ, 2/2/89).

While *Avirgan* itself is a fascinating case, the sanctions order is especially significant when compared to a similar Rule 11 ruling handed down the next day by U.S. District Judge Robert L. Carter in the Southern District of New York. Judge Carter pondered the fate of a sole practitioner facing a substantial sanctions request that the court conceded would effectively end counsel's practice. Rather than slam the lawyer for the full amount, Judge Carter assessed only $102,000 in costs against counsel, but not the documented attorney's fees of $616,000, and, in an unusual move, allocated a prior sanctions settlement of $45,000 with co-counsel as a set-off against the non-settling sole practitioner (*Humphrey v. Columbia Records*, USDC SNY, No. 86 Civ 6667 (RLC), Carter, J., 2/3/89).

Of course, observers have long predicted the day when Rule 11 would effectively kill a law practice. But what they didn't expect was a pair of rulings representing such disparate exercises of judicial discretion that it raises serious questions most lawyers simply haven't thought about yet. Is there a sliding scale standard of professionalism that becomes increasingly restrictive of counsel's conduct as his caseload draws him closer into the public eye? Do public interest lawyers have a greater duty to investigate their cases than sole practitioners? No cases to date appear to address these issues, and the orders discussed below are likewise silent on these points.

Moreover, the leniency of *Humphrey* can be construed as making an "exception" for inexperienced or impecunious counsel that in turn fosters irresponsible lawyering. On the other hand, the harshness of *Avirgan* penalizes lawyers who pass up lucrative positions for low-paying public interest work, and introduces an economic disincentive to file suit based on a lawyer's own interest in avoiding sanctions. This disincentive raises an implicit conflict of interest at the start of an attorney-client relationship, and arguably impedes citizens' access to the courts.

What prompted these two federal judges to reach such divergent conclusions? Is one conclusion, or both, an aberration—or a sign of things to come?

Background

The events behind both suits can be summarized quickly.

Janice Noble is a sole practitioner in New York. Her client, characterized by the court as a "nineteen-year-old youngster," claimed that he had written the music and lyrics appearing on a CBS album called "Radio." The client claimed that he was L.L. Cool J., the purported artist on the album, that the L.L. Cool J. promoted by defendants was James Todd Smith, a grammar school classmate, and that he (the client) wrote the lyrics and made the recording in Smith's basement, which CBS later reproduced as the "Radio" album.

Noble, who conceded inexperience, secured co-counsel familiar with copyright litigation. But co-counsel never took charge, and served instead as a "resource for assistance and advice."

From its inception, the case was marked, in the court's words, "by an astonishing amount of vitriol and vituperation, barely kept in check in the court's presence." Judge Carter ultimately dismissed the action, calling it "outrageous" and "unwarranted." In subsequent sanctions litigation, Noble's co-counsel agreed to pay the defense $30,000 immediately and another $15,000 over time. Noble refused to settle. Defendants then sought more than $800,000 in costs and fees from Noble.

Judge Carter called it a "very difficult case, not because sanctions are not clearly warranted, but because plaintiff's counsel is, I believe, a lone practitioner and even if an award includes plaintiff, the burden will be Noble's because plaintiff is virtually judgment proof. Moreover, a sizable monetary award against plaintiff's counsel could

0-87179-486-1/89/$0+.50

BNA Criminal Practice Manual

The *BNA Criminal Practice Manual* does for the criminal justice system what the *BNA Civil Trial Manual* does for the civil litigation process: it takes the user step by step through the intricacies of the criminal justice process from arrest through sentencing, and it provides practical information and strategic advice for both the new and the experienced practitioner of criminal law.

The service follows the format of the *BNA Trial Practice Series*. The "Manual" binder is a continually updated, looseleaf reference tool on all aspects of criminal practice, while the biweekly "Current Reports" notify criminal lawyers of recent events, tactics, and strategies affecting their practice.

Together the two components of this service serve as a ready source of information on both the basic aspects of a criminal law practice, such as motions and defenses, and the newer innovative techniques being devised by the best criminal lawyers in the country. As such, the publication can be used both by experienced trial lawyers and by law students in clinical programs.

This service's Manual is a compendium of practical information and strategic insights on every aspect of a criminal case. Filled with looseleaf pages that can be removed individually and updated whenever necessary, the binder takes the user from the early stages of every criminal case—the initial contact with the client and the first court appearance—through motions and on to a case's possible resolutions of plea bargaining, trial, and sentencing.

Each tabbed division of the Manual binder covers a distinct area of criminal practice and is itself divided into several chapters, each covering a more specific topic. For example, the Motions tab contains individual chapters on the various motions that might be filed during a criminal case, including those seeking the suppression of physical evidence, confessions, and identification testimony and those involving speedy trial rights, joinder and severance, venue changes, and the recusal of judges.

Chapters, in turn, are divided into distinct sections to make their use easier. The Overview leads into the topic covered in the chapter and highlights the critical concerns. The Commentary, the core of the chapter, analyzes the subject in detail, with full citations to the leading authorities, including court decisions, rules, and other sources. The Bibliography, which ends each chapter, pulls together other resources for further research and reading.

Many chapters also contain a Practice Aid, representing a real-world application of the legal principles discussed in the chapter. For instance, in the chapter entitled "Evidence of Other Crimes" behind the Evidence tab, there is a sample motion to suppress other crimes evidence and a sample legal memorandum in support of the motion.

No. 29 51:1501

MOTIONS
SUPPRESSION OF EVIDENCE

Roadblocks

OVERVIEW

Local governments are resorting with increasing frequency to the use of roadblocks to detect and arrest motorists who are operating vehicles while under the influence of alcohol. These checkpoints have permitted officials to respond energetically to the public outcry over the death, injuries, and destruction of property on the highways caused by drunk drivers. However, perhaps inevitably, the roadblocks have spawned a number of constitutional challenges.

Traditionally, the effectiveness of the roadblock has been a substantial factor in upholding its constitutionality. Courts have sanctioned checkpoints designed to cope with extraordinary situations that demand an intrusive stop to satisfy compelling state interests. For example, officials have been permitted to erect traffic stops to apprehend fleeing felons and to prevent the interstate transportation of the Mediterranean fruit fly. Similarly, the police may set up a vehicle checkpoint at the border in order to screen aliens who are seeking to enter the country illegally. The underlying theme in these cases is that the checkpoints are justified because of the significance of the state's interest and the fact that the only reasonable way for the state to accomplish its goals is to establish a roadblock. But the effectiveness of a sobriety checkpoint, as opposed to other methods of detecting drunk drivers, has been questioned by some courts.

Moreover, roadblocks are suspect if they give the police too much discretion in determining whom to stop and when to detain. In *Delaware v. Prouse*, 440 US 648 (1979), the Supreme Court held unconstitutional the common police practice of randomly stopping vehicles to check the driver's license and registration. In a postscript to the opinion, however, the Court suggested that systematic stops of *all* oncoming traffic at roadblocks might not run afoul of the Constitution. The stops in *Prouse* were deemed objectionable because policemen were allowed too much discretion in determining *which* motorists were detained.

The majority of courts say that a sobriety roadblock can pass constitutional muster so long as it is conducted "properly." A drunk driving roadblock will likely be deemed "proper" if:

(1) The site, duration, time of operation, and guidelines for questioning motorists are determined in advance by administrative law enforcement authorities, not by the officers at the roadblock;

4-89 5
0-87179-912-X/89/$0+.50

The Overview explains the scope of a *BNA Criminal Practice Manual* chapter and summarizes the current state of the law and practice on the topic. It is followed by a Commentary section that spells out in more detail the law and the procedural considerations.

This typical Practice Aid begins with a checklist of factors to consider in filing a motion to suppress and concludes with a sample suppression motion.

51:1514 MOTIONS No. 29

sobriety checkpoints do not comport with Art. I §9 of the state constitution inasmuch as there is no specific legislative authorization for them. The broad authority that state law gives the police to enforce the criminal laws does not permit police to conduct drunk driving roadblocks, according to the plurality. Because such a stop involves a seizure of the person and his effects, the authority to conduct it cannot be implied. The fact that the roadblock in issue was conducted in accordance with a state police manual setting out procedures did not validate the stop.

The *Nelson* plurality also indicated that properly designed drunk driving roadblocks may be permissible as "administrative" searches. But only if a roadblock is intended merely to facilitate non-criminal sanctions, and sufficiently limits the officers' discretion, can it be upheld as a lawful administrative search, according to the majority.

In *Ingersoll v. Palmer*, 743 P2d 1299 (Cal 1987), petitioners, California taxpayers seeking to prohibit the operation of sobriety checkpoints in the state, mounted a three-point argument that such roadblocks are impermissible in the absence of specific authorizing legislation. They failed on all three.

First, they argued that the police may not enforce traffic laws in any manner not authorized by statute. The court concluded, however, that the requisite authority is implicit in law enforcement's statutory authority to enforce criminal laws generally or traffic laws specifically.

Second, they contended that the Vehicle Code provides for uniform statewide rules governing vehicle use and police regulation of it, so that to allow municipalities to set up roadblocks on an ad hoc basis would allow a balkanization of vehicle use regulation not intended by the legislature. While the Vehicle Code generally preempts the field of traffic regulation vis-a-vis local ordinances and thus might prevent municipalities from establishing permanent drunk driving roadblocks, the court said, it would not affect the authority of the highway patrol and local police to enforce the code with checkpoints at temporary locations.

Finally, they argued that since the Vehicle Code specifically permits roadblocks in certain circumstances, roadblocks in other circumstances are impermissible, an argument the court found untenable. "Indeed, it may be more reasonable to assume the Legislature would not feel obliged to enact specific legislation authorizing conduct it deemed to be constitutional and appropriate within the scope of existing police power." 743 P2d at 1318.

PRACTICE AID

Sobriety Roadblock Checklist

(1) *Degree of supervisory control.* Who selects the checkpoint site? What criteria were used when choosing the location? Who decides the time and duration of the roadblock? Are the standards set by superior officers? County officials? Magistrates (warrant)? Who decides what questions may be posed and how long the motorists may be detained? Is there a standardized set of procedures? Were any supervisors present at the roadblock in order to insure compliance with the procedures? Were written records kept? E.g.: (a) the number of cars passing through the checkpoint; (b) the number of cars actually stopped; (c) the number of cars further detained; (d) the number of arrests?

(2) *Degree of fear and anxiety.* What does the checkpoint look like to the approaching motorist? Was there any advance warning to the motorist as he approached the checkpoint? Did the roadblock appear "official?" For example, was it apparent that

4-89 BNA Criminal Practice Manual 18
0-87179-912-X/89/$0+.50

A separate Appendix binder contains full text of a large number of federal provisions affecting the practice of criminal law: the major amendments to the U.S. Constitution, the Federal Rules of Criminal Procedure and of Evidence, and a variety of selected federal statutes both defining crimes and establishing procedures.

The Manual is fully indexed to ease research. Users can also go directly to a topic by using the Manual's system of tabs and tables of contents, which introduce each tabbed section.

The service's biweekly Current Reports are housed in a separate binder and cumulate into annual volumes, which also are indexed. These reports cover recent news events and innovative strategies and techniques that affect criminal law practices. There are reports on recent trials, pleas, and sentencing proceedings, with information gleaned from interviews with the various participants and often including key portions of the proceedings, e.g., jury instructions, motions, sentencing memorandums. Various continuing legal education programs and the meetings of organizations such as the National Association of Criminal Defense Lawyers are covered. A Practice Aids section delves into the purely practical: defenses, motions, jury instructions, and scientific evidence, for example. In the Court Developments section, court decisions are analyzed and synthesized with the focus on their practical implications.

This service's Manual binder contains practical guidance on every phase of a criminal case. The various tabbed sections take the user through the criminal process from arraignment to sentencing.

Chapters covering specific topics in the Manual typically consist of:

- *Overview*
- *Commentary*
- *Practice Aid*
- *Bibliography*

By emphasizing the practical and strategic aspects of a criminal law practice, these Current Reports complement not only this service's Manual but also The Criminal Law Reporter, *which takes a more case-reporter type of approach to the subject.*

TRIAL PRACTICE SERIES

BNA CRIMINAL PRACTICE MANUAL

Vol. 3 No. 2 January 25, 1989

CURRENT REPORTS

PROSECUTORS SANCTIONED FOR DISCOVERY GLITCHES

A federal judge in California imposed personal sanctions on two prosecutors who failed to abide by a court order guiding discovery in a drug prosecution involving eight defendants. Once the trial is over, the prosecutors will have to perform community service work set up and supervised by the probation department. A spokeswoman for the United States Attorneys office involved said the failure to comply resulted from the prosecutors' heavy caseload. (Page 27)

SUPREME COURT GIVES NOD TO SENTENCING GUIDELINES

Players in the federal criminal justice system need wonder no longer whether the sentencing guidelines will withstand United States Supreme Court scrutiny. The Court ruled that the guidelines violate neither the nondelegation clause nor the separation of powers doctrine. Justice Scalia was the lone dissenter, arguing that the Sentencing Reform Act, which established the Sentencing Commission and gave it the task of drafting the guidelines, wantonly created a junior-varsity Congress. (Page 36)

WILL *YOUNGBLOOD* DECISION CAUSE FORENSIC TOMFOOLERY?

The United States Supreme Court's decision in *Arizona v. Youngblood* that police failure to preserve evidence does not result in a violation of due process unless the defendant can prove bad faith prompted cries of dismay in defense circles. At the same time, there are predictions that as forensic art evolves, forensic procedures requiring retention of potentially exculpatory evidence will improve. One defense attorney urges the passage of national uniform standards for forensic laboratories. (Page 38)

DNA FINGERPRINTING: PROBED BY N.Y. JUDGE; WINS PARDON IN VA.

Last fall a Queens County (N.Y.) trial judge held an extensive *Frye* hearing on the admissibility of DNA fingerprinting in a rape/burglary trial and ruled the evidence admissible. In a written opinion just released, he explains the evidence with which he was presented and how it withstood the *Frye* test, and provides his judicial brethren with an outline of factors which should be considered. (Page 44)

In Virginia, a defendant who had pled guilty in a 1984 rape/murder case, opting for a life sentence rather than risking a capital conviction, was pardoned by the governor on the strength of new evidence, including DNA fingerprinting, linking another man to the crime. (Pages 31)

PANELISTS ADVISE ON MOTIONS, TRIAL TACTICS IN COMPLEX CASES

Motions practice in complex criminal cases involves a virtually limitless array of possibilities, ranging from a motion raising esoterica such such duplicity and multiplicity to a motion to dismiss based on prosecutorial misconduct, which may amount to a declaration of war against the government. Even motions that don't "win" in the sense of actually yielding the remedy sought, e.g., dismissal, may have side benefits such as sensitizing the judge to the dynamics of the case, yielding discovery material, and pre-trying the case to some extent. A motions checklist and advice from panelists at a recent seminar on complex criminal cases are contained in the Practice Aids section. (Page 32)

Another panel at the program, sponsored by the Georgetown University Law Center CLE Division, advocated the use of jury consultants and offered tips on deciding whether the client takes the stand at trial. (Page 28)

0889-9312/89/$0+.50

The front page of each biweekly Current Reports for the *BNA Criminal Practice Manual* highlights the most significant reports in the rest of the issue.

fingerprinting evidence in Virginia should be handed down within four to six months.

News Briefs

Bush Designates Drug Czar. William Bennett, former secretary of education, was designated Jan. 12 by [then] President-elect Bush to head the Office of National Drug Control Policy, created by Congress as part of the 1988 Anti-Drug Abuse Act. Bush said Bennett's job will be to "develop a national strategy against drug trafficking and drug abuse." Bush also said he is "grappling with" the question of how to fund fund the war on drugs under his flexible budget freeze plan, warning that given the current budget crunch there may be no additional funding available for drug interdiction and drug abuse programs.

Judge Sentences Man to Prison in Mercy Killing. A retired Washington attorney was sentenced Jan. 5 to a year and a day for killing his severely-disabled wife. Although Walter L. Jones was charged with first degree murder, the jury found him guilty of a lesser included offense: second degree manslaughter. *State v. Jones*, Spokane Cty (Wash) SuperCt, No. 88-1-00622, Merryman, J., 1/5/89. See 2 BNA CrimPracMan 603.

Under Washington's sentencing guidelines, Jones faced a sentence of between 12 and 14 months. Jones' attorney, Richard L. Cease, Chief Public Defender in Spokane, told BNA that he argued for an exceptional sentence, analogizing Jones' diminished capacity defense to two of his previous cases which involved the battered woman defense and which resulted in exceptional sentences. However, the judge rejected both Cease's analogy and a presentence investigation report recommendation that community service be imposed instead of jail time.

Jones will receive credit for time served (56 days), and could be granted good time at the rate of one day for every three days served. Cease said that he could not "see hauling a 66-year-old gentleman across the state" to prison, and told BNA that the local paper had condemned the judge's sentence in an editorial, concluding that it did not constitute justice. Cease said he doubts that his client will appeal.

PRACTICE AIDS

GOING THROUGH THE MOTIONS FOR COMPLEX CRIMINAL CASES

In defending a complex criminal case, do you throw every motion in the book at the government? Or does the extended give-and-take with the prosecutor during the early phases of the case—greater than is typical with the average drug case—obviate the need for a flood of motions?

Aubrey B. Harwell Jr., of Neal & Harwell, Nashville, co-chair and panelist at a recent program on complex criminal cases sponsored by the Continuing Legal Education Division of the Georgetown University Law Center, said he applies the "basic theory that you don't waive anything in a criminal case, regardless of whether you feel confident with your knowledge of the facts."

Paul Perito, of Laxalt, Washington, Perito & Dubuc, Washington, taking a position he termed "parallel" to Harwell's, added that "implicit" in that position is the fact that "you are now in front of a new forum [and you have to] educate the district court judge."

"Don't be scattergun" in filing motions, Perito advised. "Be specific." He likened motions practice to "laying out a game plan for how the case is going to be tried."

That game plan must take into account the question "Is there life after *Mechanik*?" In *U.S. v. Mechanik*, 475 US 66 (1986), Justice Rehnquist, writing for the majority, essentially concluded that any potential undue influence that a breach of Rule 6(d) may have had on the grand jury's decision to indict was "cured" or rendered harmless by the petit jury's verdict. The Court applied a Rule 52(a) analysis to "errors, defects, irregularities or variances" occurring before the grand jury.

In *Bank of Nova Scotia v. U.S.*, 108 SCt 2369 (1988), the Court found that dismissal of an indictment is appropriate in a case alleging prosecutorial misconduct before the

0889-9312/89/$0+.50

Inside the Current Reports are articles on strategies and techniques being used in current criminal cases. This Practice Aid from one Current Reports offers the advice of experienced practitioners on using motions in complex criminal cases.

Toxics Law Reporter

The *Toxics Law Reporter* is one of two similar BNA services that weekly notify subscribers of developments in specific areas of tort litigation. This service covers toxic tort, hazardous waste, and related insurance litigation. The other service, *Product Safety & Liability Reporter*, covers product liability lawsuits and relevant regulatory developments.

The *Toxics Law Reporter* is designed to keep lawyers informed about the latest developments affecting toxic tort, hazardous waste, and related insurance litigation. It reports on pending litigation, court decisions, verdicts and settlements, and other news events. Another regular feature is the Analysis and Perspective section, which features analytical articles by expert practitioners on strategies, tactics, and techniques used in litigating toxic tort and hazardous waste cases.

The weekly issues are housed in a three-ring binder and are regularly indexed by the topical-word approach. The issues cumulate into yearly volumes (June-May) with a final topical index and table of cases.

The latest legal developments in the field of toxic tort, hazardous waste, and related insurance litigation are reported each week in BNA's *Toxics Law Reporter*. The service summarizes recent court decisions and reports on developments in pending litigation, verdicts, and settlements. Analytical pieces by lawyers and other experts practicing in the field are another regular feature of the service, offering readers insights into important current issues and trends.

Each self-contained weekly issue is divided into a number of sections. The front, Highlights page summarizes the week's most important developments, while the second, Topical Summary page summarizes the issue's entire contents.

Each issue is then divided into two main sections, covering Toxic Torts and Hazardous Waste Law respectively. Each of these is further divided into subsections reporting on pending litigation (pleadings, discovery, evidence and other pretrial preparations, briefs and motions, and court orders), court decisions (summaries of state and federal court opinions that set precedents or indicate important new trends), and verdicts and settlements (in the case of toxic torts) and enforcement and settlements (in the case of hazardous waste law).

The Toxic Torts section reports on personal injury, property damage, and insurance litigation involving exposure to toxic substances. Litigation involving either environmental or occupational exposure is followed, as are related product-liability lawsuits.

Toxics Law Reporter illustrates a format commonly used by BNA notification services. Each self-contained issue begins with a Highlights page summarizing the issue's most noteworthy contents.

THE BUREAU of NATIONAL AFFAIRS, INC.

TOXICS LAW REPORTER

A WEEKLY REVIEW OF TOXIC TORTS, HAZARDOUS WASTE, AND INSURANCE LITIGATION

Volume 3, Number 45 April 12, 1989

HIGHLIGHTS

THE ALASKA OIL SPILL seriously harmed fishermen and others in related industries, according to suits filed in Alaska seeking billions of dollars in damages. The spill of 10 million gallons of crude oil in the Prince William Sound, which occurred after an Exxon Corp. tanker ran aground, contaminated miles of fisheries and damaged other natural resources relied on by fishing-related industries, the suits claim. Two separate putative class action suits are filed by attorneys Melvin Belli and David Berger (p. 1415).

A DEDHAM WATER CO. ATTORNEY urges the U.S. Court of Appeals for the First Circuit to reverse a lower court decision on the type of causal nexus required to establish liability in a private cost recovery action under the superfund law (p. 1429).

SUPERFUND PLAINTIFFS, seeking to avoid a possible constitutional problem in a contribution suit against Arizona, move for a declaration that Arizona consented to federal jurisdiction by removing a state court action filed against it (p. 1430).

THE MARKET SHARE LIABILITY THEORY is adopted by the New York Court of Appeals, which upholds the constitutionality of New York's toxic tort revival law and rules that a diethylstilbestrol manufacturer can be liable even if it did not produce the particular drug that allegedly caused the plaintiff's injury (p. 1424). . . . In another case, attorneys for a plaintiff in a DES case say they will appeal a ruling that New York's revival statute does not apply to plaintiffs who were not residents of the state when their claims accrued (p. 1421).

THE BHOPAL CASE CONTINUES, as the Indian Supreme Court orders Union Carbide Corp. and the Indian government to produce all documents relevant to the $470 million settlement of the Bhopal gas leak case. The court also rules that Carbide must continue to submit to the jurisdiction of the Indian courts (p. 1416).

THE ALLOCATION OF SUPERFUND RISKS is now a principal preoccupation of many environmental lawyers, according to attorney Alfred R. Light in this week's Analysis and Perspective section. The author, who will be on a panel of distinguished experts at an upcoming BNA conference on corporate liability issues, argues that potentially responsible parties should become principled participants in the evolution of the law governing hazardous waste cases (p. 1439).

NINE SUITS IN KANSAS against asbestos manufacturers will have to be dismissed as a result of a recent Kansas Supreme Court ruling that the state's 10-year statute of repose applies to latent injury claims, according to the plaintiffs' attorney. Meanwhile, 13 former railroad workers or their estates settle asbestos claims against a railroad filed in a federal court in Kansas (p. 1420).

TORT AND SUPERFUND CLAIMS are asserted in two separate landfill suits. A case in Pennsylvania seeks $55 million in damages, as residents near a landfill say pollution from the waste site contaminated the area's land and water (p. 1417). . . . An Oklahoma couple whose home is adjacent to a landfill seeks more than $10 million for alleged injuries to their health and property (p. 1418).

A WASHINGTON COURT REJECTS an invitation to broaden exceptions to the rule that an asset purchaser is not liable as a successor. The court also dismisses, with prejudice, a company's claims against a purchaser for a selling corporation's superfund liability (p. 1431).

A PERMANENT CLOSURE ORDER and a $2.78 million penalty for Resource Conservation and Recovery Act violations are issued by a federal court in Indiana. The case marks the first time a federal court issued a permanent closure order of a landfill for loss of interim status under RCRA, according to an attorney in the case (p. 1433).

The second page, the Topical Summary, lists the entire contents of the issue.

TOPICAL SUMMARY

TOXIC TORTS

Environmental Exposure

1,2-DIBROMO-3-CHLOROPROPANE
Shell asks California court to republish opinion to enable state supreme court to review medical monitoring issue . . . 703
PESTICIDES
FIFRA pre-empts claims, federal court in Maine decides . . . 705
TOXIC CHEMICALS
U.S. Supreme Court refuses to review decision applying collateral estoppel in *Stringfellow* . . . 704

Occupational Exposure

ASBESTOS
Product not identified, Ninth Circuit finds . . . 711
Third Circuit agrees to rehear punitive damages case . . . 704
U.S. Supreme Court declines to review ruling allowing multiple punitive awards . . . 711
RADIATION
Ohio jury awards $100,000, no punitives, to nuclear worker 712

Outside the Courtroom

JUDICIAL REFORM
Group named to study New York commercial court idea . . . 713
PESTICIDES
DuPont says it will stop paying claims for alleged crop damage from Benlate DF . . . 712

Product Liability

AIDS
Seventh Circuit asks Wisconsin Supreme Court to decide limitations period for blood banks . . . 705
New York court dismisses suit against blood bank . . . 709
HALCION
Missouri court reinstates protective order for papers produced to criminal defendant . . . 708
INTRAOCULAR LENSES
U.S. Supreme Court declines to review ruling barring tort suit against optical lens maker . . . 710
TOBACCO
Cipollone voluntarily dismissed; experts predict little effect on cigarette litigation . . . 706

HAZARDOUS WASTE LAW

Insurance Law

CALIFORNIA
U.S. Supreme Court should affirm continuous trigger, but not address allocation issue, amici argue . . . 714
DUTY TO DEFEND
Fifth Circuit says missing policies no basis for coverage . . . 716
POLICY COVERAGE
Sixth Circuit says PRP letter not a "suit" under CGL policy 717

Outside the Courtroom

SUPERFUND
Conference advises changes to de minimis settlement process 720
WASTE DISPOSAL
Greenpeace cites Arkansas dioxin burn as largest intentional release in history . . . 721

State and Local Laws

BANKRUPTCY
Claim filed too late, federal court in Florida says . . . 716
CONSENT DECREES
Companies, Manitowoc agree in federal court in Wisconsin to clean up site for $19 million . . . 719
MINNESOTA
Company to pay fine in state court for criminal dumping . . . 719
PENNSYLVANIA
Legal, medical cost recovery permitted under state superfund law, state court says . . . 715

Superfund Litigation

COST RECOVERY
Fourth Circuit rejects claim of PCB threat . . . 718
REMEDIAL ACTIONS
EPA says superfund cleanups hit record level in 1992 . . . 718

ANALYSIS AND PERSPECTIVE

Perspective

ALFRED R. LIGHT
Illuminating Irrationality: Self-Deception and Superfund Litigation . . . 722

TABLE OF CASES

Listing of cases reported . . . 726

The Hazardous Waste Law section contains concise reports on civil and criminal suits brought by private parties or governments involving liability for cleanup, cost recovery, or natural resource damage related to hazardous waste. Such suits include those brought under the Superfund law (or CERCLA, the Comprehensive Environmental Response, Compensation, and Liability Act) and under the Resource Conservation and Recovery Act (RCRA).

A third regularly featured section of this service is Analysis and Perspective, which contains the lengthier analytical pieces offering the perspectives of outside experts on recent trends and developments.

Although the service is primarily designed to notify subscribers of recent developments in the field, it also can be effectively used for research purposes. The weekly issues are housed in a three-ring binder and cumulate into yearly volumes that may be kept in separate storage binders. In order to research a question in the *Toxics Law Reporter*, simply go to the Index in the current binder and use the major topical entries, and the entries under them, to find material reported in the service that will help answer the question. This process can be repeated for older volumes retained in the storage binders.

This notification service regularly updates readers on pending litigation. The weekly issues contain reports not only about decided cases but also about lawsuits just filed or in the midst of trial. Litigation tactics and techniques are a major part of the service's focus. The advice of experts in the field is also a regular feature of the Analysis and Perspective section.

1415

TOXIC TORTS

PENDING LITIGATION

ENVIRONMENTAL EXPOSURE

Alaska Oil Spill

LAWSUITS ALLEGE BILLIONS IN DAMAGES FROM EXXON OIL SPILL, CLEANUP IN ALASKA

Lawsuits seeking billions of dollars in damages have been filed by fishermen and others in related industries alleging they have been seriously harmed by the March 24 oil spill in the heart of Prince William Sound in Alaska (*Butcher v. Exxon*, Alaska SuperCt, No. 3AN-89-2672 Civil, 3/30/89).

The principal defendant in the lawsuits is Exxon Corp., whose tanker, the *Exxon Valdez*, released more than 10 million gallons of crude oil after running aground in the sound.

The spill, considered the worst oil-tanker spill in United States history, has contaminated miles of the sound's fisheries and has damaged other natural resources relied on by fishing-related industries for subsistence and economic purposes, the lawsuits said.

A putative class action filed by San Francisco attorney Melvin Belli, sought more than $2 billion in damages against Exxon and other defendants. Potential class members include at least 1,600 Alaskan residents who are commercial fishermen, deckhands, processors, longshoremen, and fish buyers, or who work in other positions linked to the fishing industry, the complaint said. The complaint was filed March 30 in the Superior Court for the State of Alaska, Third Judicial District.

The state of Alaska also is named as a defendant in Belli's suit. The state, according to the complaint "is responsible to the citizens of the state to monitor, inspect, and approve of contingent plans for the cleanup and containment of oil spills caused or potentially caused by the defendants."

Other defendants in the suit include: Alyeska Pipeline Service Co., an association of holders of the pipeline right-of-way system; Exxon Shipping Co., a subsidiary of Exxon Corp.; and the Trans-Atlantic Pipeline Liability Fund, a non-profit corporate entity established by the Trans-Alaska Pipeline Authorization Act.

Belli's suit alleged the defendants were negligent and strictly liable for damages caused by the spill and by their failure to respond to it immediately. The plaintiffs alleged the defendants violated provisions of the Maritime Liability Act because the oil tanker was operated in a negligent or reckless manner. The plaintiffs also alleged violations of the Alaska Environmental Conservation Act, which defines oil as a hazardous substance.

The plaintiffs alleged the presence of oil in the sound and its subsequent spreading to nearby islands presents an "imminent and substantial danger to the public health or welfare, including, but not limited to fish, animals, vegetation, and/or any part of the natural habitat in which they are found."

The plaintiffs also sought injunctive relief against the defendants that would require them to protect areas of Prince William Sound not currently affected by the spill.

'A Community Of Interest'

"There is a community of interest in obtaining equitable relief concerning the stoppage of the oil slick spreading to all areas of the Prince William Sound and in obtaining adequate compensation for the damages, lost wages, injuries, emotional distress, pain and suffering, property damage, and damage to livelihood and ecology, which defendants' action have inflicted upon the class," the complaint stated. The plaintiffs also sought all costs for cleanup and protection of property and equipment.

Exxon and the other defendants, including the state, have been criticized as responding too slowly to the spill. Those complaints are reflected in Belli's suit.

"Defendants Alyeska and Exxon have continuously reassured environmentalists and others, including the plaintiffs and the plaintiffs class, at all times prior to the accident that there existed an emergency cleanup plan by which any major oil spill could be successfully contained within five hours of occurrence," the complaint said. "Yet a day after the spill, little had been done to contain it other than an unsuccessful attempt to spray chemical dispersants."

The plaintiffs alleged it took nearly an entire day for Alyeskan, Exxon, and state officials to begin placing barrier booms in the sound in an effort to contain the spill.

For customized research and copies of documents or court decisions referenced in this issue, **call BNA PLUS toll-free (800) 452-7773 Nationwide; (202) 452-4323 in Washington, D.C.** Cost estimates for services and additional information about BNA PLUS services provided upon request.

4-12-89

Toxics Law Reporter
0887-7394/89/$0+.50

The material inside each issue of the *Toxics Law Reporter* is divided up according to subject matter. This is a lead article in the Toxics Torts section.

This is a lead article in the Hazardous Waste Law section. Many issues of the service also contain an Analysis and Perspective of recent trends and developments, written by an experienced practitioner.

1429

HAZARDOUS WASTE LAW

PENDING LITIGATION

SUPERFUND LITIGATION

Liable Parties

DEDHAM WATER ARGUES TO FIRST CIRCUIT SEEKING REVERSAL OF CAUSATION STANDARD

BOSTON—(By a BNA Staff Correspondent)—An attorney representing the Dedham Water Co. April 3 urged the U.S. Court of Appeals for the First Circuit to reverse a lower court decision on the type of causal nexus required to establish liability in a private cost recovery action under the superfund law (*Dedham Water Co. v. Cumberland Farms Dairy Inc.*, CA 1, No. 88-1020, oral argument 4/3/89).

Dedham Water Co. claimed it incurred costs to protect a public water supply from actual and threatened releases of hazardous substances from the property of Cumberland Farms Dairy Co. The company sought $19 million in compensatory damages, including $6.5 million to design, build, and maintain a water treatment plant, and money to operate it for years to come. A count seeking treble damages brought the final figure to $57 million.

Although evidence showed that a truck maintenance area on Cumberland Farm's property was once the scene of numerous disposals of solvents containing volatile organic compounds, the U.S. District Court for the Western District of Massachusetts said the evidence also showed these substances were prevented from reaching the water company's property.

In a July 4, 1988, decision on the nature of a prima facie case under Section 107 of the Comprehensive Environmental Response, Compensation, and Liability Act, Judge Joseph L. Tauro denied Dedham Water's claims, writing that the plaintiff "failed to prove by a preponderance of the evidence that Cumberland Farms was responsible for any groundwater contamination" that affected Dedham Water's wells (3 TXLR 283). The wellfield actually was contaminated by a third party, the court concluded.

"[The plaintiff] confuses the principle of strict liability for the effects of a release, with the antecedent questions whether the release has any effects at all. While the two questions may merge in some traditional [one-site] CERCLA cases, in the instant [two-site] case they remain distinct," the court said.

Actual Contamination 'Not Required'

In arguing for a reversal of the decision, Thomas F. Holt Jr. told the court of appeals Tauro was wrong to require Dedham Water to prove the contamination in its wells came from Cumberland Farms. Holt argued that Dedham Water should be reimbursed for its costs even if the contamination did not originate at the dairy. Under CERCLA, the liability-creating event is "the release or threatened release of hazardous substances and the incurrence of response costs, not migration and actual contamination," he said.

Dedham Water is entitled to compensation under CERCLA without having to prove common law causation, Holt stressed. The question before the First Circuit is "whether the standard of causation under CERCLA is identical to a common law standard under nuisance or trespassing," he said. "If common law remedies were adequate we wouldn't need CERCLA at all," Holt said.

"CERCLA was enacted . . . to allow for recovery of 'response costs,' which are defined in a manner very different from damages," he explained. According to the company's brief:

> [T]he requisite causal connection is established when the plaintiff has a reasonable basis to believe that a release or a *threat of release* of hazardous substances necessitates the incurrence of response costs. Courts considering this question have properly articulated a rule of reason approach which is dependent on proof of 'the circumstances existing when the costs were incurred.' *Williams v. Allied Automotive*, 28 ERC 1223, 1225 (N.D. Ohio, Aug. 3, 1988) [3 TXLR 423]; *see also Artesian Water v. Gov't of New Castle*, 851 F2d at 643, 651 (3d Cir. 1988) [3 TXLR 251).

To hold otherwise is to "eviscerate the statute," the brief said, citing the opinion of the U.S. Court of Appeals for the Second Circuit in *New York v. Shore Realty Corp.*, 759 F2d 1032 (1985), for the conclusion that CERCLA Section 107(a) "does not contain a common law causation requirement of migration and subsequent actual contamination."

Water Company Sued 'Wrong Party'

In oral argument, Cumberland Farms' counsel, Allan van Gestel, charged that Dedham Water pursued the wrong party. Van Gestel noted that in his decision Tauro stated that a third company—the Shields Chemical Co.—and a broken sewer line were the probable causes of contamination in the wells of both Cumberland Farms and Dedham Water. He argued that the district court ruling was therefore correct in finding Dedham Water's costs were not in response to any action by Cumberland Farms.

4-12-89

Toxics Law Reporter
0887-7394/89/$0+.50

Product Safety & Liability Reporter

Product liability litigation is the focus of BNA's *Product Safety & Liability Reporter*, a weekly notification and reference service that also provides in depth coverage of administrative and legislative regulation of product safety. The service's weekly Current Reports notify subscribers of the latest developments in important product liability cases and contain summaries of the major court decisions in the area. They also report on congressional activities affecting product liability and safety, as well as those of administrative agencies such as the Consumer Product Safety Commission and the National Highway Safety Administration.

This service also cumulates in its separate Reference File all the relevant federal statutes and regulations affecting product liability and safety.

The *Product Safety & Liability Reporter* consists of four binders. Two house the weekly Current Reports in six-month increments; the other two are the Reference File. Each Current Reports binder contains an index; the Reference File's separate index is found in the first Reference File binder. Back issues of Current Reports may be retained in storage binders, which also contain indexes.

BNA's *Product Safety & Liability Reporter* provides start-to-finish coverage of major product liability litigation, culminating in complete reports of all important court decisions. Together, the service's Current Reports and Reference File also serve as a single source of information for the statutes and regulations that control the product safety and liability field.

Each weekly Current Reports begins with a Highlights page summarizing the most important articles in that week's issue. The second page summarizes the issue's entire contents, dividing the coverage into the service's two major subject areas: product liability and product safety.

The first major section in each week's issue falls under the banner Product Liability and contains reports on ongoing product liability litigation and summaries of court decisions in the area. This section also covers legislative developments in product liability law.

The second major Current Reports section, Product Safety, follows the activities of the relevant federal agencies and congressional committees and subcommittees, including the Consumer Product Safety Commission. Other sections that regularly appear in Current Reports are Analysis and Perspective, which contains the views of experts in the field, and Recall Report, which is a monthly list of consumer products that have been recalled.

The service's two-binder Reference File provides full text of major consumer product safety laws, standards, rules, regulations, and enforcement procedures.

Product Safety &
Liability
REPORTER

Volume 20, Number 34 | THE BUREAU OF NATIONAL AFFAIRS, INC. | August 28, 1992

HIGHLIGHTS OF CURRENT REPORT

FEDERAL LAW PRE-EMPTS claims against pesticide makers based on failure to warn and inadequate labeling, the Nevada Supreme Court unanimously decides. The decision, the first post-*Cipollone* state high court ruling to address the effect of federal pesticide labeling law, came in a suit involving chlordane (p. 935).

A FAMILY'S EVIDENCE that exposure to soap containing hexachlorophene caused a child's mental retardation is not admissible, a New Jersey trial court rules, saying the plaintiffs' theory is not generally accepted in the scientific community. The court holds that the state high court's looser standard of admissibility in toxic tort cases does not apply to suits involving pharmaceuticals (p. 936).

A CALIFORNIA APPEALS COURT sets aside a discovery order, saying a trial court applied the wrong standard in requiring a tire manufacturer to disclose trade secret information to plaintiffs in a product liability suit (p. 937).

POST-MANUFACTURE DESIGN CHANGES to a forklift are inadmissible in a federal product liability suit even though the federal rules of evidence conflict with a state law allowing such proof, the U.S. Court of Appeals for the Third Circuit says (p. 938).

AN ELECTRICIAN shocked while working on a motor control unit appeals a judgment that his contributory negligence superseded an Alabama federal court jury's finding that the unit was defective and unreasonably dangerous (p. 939).

THE 'TWO-DISEASE RULE' should apply in asbestos cases, a Pennsylvania appeals court rules, joining the majority of jurisdictions that have said one injury does not trigger the limitations period for a separate, later-occurring disease (p. 940).

A WRONGFUL DEATH CLAIM brought more than three years after diagnosis of a fatal disease, but within two years of the date of death is timely, the North Carolina high court says (p. 942).

PRODUCT HAZARD REPORTING RULES issued by the Consumer Product Safety Commission illustrate the importance of tracking product liability suits and related information, authors Samuel Goldblatt and Eric L. Stone say in this week's **Analysis and Perspective** section. The authors discuss the CPSC regulations and their ramifications for manufacturers (p. 954).

THE *CIPOLLONE* DECISION will lead to increased dispute over the pre-emption defense in failure-to-install airbag cases, attendees at an American Bar Association panel are told (p. 940) . . . Meanwhile, speakers at another session discuss special ethical problems encountered by attorneys who practice product liability law (p. 941).

A BAN OF BABY WALKERS is requested by Consumer Federation of America and pediatricians who claim the play seats are nothing more than tiny injury vehicles for the nation's infants. In a petition filed with the Consumer Product Safety Commission, the groups ask the agency to prohibit the sale and manufacture of baby walkers in the United States (p. 946).

A SURVEY OF MANUFACTURERS of swimming pools, spas, and hot tubs will be conducted by the CPSC to determine the level of compliance with the labeling provisions of a voluntary standard for pool covers. The CPSC may issue a mandatory standard if it determines the conformance with the labeling provisions is inadequate (p. 946).

A PUBLIC SERVICE AD CAMPAIGN to promote the use of residential smoke detectors is planned by the CPSC for September (p. 947).

SATISFACTORY PROGRESS is reported for 36 out of 38 voluntary standard projects for which the CPSC has provided technical support (p. 948).

AN INVESTIGATION of alleged problems in 1.4 million General Motors vehicles with throttles that can stick is initiated by the National Highway Traffic Safety Administration (p. 949).

Section 1

0092-7732/92/$00.50

The front page of the *Product Safety & Liability Reporter* highlights the week's most important news and court decisions in the product liability field. All are given full treatment inside the issue.

283

BNA

Product Liability

Tobacco

ORAL ARGUMENTS IN CIPOLLONE BEGIN AS ATTORNEYS ADDRESS THIRD CIRCUIT

PHILADELPHIA—(By a BNA Staff Correspondent)—Rose Cipollone knew long before she contracted fatal lung cancer that she could have reduced the risk of cancer to zero if she had quit smoking, tobacco company attorneys argued March 28 in oral arguments in the appeal of the *Cipollone* case (*Cipollone v. Liggett Group Inc.*, CA 3, No. 88-5732, argued 3/28/89).

"The jury found that Rose Cipollone knew [of the risk] and made a conscious choice to injure herself by smoking," Donald J. Cohn, attorney for Liggett Group Inc., argued. He asked the U.S. Court of Appeals for the Third Circuit to vacate the jury's $400,000 award to Cipollone's husband, Antonio, for breach of an express warranty in cigarette advertising that smoking was not hazardous (17 PSLR 212).

The case, the first personal injury damage award involving cigarette smoking, is being closely watched by product liability litigators, particularly those involved in tobacco litigation.

The jury in the 1988 trial in the U.S. District Court for the District of New Jersey found Rose Cipollone 80 percent responsible for her own injury and made no award to her estate (16 PSLR 556). It also absolved Liggett and co-defendants Lorillard Inc. and Philip Morris Inc. of conspiring to suppress information about the risks of cigarette smoking, and absolved Liggett of failing to warn Rose Cipollone of the hazard of smoking. Although they were not found liable, Lorillard and Philip Morris joined Liggett's appeal of the award to Antonio Cipollone, citing "contingent issues" that could affect other tobacco companies.

Plaintiffs' Attorney Criticizes Advertising

Marc Z. Edell, an attorney for the estate of Rose Cipollone and for Antonio, told the appeals court panel that Liggett's advertising contained a "strong suggestion that while other cigarettes might be harmful, Chesterfields are not." As an example, Edell cited commercials by the late entertainer Arthur Godfrey that said Chesterfields do not affect the nose, throat, or other organs. To find Liggett liable, "you do not need reliance [on the warranty] on the part of a specific buyer," he said.

Both sides appealed different aspects of the lower court ruling, contending that Judge H. Lee Sarokin made various errors in his charge to the jury. Edell is appealing the lower court's dismissal of a claim for damages under the common law tort theory of "generic utility risk." He also seeks a new trial on the jury's finding that Rose Cipollone was 80 percent responsible for her injury by continuing to smoke even after the federal government imposed health warnings on cigarettes in 1966.

Firms Claim Business Loss

Cigarette manufacturers would have to go out of business if the plaintiffs prevailed under a "generic risk utility" claim, according to Robert E. Northrip, attorney for Lorillard. "It could result in the total prohibition of cigarettes," Northrip added, likening the theory to telling someone "not to surface after you go underwater."

Commenting that Rose Cipollone "used the cigarettes the way Liggett intended her to use them," Judge Edward R. Becker asked Edell what difference that made as a matter of law.

"Manufacturers should not be able to say that 'you were unreasonable in using the product the way we intended you to use it,'" Edell replied. Pervasive cigarette advertising for many years contained an implied warranty that smoking was not hazardous until the federal government required health warnings in 1966, he said. In requiring warnings, the Federal Cigarette Labeling and Advertising Act of 1966 exempted manufacturers from further liability for failure to warn.

If the utility risk claim survives, "it should be pre-empted" by the 1966 federal bar to warning liability, which was enacted to "draw a balance" on the issues of protecting public health, warning smokers of the hazard, and preserving commerce, Northrip contended. He also said the Appellate Division of New Jersey Superior Court has ruled that damages on a generic utility risk claim can be awarded only of there is a manufacturing defect, a failure to warn, or a design defect, and that this rule should be applied retroactively. "There is no case where the plaintiff has collected" without proving one of those elements, he added.

"You're not suggesting we not wait until the New Jersey Supreme Court has ruled?" Becker asked, noting that an appeal is pending on the Appellate Division ruling. "It really wouldn't make sense for us to tell them how to construe a New Jersey statute."

At another point, Becker asked, "isn't this really a product liability case? Wouldn't the New Jersey Supreme Court say that someone who smoked and knew [of the risk] shouldn't be able to collect damages? Why isn't it reasonable to say the New Jersey Supreme Court, if faced with this case, would say that contributing fault is a defense against an express warranty claim?"

Husband's Warning Disputed

Edell disagreed that Rose Cipollone's knowledge of the risk barred a claim on breach of express warranty. Disputing a claim in the defense appeal brief that Cipollone's husband had warned her "these cigarettes are going to kill you," Edell said, "that's not found anywhere in the [trial] transcript." Asked by Becker if such a "smoking gun" quote was in the transcript, Cohn said, "It is, your honor. I can't find it in the record at this moment." Testimony also showed that several of

3-31-89

Product Safety & Liability Reporter
0092-7732/89/$00.50

The articles inside provide in-depth accounts of ongoing and just completed product liability litigation.

Labor Relations Reporter

Labor Relations Reporter combines virtually every known reporter-services format in order to fully cover its broad subject: labor and employment relations law. The service's decisional and reference materials pull together labor and employee relations documents dating back to 1935, while its notification elements keep subscribers abreast of current developments.

The service is divided into six major parts, each treating a separate subject area of labor law: labor-management relations, wages and hours, labor arbitration, fair employment practices, individual employment rights, and disability laws.

The key to this whole multi-binder service is the Master Index Binder, the starting point for reference and research. For quick answers to labor law questions, there is also the Labor Relations Expediter, which consists of two looseleaf reference binders. The first provides a full editorial explanation of the current state of labor law as interpreted by the courts, agencies, and arbitrators. The second binder contains the full text of federal statutes and regulations.

This multi-part notification and legal reference service covers the vast field of employer-employee relations. It is designed to provide current labor and employee developments, quick answers to the day-to-day questions encountered in the labor and industrial relations field, and a complete reference library for locating all rulings, data, and other background information regarding a particular case or problem.

The service is divided into five major parts, each covering a specific area of labor law. Most of these parts consist of more than one binder, and each part cumulates court and agency decisions into bound volumes with a permanent reference value. Subscribers, including libraries, may purchase the entire service or only a single part.

The service's first major subdivision, Labor-Management Relations, covers the basic federal laws of labor relations—the Taft-Hartley Act (National Labor Relations Act, as amended) and the Landrum-Griffin Act (Labor-Management Reporting and Disclosure Act)—as well as other significant labor laws. In one of its binders are housed summaries of all decisions of the National Labor Relations Board and full text of federal and state court decisions.

These decisions and summaries are headnoted and supplied with numbers that tie them into the service's indexing system. They are issued weekly in the form of looseleaf pages, which are stored in the binder until they are reprinted in a hard-bound volume. Volume 1 of these Labor Relations Reference Manuals, as these hard-bound volumes are called, contains decisions issued in 1935; more recent volumes are numbered in the hundreds.

Labor Relations Reporter publishes the full text of court decisions on labor law, as well as digests, like this one, of decisions by the National Labor Relations Board. All decisions are headnoted and assigned numbers from the service's Outline of Classifications.

ARIZONA PUBLIC SVC. CO. 130 LRRM 1385

ARIZONA PUBLIC SVC. CO. —

ARIZONA PUBLIC SERVICE COMPANY, Flagstaff, Ariz. **and** ELECTRICAL WORKERS (IBEW), AFL-CIO, LOCAL 387, Case No. 28-CA-7074, February 28, 1989, 292 NLRB No. 144 [supplementing 273 NLRB 1757, 118 LRRM 1277]

Before NLRB: Stephens, Chairman; Johansen and Cracraft, Members.

DISCRIMINATION Sec. 8(a)(3)

— Sympathy strikers — Suspension ▸52.358 ▸52.14

On remand from federal appeals court, NLRB reverses earlier finding and concludes that employer violated LMRA by suspending eight sympathy strikers, even though language of collective-bargaining contract's no-strike clause is broad enough to encompass sympathy strikes. (1) Parties did not intend clause to encompass sympathy strikes, where (a) bargaining history indicates that employer recognized there was no agreement that such strikes were covered by clause, and (b) employer's repeated acquiescence in sympathy strikes indicates that such strikes were not contractually proscribed; (2) under NLRB law existing at time parties last ratified contract, broad no-strike clause was not sufficient to establish waiver of right to participate in sympathy strikes.

[*Text*] On February 5, 1985, the National Labor Relations Board issued a Decision and Order [1] in this proceeding, finding that the Respondent did not violate Section 8(a)(3) and (1) of the National Labor Relations Act by suspending eight employees because they engaged in a sympathy strike. The Board concluded that their refusal to cross a stranger picket line contravened the no-strike provision of the parties' collective-bargaining agreement, which prohibited unauthorized work stoppages and permitted the Respondent to discipline employees who took part in them.

The Union filed a petition for review with the United States Court of Appeals for the Ninth Circuit. On May 6, 1986, the court remanded the case to the Board for consideration of evidence bearing on whether the parties intended to ban sympathy strikes through the contract's broad no-strike provision.[2]

. . .

The Board has reconsidered its original decision, the administrative law judge's decision, and the record in light of the court's remand, which the Board accepts as the law of the case, and the statements of position, and has decided to reverse the Board's prior decision.[3]

In the original decision, the Board based its analysis on the following facts. After eight of Respondent's crewmembers refused to perform work on July 28, 1982,[4] because of a stranger picket line at the worksite, the Respondent by letter dated July 29 threatened the Union with a lawsuit. By letter dated the same day the Union replied that it had not authorized the employees' refusal to work. On August 2 the respondent suspended the eight employees for 3 days, informing them that their work stoppage violate article I, section 2, of the contract, which reads as follows:

"During the term of this Agreement, and during any period of time while negotiations are in progress between the parties hereto for the extension or renewal of this Agreement, the Union agrees on behalf of itself and each of its members that there will be no authorized concerted failure to boycott, or otherwise, with the Company's business.

"The Company agrees, as part of the consideration of this Agreement, that neither the Union, its officers, representatives, or members shall be liable for damages for unauthorized stoppages, strikes, intentional slowdowns, or suspensions of work in Company's service, if:

"(a) The Union gives written notice to the Company within twenty-four 24) hours of such action that it has not authorized the stoppage, strike, slowdown, or suspension of work;

"(b) Copies of the notice described (a) above are posted immediately by the Union on the bulletin board;

"(c) The Union further cooperates with the Company in getting the employees to return and remain at work.

" It is recognized that the Company has the right to take disciplinary action, including discharge, against any employees who engage in any unauthorized stoppage, strike, intentional slowdown, or suspension of work, subject to the Union's right to present a grievance on such discipline in accordance with Article VII of this Agreement in cases in which an issue of fact exists as to whether or not any particular employee has engaged in, participated in, or encouraged any such violation."

Because the parties' contract permitted the Respondent to discipline employees who participated in "unauthorized" strikes and the Union identified the strike as unauthorized, the Board concluded that the Respondent was free to discipline sympathy strikers for participating in conduct the contract expressly prohibited. In a footnote at the end of its decision the Board cited *Indianapolis Power Co.*, 273 NLRB 1715 [118

[1] 273 NLRB 1757 [118 LRRM 1277].

[2] *Electrical Workers Local 387 v. NLRB*, 788 F.2d 1412 [122 LRRM 2304] (1986).

[3] In accordance with our decision in *New Horizons for the Retarded*, 283 NLRB No. 181 [125 LRRM 1177] (May 28, 1987), interest on and after January 1, 1987, shall be computed at the "short-term Federal rate" for the underpayment of taxes as set out in the 1986 amendment to 26 U.S.C. §6621. Interest on amounts accured prior to January 1, 1987 (the effective date of the 1986 amendment to 26 U.S.C. §6621), shall be computed in accordance with *Florida Steel Corp.*, 231 NLRB 651 [96 LRRM 1070] (1977).

[4] All dates are in 1982 unless otherwise indicted.

The classification numbers tie the decisions into the service's Cumulative Digest and Index (CDI) system.

FILE in Master Index Binder under tab (C-II) and before Final Supp. (129 LRRM) beginning with page C-II A801. **DISCARD** previous Master CDI (130 LRRM) beginning with page C-II A701.

LABOR RELATIONS REPORTER®

March 6, 1989

Master CUMULATIVE DIGEST and INDEX (CDI) Labor Relations (130 LRRM)

January 9 — February 27, 1989

(See also CDIs beginning with pages C-II A801, C-II A901, C-II 101, C-II 301 and bound CDI volumes.)

Classification numbers identified by the symbol in this CDI represent specific points of labor relations law. They are located by topic in General Index under tab (A). The Outline of Classifications under tab (C-I) provides the description of each number.

Each descriptive entry below provides the particulars in a given case relating to the classification number. See LRRM Binder 2 for latest cases.

▸ **4.05** Appeals court has jurisdiction to consider interlocutory appeal from lower court's order granting prison correctional officials and their union leave to intervene for certain discovery purposes only in action under 1871 CRA by prison inmates who allege violation of their constitutional rights by prison authorities and seek preliminary injunction. (CA 2) 2369

Summary judgment was not proper in unions' action alleging that company and town's law-enforcement officials conspired to deprive company's striking employees of their constitutional rights in violation of 1871 CRA by discriminatory enforcement of law, arresting strikers without probable cause, and setting excessive bail. (CA 9) 2353

▸ **5.10** Merger agreement permitting each local lodge to "retain" treasury after international union's merger with another labor organization did not allow lodges to retain their treasuries after lodges disaffiliated from international. (CA 3) 2528

International union is entitled to recover per capita tax from its disaffiliated local lodges until NLRB's certification of locals as affiliates of rival union. *Id.*

International union did not breach its constitution when its president ordered consolidation of two local unions, where consolidation order was not unreasonable or issued in bad faith. (DC DC) 2063

Order consolidating two local unions does not contravene international's policy regarding mergers of affiliated locals, where section of union constitution governing mergers

Section 1a

Vol. 130, No. 9

1-55871-033-7/89/$0+.50

C-II A701

Through an identical procedure of headnoting, indexing, advance sheets, and hard-bound volumes, the other major parts of the service—Wages and Hours, Labor Arbitration, Fair Employment Practices, Individual Employment Rights, and Americans with Disabilities—have put together a library of decisional law that covers virtually all aspects of labor relations. The indexing system, which is called Cumulative Digest and Index (CDI), is described later in this book, both in the description of BNA's *Media Law Reporter* and, with specific reference to the *Labor Relations Reporter*, in a chapter on Methods of Research.

Besides its decisional component, each major part of this service contains either a notification or reference element or both. There is, for example, the Wages and Hours Manual, two binders containing the current federal laws, rules, and regulations on the subject, plus editorial explanations of how they have been interpreted. The Fair Employment Practices and Individual Employment Rights parts of the service have similar reference binders. Other binders contain full text of state labor relations laws and regulations, as well as digests of state laws and regulations affecting wages and hours. Yet another binder houses the major notification element of the service, the weekly Analysis/News & Background Information, which reports and analyzes the week's most important new developments.

With weekly notification reports, constantly updated reference manuals, and regular releases of full-text court decisions, the Labor Relations Reporter *is a library of information on labor and employment relations law.*

The key to unlocking the decisional parts of the service is the Cumulative Digest and Index (CDI) system, which is explained briefly in the next couple of pages and more thoroughly in the chapter Methods of Research.

Labor Relations Reporter also contains several reference binders, covering state labor laws, wages and hours, fair employment practices, and individual employment rights. Here is a sample page from the State Labor Laws binder.

No. 732 SLL 13:301

ARKANSAS

PART III—WAGES, HOURS, CHILD LABOR (DIGEST)

1. WAGES: LAWS

Source: Arkansas Code, Annotated, Secs. 11-4-201 to 11-4-219, as amended by Act 360, L. 1989, effective July 2, 1989 (unless otherwise indicated).

1.05 ADMINISTRATIVE AGENCY

Department of labor. (Secs. 11-4-203(1) and 11-4-209)

1.10 COVERAGE

Any individual employed by any individual, partnership, association, corporation, business trust or any person or group of persons acting directly or indirectly in interest of employer in relation to employee which employs four or more persons. (Sec. 11-4-203(5), as amended by Act 360, L. 1989, effective July 2, 1989)

1.20 EXEMPTIONS

Employers covered by Fair Labor Standards Act; individuals employed in bona fide executive, administrative, or professional capacity; as outside commission paid salesman, who customarily performs services away from employer's premises, taking orders for goods or services; in employment by U.S. or state or political subdivision except public schools and school districts in activities of educational, charitable, religious, or nonprofit organization where employee-employer relationship does not in fact exist; as independent contractor (one who contracts to perform work away from employer's premises, uses own methods to accomplish work, and is subject to control of employer only as to result of own work); employed by agricultural employer who did not use more than 500 man-days of agricultural labor (any day during which employee performs any agricultural labor, and any person otherwise excluded shall be considered to be employee in computation of man-days) in any calendar quarter of preceding calendar year; in range production of livestock; in planting, or tending trees, cruising, surveying, or felling timber, or in preparing or in transporting logs or other forestry products to mill, processing plant, railroad, or terminal by employer of less than eight employees. Also exempt are (1) parent, spouse, child, or other member of agricultural employer's immediate family; (2) individual (a) employed as hand harvest laborer and paid on piece-rate basis in operation which has been, and customarily and generally recognized as having been, paid on piece-rate basis in region of employment, (b) commutes daily from permanent residence to farm on which is employed, (c) has been employed in agriculture less than 13 weeks during preceding calendar year; (3) migrant (a) 16 years or under and employed as hand harvest laborer, (b) paid on piece-rate basis in operation which has been, and customarily and generally recognized as having been, paid on piece-rate basis in region of employment, (c) employed on same farm as parents, and (d) paid same piece-rate as employees over age 16 are paid on same farm. (Sec. 11-4-203(5) and (7))

1.30 RATE SET BY LAW

$3.30 per hour; and $3.35 per hour, effective Sept. 1, 1989. (Sec. 11-4-210(a), as amended by Act 360, L. 1989, effective July 2, 1989).

Gratuities: Employer or employee engaged in occupation in which gratuities have been customarily and usu-

☆4-10-89 17
1-55871-033-7/89/$0+.50

One of the notification components of the service is this weekly report on new developments. Each issue also contains an analysis of a recent case.

FILE in Binder 1 behind tab 'Analysis/News and Background Information' and after prior weekly issue ending with page 130 LRR 416.

BNA LABOR RELATIONS REPORTER®

LABOR-MANAGEMENT RELATIONS

April 10, 1989
130 LRR 417

ANALYSIS/NEWS and BACKGROUND INFORMATION
(including Summary of Developments)

SUMMARY OF DEVELOPMENTS

DOL Urged To Keep Prohibition On Homework In Women's Apparel

A proposal to lift the ban on homework in the women's apparel industry drew nothing but criticism at two days of Labor Department hearings in New York City. Federal and state officials joined industry and labor leaders in blasting the measure as a return to sweatshop conditions, subminimum wages, and child labor.

Though the proposal was promoted by the Reagan administration as a way to meet worker demand for greater workplace flexibility, DOL officials at the hearings did not indicate that the measure has the wholehearted support of the Bush administration. "It's merely a possibility," Bill Blackburn, the Wage and Hour Division's director of policy and analysis, told BNA. "It's something the Reagan administration pushed, but we haven't got any real signal from Bush."

"Removing the ban exposes the poorest and most vulnerable members of society to exploitation and unacceptable dangers," Harris Wofford, secretary of Pennsylvania's Department of Labor and Industry, told DOL. ILGWU President Jay Mazur testified that industrial homework—legal or not—almost always violates many local health, fire, and building laws. (130 LRR 429)

IN THIS SECTION

	Page
GRIEVANCE SETTLEMENT: Damages For Violation Of Subcontracting Clause Are Awarded To Union	424
ANALYSIS: Employment Contract That Company Handbook Created Did Not Require Cause For Discharge Of At-Will Worker	425
NEWS AND BACKGROUND INFORMATION	429

Vol. 130, No. 14
Section 1
1-55871-033-7/89/$0+.50

Media Law Reporter

The *Media Law Reporter* is a weekly full-text case service that reports court decisions affecting newspapers, magazines, radio, television, film, and other media. Subjects regularly addressed in the reported decisions are libel, invasion of privacy, newsgathering, obscenity, and broadcast regulation. The service reports all significant federal and state court decisions affecting media law. Opinions, with rare exceptions, are reported in full text.

Cases are issued to subscribers on a weekly basis. A four-page report that accompanies the cases summarizes their holdings and also provides coverage of relevant news events such as court filings, jury awards, and legislative actions.

The weekly issues are stored in a single binder where they cumulate until they are republished, with no change in the page numbers, in a bound volume. Each reported case is preceded by one or more headnotes summarizing the legal points decided in the case. Each headnote is assigned a number or numbers showing where it fits into the service's Classification Guide.

Research in the *Media Law Reporter* is made easy by the use of several finding aids, which appear in the front of both the looseleaf binder and each bound volume. The most direct method of research begins with the Classification Guide, which is the major framework for classifying decisions published in the service. The Classification Guide organizes into outline form the wide range of subjects covered in the service and provides each subject with a number. For example, the number 11.3002 is assigned to the subject of actual malice as a standard of liability in defamation actions. A quick survey of the Classification Guide reveals the breadth of the *Media Law Reporter's* coverage.

Armed with the appropriate number, the researcher then goes to the Index Digest, which also appears in the front of the binder or bound volume. Here, he or she will find reprints of every relevant headnote that appears in that binder or volume. Each headnote indicates the name of the court decision to which it refers and the page in the volume on which the full text of the decision can be found.

Another way of getting to the same point is to use yet another finding aid in the front of the volume or binder, namely, the Topical Index. This index is an alphabetical arrangement of words and phrases describing all topics covered in the *Media Law Reporter*. Each word or phrase refers the user to a Classification Guide number. For example, a researcher looking up the phrase "actual malice" is provided with the appropriate number, 11.3002, and with this number, he or she can then go to the Index Digest and on to the full-text cases themselves.

Media Law Reporter's Classification Guide offers the most direct way to find the full text of court decisions reported by this decisional service. For example, the number 5.1005 will lead you to all reported cases on prior restraints on contact with trial participants.

FILE this "Classification Guide" in your Media Law Reporter binder in page number order and directly behind the tab marked CLASSIFICATION GUIDE. The tab marked CLASSIFICATION GUIDE is the third of five tabs. **DISCARD** the Classification Guide dated Aug. 18, 1981.

BNA **MEDIA LAW REPORTER**®

February 7, 1989 THE BUREAU OF NATIONAL AFFAIRS, INC. **Vol. 16, No. 1**

CLASSIFICATION GUIDE

I. REGULATION OF MEDIA CONTENT

▸ **5. Prior restraints**
.01 In general
.03 Authority to restrain
.05 National security restraints
[.10] Fair trial restraints (for access to courtrooms, see ▸40.1105; for access to judicial records, see ▸38.15)
.1001 —In general
.1003 —Restraints on publication
.1005 —Restraints on contact with trial participants (for access to jurors, see ▸42.03)
.1007 —Restraints on third parties
.15 Obscenity restraints (see also ▸10)
.17 Commercial speech restraints (see also ▸15)
.20 Privacy restraints (see also ▸13)
[.30] Judicial review
.3001 —In general
.3002 —Standing
.3003 —Mootness
.3004 —Contempt
.3005 —Burden of proof necessary

▸ **8. Fair trial, free press** (for access to courtrooms, see ▸40.1105; for access to judicial records, see ▸38.15; for access to law enforcement records, see ▸38.17)
.01 Restrictive orders in general (for prior restraints, see ▸5; see also ▸50.17)
.02 Judicial authority
[.03] Broadcast coverage restrictions
.0301 —In general
.0303 —Camera guidelines
[.05] Restrictive orders in criminal proceedings (for prior restraints, see ▸5.10; for access to courtrooms, see ▸40.1105)
.0501 —Pre-trial
.0503 —Trial
.0505 —Post-trial
.07 Restrictive orders in civil proceedings
.20 Alternative protective measures
[.25] Judicial review

Section 1 101

Look next at the Index Digest in the current binder. There, you will find the headnote, case name, and page number of every relevant case in the binder.

FILE "Index Digest" in your Media Law Reporter binder in page number order behind the tab marked INDEX DIGEST.

BNA **MEDIA LAW REPORTER**®

March 28, 1989 THE BUREAU OF NATIONAL AFFAIRS, INC. **Vol. 16, No. 8**

INDEX DIGEST

Covering 16 Media Law Reporter 1001 — 1224

February 7, 1989 — March 14, 1989

I. REGULATION OF MEDIA CONTENT

▸ **5. Prior restraints**

Fair trial restraints

▸ **005.1005 Restraints on contacts with trial participants**

Press and public have qualified First Amendment and common law right of access to pre-trial proceedings and pleadings in civil action against Catholic priest and diocese for alleged acts of sexual abuse by priest, and complete sealing of all pleadings and pre-trial proceedings is not warranted, in view of defendants' failure to show that closure is necessary to prevent clearly defined and serious injury, or that overriding interest exists which cannot be protected except by closure, or that disclosure would prejudice defendants' right to fair trial, although pendency of priest's criminal prosecution based upon same facts warrants order limiting dissemination, by counsel in civil proceeding, of extrajudical statements as defined in Rule of Professional Conduct 3.6, and pleadings containing such information must be submitted under seal. — Hutchison v. Luddy (Pa CtCommPls, 12/23/88) 1001

▸ **005.1007 Restraints on third parties**

California trial court's order prohibiting television station from exhibiting drawing of defendant's facial features is unconstitutional prior restraint, since drawing was lawfully obtained during public arraignment, and since court's earlier order, issued pursuant to California rules governing electronic media coverage of court proceedings, which prohibited frontal photographs of defendant, does not prohibit taking or publishing artistic drawings depicting defendant. — KCST-TV Channel 39 v. Municipal Court of San Diego County (Calif CtApp, 5/13/88) 1026

▸ **8. Fair trial, free press**

Broadcast coverage restrictions

▸ **008.0303 Camera guidelines**

California trial court's order prohibiting television station from exhibiting drawing of defendant's facial features is unconstitutional prior restraint, since drawing was lawfully obtained during public arraignment, and since court's earlier order, issued pursuant to California rules governing electronic media coverage of court proceedings, which prohibited frontal photographs of defendant, does not prohibit taking or publishing artistic drawings depicting defendant. — KCST-TV Channel 39 v. Municipal Court

Section 3

0148-1045/87/$0+.50
701

Two final finding aids are the Table of Cases and the Table of Cases by Jurisdiction. The Table of Cases lists alphabetically, both by plaintiff and by defendant, the name of each case appearing in the volume or binder. It also provides any relevant case history and any parallel citations to other reporters that are available at the time of publication. The Table of Cases by Jurisdiction lists the cases in the volume by the federal court or state in which they were decided.

A full library of the *Media Law Reporter*, which began publication in 1977, brings together in one place virtually every important media law case decided since that time. Moreover, the very first volume of the service reproduces over 150 relevant decisions handed down prior to 1977.

New decisions, as they are issued, are filed in a ring binder. In the front of the binder are all the finding aids described above. The Index Digests and the tables of cases are reissued every two months. When space in the ring binder dictates, which usually is every 10 months, all the material in the binder—finding aids and full-text decisions—are reprinted, bound into a volume, and sent automatically to subscribers.

With each week's worth of new decisions, subscribers receive a four-page report summarizing the decisions' holdings and notifying subscribers of other noteworthy events. This latter aspect of the report, the "News Notes" section, alerts readers to court decisions before they are published in full text and also to such developments as court filings, jury awards, agency rulings and regulations, and federal and state legislative actions. These four-page reports, which serve a purely notification function, are stored in the current ring binder but are not reprinted in the bound volumes.

Media Law Reporter *follows the Cumulative Digest and Index system common to BNA decisional services. By simply finding the most appropriate CDI number for the topic in question, a researcher can find digest summaries and the full text of relevant court decisions both in the current binder and in the bound volumes.*

Text of Decisions of the Federal and State Courts Involving Media Law

HUTCHISON v. LUDDY

**Pennsylvania Court of Common Pleas
Somerset County**

SAMUEL C. HUTCHISON v. FATHER FRANCIS LUDDY, BISHOP JAMES HOGAN, MONSIGNOR THOMAS MADDEN, MONSIGNOR ROY F. KLINE, MONSIGNOR PAUL PANZA, MONSIGNOR IGNATIUS WADAS, DIOCESE OF ALTOONA - JOHNSTOWN, ST. MARY'S CATHOLIC CHURCH, CARDINAL JOHN KROL, and the ARCH-DIOCESE OF PHILADELPHIA, No. 445 Civil 1988, December 23, 1988

REGULATION OF MEDIA CONTENT

1. Prior restraints—Fair trial restraints—Restraints on contact with trial participants (§5.1005)

Fair trial/free press—Restrictive orders in civil proceedings (§8.07)

NEWSGATHERING

Access to records—Judicial—Civil—Pre-trial/discovery (§38.1505.04)

Access to places—Public institutions—Courtrooms—Civil actions—Pre-trial (§40.1105.0301)

Press and public have qualified First Amendment and common law right of access to pre-trial proceedings and pleadings in civil action against Catholic priest and diocese for alleged acts of sexual abuse by priest, and complete sealing of all pleadings and pre-trial proceedings is not warranted, in view of defendants' failure to show that closure is necessary to prevent clearly defined and serious injury, or that overriding interest exists which cannot be protected except by closure, or that disclosure would prejudice defendants' right to fair trial, although pendency of priest's criminal prosecution based upon same facts warrants order limiting dissemination, by counsel in civil proceeding, of extrajudicial statements as defined in Rule of Professional Conduct 3.6, and pleadings containing such information must be submitted under seal.

REGULATION OF MEDIA CONTENT

2. Fair trial, free press—Restrictive orders in civil proceedings (§8.07)

NEWSGATHERING

Access to records—Civil—Pre-trial/discovery (§38.1505.04)

Access to civil discovery material is governed not by First Amendment but by application of Pennsylvania Rules of Civil Procedure, and thus defendants seeking protective order must demonstrate only good cause, which has been shown by Catholic priest who is defending not only civil action arising out of charges of sexual abuse but also criminal action, but blanket protective order sealing all discovery material relating to defendants other than priest is not warranted.

Motion by defendants in civil action to seal pre-trial proceedings and records.

Motion granted in part and denied in part.

Richard Serbin and Joseph Nypaver, Altoona, Pa., for plaintiff.

L. Edward Glass, Johnstown, Pa., for defendant Luddy.

John P. O'Dea, Philadelphia, Pa., for defendants Krol and Archdiocese of Philadelphia.

Carl A. Eck and Maria Zulick, Pittsburgh, Pa., for remaining defendants.

Scott Henderson, of Thorp, Reed & Armstrong, Pittsburgh, for intervenor Pittsburgh Press.

Full Text of Opinion

Fike, J.:

This case is before the court on a motion filed by defendants, Bishop James

1001

By turning to the page number mentioned in the *Media Law Reporter* Index Digest, you find the full text of the case on point. For older cases, repeat the process in the bound volumes, using the same classification number.

A four-page notification report comes with each week's release of new court decisions. The report summarizes the holdings of the decisions and also contains one or more news stories about ongoing litigation.

DECISIONS

MEDIA LAW REPORTER®

April 11, 1989 THE BUREAU OF NATIONAL AFFAIRS, INC. Vol. 16, No. 10

OPINIONS IN THIS ISSUE

To Be Cited 16 Med.L.Rptr.

OBSCENITY—SEIZURE

The pretrial seizure of the total inventory of materials presumptively protected by the First Amendment, on a mere finding of probable cause that an Indiana racketeering law is being violated by distribution of obscene materials, and without an adversarial hearing resulting in a determination of the materials' obscenity, is an unconstitutional prior restraint, the U.S. Supreme Court holds (Fort Wayne Books v. Indiana, 2/21/89).

NEWSRACKS—PERMITS

The First Amendment is not violated by a Lincoln, Neb., ordinance that requires anyone wishing to locate a newsrack on city property to complete a permit application, to pay a permit fee, and to obtain liability insurance, and that restricts newsracks' size, type, and location, the U.S. Court of Appeals for the Eighth Circuit rules, since the ordinance is a legitimate time, place, and manner restriction that is designed to promote significant governmental interests (Jacobsen v. Harris, 3/16/89).

ALSO IN THIS ISSUE—

The determination of whether a retraction appeared in "substantially as conspicuous a manner" as the allegedly defamatory statement is a question of fact for the jury (Twin Coast Newspapers Inc. v. Los Angeles County Superior Court, 3/7/89); a labor union's exclusion of NBC from its convention, held in a city-owned convention center leased by the union, is not state action and thus does not violate the First Amendment (NBC v. Communications Workers of America, 11/28/88); newspapers that share offices and personnel but that have distinct corporate and editorial identities must both be designated as "official" newspapers (Albia Publishing Co. v. Klobnak, 1/25/89); a genuine issue of material fact exists as to whether a mental patient was sane during a particular period, for purposes of tolling the statute of limitations, and thus precludes summary judgment for a magazine in an invasion of privacy action based upon publication of the patient's name and photograph (Pederson v. Time Inc., 1/19/89); photograhs of public officials and candidates taken in public places with persons who either pose with them or who inadvertently appear in such pictures do not give rise to a cause of action for invasion of privacy (Cox v. Hatch, 7/18/88).

TABLE OF CASES

Albia Publishing Co. v. Klobnak (Iowa SupCt) 1377
Cox v. Hatch (Utah SupCt) 1366
Fort Wayne Books Inc. v. Indiana (US SupCt) 1337
Jacobsen v. Harris (CA 8) 1380
NBC v. Communications Workers of America (CA 11) 1356
Pederson v. Time Inc. (Mass SupJudCt) 1382
Twin Coast Newspapers Inc. v. Superior Court (Calif CtApp) 1374

0148-1045/89/$0+.50

United States Patents Quarterly

First published in 1929, *United States Patents Quarterly* is BNA's oldest service. It is a full-text decisional service that reports all important decisions dealing with patents, trademarks, copyrights, unfair competition, trade secrets, computer chip protection, and other intellectual property issues.

Among the courts and agencies whose decisions are regularly reported in this service are the U.S. Supreme Court, the U.S. Court of Appeals for the Federal Circuit and the other federal circuits, the federal district courts, the U.S. Court of Claims, the Commissioner of Patents and Trademarks, the Patent and Trademark Office Board of Patent Appeals and Interferences, and the Patent and Trademark Office Trademark Trial and Appeal Board.

Each full-text decision is preceded by one or more headnotes spelling out the decision's holdings. Classification numbers that accompany the headnotes tie the decision into the service's Classification Outline.

The service consists of weekly advance sheets, quarterly bound volumes, annual cumulative digests, and five-year cumulative indexes.

United States Patents Quarterly publishes the full text of court and administrative agency decisions in the field of intellectual property law. Through the issuance of weekly advance sheets and the headnoting, indexing, and cumulation of the decisions, the service fulfills both of the traditional functions of reporter services: notification and research.

Each week, the service issues advance sheets of about 15 to 20 recent decisions with headnotes summarizing each point of law decided. News Notes supplement the advance sheets with brief reports of topics of interest.

The advance sheets are stored in three-ring binders until a hard-bound book cumulating three months of advance sheets is issued. Each bound quarterly volume begins with a Topical Index and then a reprinting of the service's Classification Outline. With these two tools, both the novice and the experienced user of the service can quickly proceed to the next section of the bound volume—the Index Digest, which contains, in a topically organized manner, the headnotes of all the full-text decisions published in that particular volume.

Also, once a year, a soft-bound Annual Digest cumulates all the headnotes for the decisions reported that year. This Annual Digest also contains a Table of Cases and a Topical Index.

In January 1987, almost 50 years after it first began publication, *United States Patents Quarterly* began its second series (USPQ2d), which features a completely revamped Classification Outline. A Conversion Table allows users to research points of law using both the old outline and the new one.

THE UNITED STATES PATENTS QUARTERLY

USPQ

Second Series

Covering intellectual property law

February 27, 1989 | Pages 1673-1752 | Vol. 9, No. 9

HIGHLIGHTS

COPYRIGHTS

Works Made For Hire: Term "employee," in first section of "work for hire" provisions of 17 USC 101, must be construed to apply only to formal, salaried employees, and works of art produced by artist under contract therefore are not works made for hire under that section (Dumas v. Gommerman, CA 9, 1/13/89, p. 1701).

Publication: Videotape of television news broadcast segment that has not been offered for public sale by station for purposes of further distribution, public performance, or public display has not been "published" within meaning of 17 USC 101 (KCNC-TV Inc. v. Broadcast Information Services Inc., DC Colo, 12/21/88, p. 1732).

Defenses: Infringement defendants' assertion that ASCAP refused to provide complete list of music it licensed, which consists of approximately 3 million songs, is without merit since actual knowledge of infringement is not necessary to create liability (Billy Steinberg Music v. Cagney's Pub, DC NIll, 4/8/88, p. 1749).

PATENTS

Mootness: Settlement agreement that transfers ownership and control of defendant corporation to plaintiff renders moot plaintiff's action for patent infringement and therefore Federal Circuit is without jurisdiction to hear plaintiff's appeal from district court's final judgment (Gould v. Control Laser Corp., CA FC, 1/30/89, p. 1718).

Royalties: Royalties must be paid on crossbow's prod, stock, camouflage paint, and overdraw mechanisms under license agreement which exempts accessories from royal-

(Continued on inside front cover)

TABLE OF CASES

Allen Archery Inc. v. Precision Shooting Equipment Inc. (CA 7) 1728
Billy Steinberg Music v. Cagney's Pub (DC NIll) 1749
Boston Athletic Association v. Sullivan (CA 1) 1690
Celebrity Service International Inc. v. Celebrity World Inc. (DC SNY) 1673
Dumas v. Gommerman (CA 9) 1701
First National Bank of Omaha v. Autoteller Systems Service Corp. (TTAB) 1740
Gould v. Control Laser Corp. (CA FC) 1718
Holloway v. Quigg (DC DC) 1751
KCNC-TV Inc. v. Broadcast Information Services Inc. (DC Colo) 1732
Keebler Co. v. Murray Bakery Products (CA FC) 1736
Maas, Ex parte (BdPatApp & Inter) 1746
Playskool Inc. v. Product Development Group Inc. (DC ENY) 1712
Scotch Whiskey Association v. Majestic Distilling Co. (DC Md) 1723
Spindelfabrik Suessen-Schurr v. Schubert & Salzer Maschinenfabrik (CA FC) 1743

Each week, USPQ subscribers receive a set of new court decisions on patents and other intellectual property issues. They cumulate in a binder until republished in a bound volume.

INDEX DIGEST

Covering 4 USPQ2d 1001 - 4 USPQ2d 1976

DIVISION I - PATENTS

▸ 105. Patent Grant

▸ 105.01 In general

Patent law does not preclude application of state contract law to provide relief for patent licensee's breach of contractual provision by which licensee agreed that, after its license to manufacture licensor's product had terminated, licensee would not include licensor's features and designs in its products, even though agreement prevented licensee from using information that it had previously obtained by reverse engineering, since parties to contract may limit their right to take action that they previously had been free to take. — Universal Gym Equipment Inc. v. ERWA Exercise Equipment Ltd. (CA FC, 9/2/87) 1035

▸ 105.12 Design patents

Design patents for upper and outsole of athletic shoe which incorporated some functional elements are not invalid for functionality, since function performed by any given design element could be performed by other types of design, and since overall impression created by combination of design elements is ornamental or aesthetic rather than functional. — Pensa Inc. v. L. A. Gear California Inc. (DC CCalif, 6/15/87) 1016

▸ 110. Practice and Procedure in Patent and Trademark Office

▸ 110.07 Attorneys and agents

Requirement of 37 CFR 10.6(d) that attorneys employed by federal government be endorsed as "inactive" on Patent and Trademark Office register during their government service is waived as to attorney who challenged PTO's initial denial of his request for registration with inactive designation and who obtained federal district court ruling that such denial was arbitrary and capricious. — Athridge, In re (ComrPats, 10/2/87) 1656

Attorney who recognized high level of materiality of prior art patent was not at liberty, under state of law in 1971, to attempt to draft claims around such reference or to justifiably believe that there was no duty to bring that reference to examiner's attention, and his failure to disclose such highly material reference constitutes gross negligence warranting finding of inequitable conduct. — Kesten, Ex parte (Bd Pat App & Inter, 11/26/86) 1609

Neither attorney's declared ignorance of his duty, nor his particular education and experience, lessen test for satisfying duty of candor from that which would be applied to hypothetical actor in particular position, specifically competent registered patent attorney preparing application for client. *Id.*

Prosecution

▸ 110.0903 Duty of candor

Attorney who recognized high level of materiality of prior art patent was not at liberty, under state of law in 1971, to attempt to draft claims around such reference or to justifiably believe that there was no duty to bring that reference to examiner's attention, and his failure to disclose such highly material reference constitutes gross negligence warranting finding of inequitable conduct. — Kesten, Ex parte (Bd Pat App & Inter, 11/26/86) 1609

Neither attorney's declared ignorance of his duty, nor his particular education and experience, lessen test for satisfying duty of candor from that which would be applied to hypothetical actor in particular position, specifically competent registered patent attorney preparing application for client. *Id.*

Applicant for patent on method of inhibiting mineralization of implanted tissue by use of quaternary ammonium salt having at least one alkyl group containing from 7 to 15 carbon atoms is not guilty of inequitable conduct for failing to disclose unsuccessful tests of "16-carbon compounds," since 16-carbon compounds are to some extent effective as inhibitors and withheld test data involves compounds outside applicant's

Section 4 201

The grandparent of BNA decisional services, USPQ uses a Cumulative Digest and Index (CDI) system.

BNA's Patent, Trademark & Copyright Journal

BNA's Patent, Trademark & Copyright Journal is a weekly notification service on developments in intellectual property law. The service provides timely and comprehensive reporting of court decisions, legislation, and regulatory actions in the patent, trademark, and copyright fields. The scope of the service is much broader than its name implies, encompassing other "intellectual property" concerns as well, such as trade secrets. To keep tabs on the protection of intellectual property, the service also pays close attention to the antitrust laws, the laws of unfair competition, and government contracts.

All important federal and state judicial, administrative, and legislative developments are covered. Special emphasis is placed on the activities of the U.S. Court of Appeals for the Federal Circuit, the Patent and Trademark Office, and the Copyright Office.

The contents of the weekly, self-contained issues are organized as follows: Highlights, News & Comment, Text, and Calendar of Events. The issues are stored in two binders, each covering six months of reports.

The weekly issues of this notification service provide an in-depth review of significant developments in the intellectual property field. The publication covers congressional activity, court decisions, relevant conferènces, professional associations, and international developments, plus actions of the Patent and Trademark Office and the Copyright Office. Complex subjects are reduced to brief, readable summaries, which at the same time provide sufficient detail for the legal professional.

Each issue begins with a Highlights page that briefly summarizes the most important stories reported elsewhere in the issue. The second page summarizes the issue's entire contents and also contains a table of cases reported in the issue.

The major section in each week's issue is News & Comment, which contains the reports on recent judicial, legislative, regulatory, and other activities. Decisions of the U.S. Court of Appeals for the Federal Circuit, which next to the U.S. Supreme Court is the primary judicial authority for interpreting U.S. patent law, are reported usually in the same week in which they are issued. The service's legislative coverage is detailed, thorough, and extensive, as bills are followed from introduction through to hearings and enactment. Coverage of the Patent and Trademark Office and of the Copyright Office focuses on their rulemaking activities and also on the PTO's adjudication function. The actions of other government agencies are reported as well, when they affect intellectual property rights. The publication also covers the meetings of several professional groups, including the American Intellectual Property Law Association, the U.S. Trademark Association, the Copyright Society of the United States, and the Intellectual Property Owners Inc.

The service takes a notification approach to the intellectual property, field, beginning with its front page Highlights of each issue's most noteworthy contents.

BNA's
PATENT, TRADEMARK & COPYRIGHT JOURNAL

ROUTE TO

Vol. 37, No. 916 **HIGHLIGHTS** February 2, 1989

WORK FOR HIRE provisions of Section 101(1) of the Copyright Act apply only to formal, salaried employees, according to the U.S. Court of Appeals for the Ninth Circuit. The Jan. 13 decision concluded that the drafters intended to create a bright line between employees and independent contractors. page 293

ANIMAL PATENTS RULE was properly issued by the Patent and Trademark Office without prior notice and a period for comments, the U.S. District Court for the Northern District of California held Jan. 26. Dismissing a challenge to the agency action, the court reasoned that the rule was not subject to notice and comment requirements under the Administrative Procedure Act because it is interpretative of PTO and Supreme Court decisional law. page 295

SECTION 112 of the Patent Act does not require an invention to be described with the identical words used in the patent claims, the U.S. Court of Appeals for the Federal Circuit ruled Jan. 24. The court reversed a PTO rejection of an application whose specification did not include the words "not permanently fixed," added later to the patent claims. page 296

PTO RULE concerning the involvement of PTO employees in litigation was issued Jan. 26. The new regulation provides comprehensive guidelines for service of process, the scope of testimony permitted by PTO employees, and the production of documents. pages 297, 314

SOFTWARE RENTAL BILL (S 198) introduced Jan. 25 by Senator Orrin G. Hatch (R-Utah) would create copyright infringement liability for the unauthorized rental of a copy of copyrighted computer software. Patterned after the 1984 Record Rental Amendments, the bill would amend Sections 109(b)(1) and (b)(3) of the Copyright Act. page 298

ATTORNEY'S FEES LEGISLATION (HR 671) introduced Jan. 25 by Representative Howard L. Berman (D-Calif) would impose a mandatory fee award in copyright infringement cases when the prevailing party owns the rights to the infringed work and either a small business concern or an individual is the author of the work. page 299

DISCOVERY MOTION was properly denied by the Trademark Trial and Appeal Board in favor of an adverse party's motion for summary judgment, the U.S. Court of Appeals for the Federal Circuit held Jan. 25. The court ruled that the stated need for "certain information" by the movant for discovery does not state "reasons" under Fed.R.Civ.P. Rule 56(f) why he cannot present facts essential to justify opposition to a summary judgment motion. page 300

ANALYSIS SECTION of PTCJ examines the possible effects of a Ninth Circuit decision on copyright protection for derivative works on the development of computer software enhancements. The article was prepared by Richard H. Stern, a member of the PTCJ Advisory Board. page 305

This issue contains pages 293–320

0148-7965/89/$0+.50

Articles inside report in detail recent court decisions and legislative and agency actions.

NEWS & COMMENT

BNA's
PATENT, TRADEMARK & COPYRIGHT JOURNAL

Copyrights

§101(1) WORK FOR HIRE COVERS ONLY FORMAL, SALARIED EMPLOYEES

With an extensive analysis of the legislative history of the 1976 Copyright Act, the Ninth Circuit concluded that the "work made for hire" provisions at 17 USC 101(1) apply only to formal, salaried employees. The drafters intended to create a bright line between employees and independent contractors to avoid mistakes in the parties' appraisal of the contracted work's status, the court explained, and to protect the artist's right to renegotiate transfers at a later date under 17 USC 203(a). (*Dumas v. Gommerman*, CA 9, No. 87-6542, 1/13/89)

Background

Jennifer Dumas is the widow of Patrick Nagel, a graphic artist and commercial illustrator who died in 1984. In 1979, Nagel was commissioned by ITT Canon, through the advertising agency of D'Arcy, McManus and Masius Inc., to create four works of art. ITT intended to give out lithographs of the Nagel works to its distributors as part of a promotional campaign.

Because the promotional giveaway was less than successful, ITT was left with many extra sets of lithographs and threw away the four original paintings. In 1985, Gommerman, an owner of an art gallery and art publishing company, purchased the remaining lithographs from ITT, as well as any copyrights ITT may have held in the works. In 1986, Gommerman obtained a copyright registration for the works in his name, and produced and sold posters from one of the works.

Dumas learned of the purported copyright transfer in 1986, notified Gommerman of her claim to the copyright in the works, and in 1987 obtained a copyright registration of her own in the works. Dumas then filed suit for copyright infringement, and the district court granted Dumas' motion for preliminary injunction.

Gommerman appealed.

Arguments on Appeal

The district court found that Nagel was not an "employee" of ITT for copyright purposes because ITT did not exercise sufficient direction and control over Nagel's creation of the works. The sole issue raised on appeal, Judge Fletcher began, is whether the district court applied the correct legal standard in determining whether Nagel was an employee producing "works made for hire" under 17 USC 101. (Ed. Note: In footnote 3, the Ninth Circuit declined to consider Gommerman's "joint authorship" argument because it was not raised before the trial court.)

On appeal, Gommerman agreed with the "supervision and control" test, but maintained that the district court was too strict in requiring proof of significant control. Dumas also accepted the district court test, but preferred the narrower "literal interpretation" of the statute employed by the Fifth Circuit in *Easter Seal Society for Crippled Children v. Playboy Enterprises Inc.*, 815 F2d 323, 2 USPQ2d 1585 (CA 5 1987), 34 PTCJ 5.

1909 Act and 1976 Act

Under Section 26 of the 1909 Copyright Act, Judge Fletcher explained, the employer was considered the "author" and initial copyright holder of "works made for hire." The 1909 Act contained no definition of "works made for hire," and courts presumed contracts commissioning works to assign copyrights to the patron unless there was an agreement to the contrary. This rule was expanded into a presumption that anyone who paid an artist to create a copyrightable work was the statutory author under the work for hire doctrine, the court related.

Section 201(a) of the 1976 Act vests copyright initially in the author, and Section 201(b) provides as follows:

> the employer or other person for whom the work was prepared is considered the author for purposes of this title, and, unless the parties have expressly agreed otherwise in a written instrument signed by them, owns all of the rights comprised in the copyright.

Section 101 of the 1976 Act provides two definitions of "work made for hire": (1) a work by an employee within the scope of his employment; and (2) a work specially ordered or commissioned for certain specified uses. The Act nowhere defines "employee," "employer," or "scope of employment," Judge Fletcher pointed out.

A particularly important effect of imputing authorship to an employer under Section 201(b), the Ninth Circuit continued, is the elimination of Section 203(a) termination rights. If the copyright were owned by the employee ab initio and were transferred to the employer, Section 203(a) would permit the employee to terminate the transfer 35 years into the copyright term. These termination rights, according to the court, were intended to adjust for the unequal bargaining position of authors, resulting in part from the impossibility of determining a work's value until it has been exploited. (Ed. Note: In footnote 10, the court observed that the scope of the work for hire doctrine was closely linked with the "termination of transfers" question.)

Legislative History

The 1976 Act embodies a clear break with prior doctrine, according to the Ninth Circuit, and no appellate decision thereunder has continued the employer-oriented approach of the cases decided under the 1909

0148-7965/89/$0+.50

Most weekly issues contain a Text section, which reprints important documents in full text. U.S. Supreme Court decisions, proposed or enacted legislation, legislative committee reports, and agency rulings and announcements are examples of material appearing in this section.

Issues also contain a calendar of professional conferences and regulatory deadlines, as well as occasional analysis pieces by experts in the field.

Periodic indexes to the issues complement the publication and provide an easy means of performing research. The indexes are organized by topic with each entry providing a brief summary of the contents of the report or article and the page number where it can be found. The indexes also contain a Table of Cases..

The weekly issues cumulate into six-month volumes, which are housed in separate binders. Individual indexes cover each volume.

This notification service complements the full-text decisional coverage United States Patents Quarterly *gives to the intellectual property field.* BNA's Patent, Trademark & Copyright Journal *provides weekly notification of many of the decisions later printed in USPQ. Plus it reports on legislative and regulatory actions, as well as the activities of bar and private organizations. Text of the most significant documents discussed in any issue is also provided.*

Important documents are reprinted in full text in *BNA's Patent, Trademark & Coyright Journal.*

314 (Vol. 37)

TEXT

BNA's
PATENT, TRADEMARK & COPYRIGHT JOURNAL

PTO FINAL RULE ON SERVICE OF PROCESS AND TESTIMONY OF PTO EMPLOYEES

57 FR 3976

DEPARTMENT OF COMMERCE

Patent and Trademark Office

37 CFR Parts 15 and 15a

[Docket No. 9106–9006]

Service of Process and Testimony of Employees of the Patent and Trademark Office and Production of Documents in Legal Proceedings

AGENCY: Patent and Trademark Office, Commerce.

ACTION: Final rule.

SUMMARY: The Patent and Trademark Office is adding 37 CFR Parts 15 and 15a to supplement 15 CFR Parts 15 and 15a. These new parts prescribe policies and procedures to be followed with respect to service of process on the Patent and Trademark Office, the Commissioner of Patents and Trademarks, and employees of the Office, the testimony of Office employees regarding official matters, and the production of official documents in legal proceedings. These regulations serve as a statement of Office policy and provide comprehensive guidelines for the Office and its employees, outside agencies, and other persons regarding the appropriate procedures for service of process, testimony, and production of documents.

EFFECTIVE DATE: January 26, 1989.

FOR FURTHER INFORMATION CONTACT: Associate Solicitor John W. Dewhirst by mail at Box 8, U.S. Patent and Trademark Office, Washington, DC 20231 and by phone at (703) 557–4035.

SUPPLEMENTARY INFORMATION: These regulations are designed to supplement, and be construed consistent with, 15 CFR Parts 15 and 15a. The regulations in Part 15a state the views of the Office with respect to the permissible scope of testimony which may be given by Office employees in connection with their performance of quasi-judicial patent and trademark matters. These Office views are consistent with *United States v. Morgan*, 313 U.S. 409, 422 (1941); *Western Electric Co., Inc. v. Piezo Technology, Inc. v. Quigg*, No. 88–1216, 860 F.2d 428, 8 USPQ 2d 1853 (Fed. Cir. Nov. 1, 1988); *In re Mayewsky*, 162 USPQ 86, 89 (E.D. Va. 1969), and *Shaffer Tool Works v. Joy Mfg. Co.*, 167 USPQ 170 (S.D. Tex. 1970).

Because these regulations concern agency management and personnel, they are not rules or regulations within the meaning of section 1(a) of Executive Order 12291, and they are not subject to the requirements of that Order. Accordingly, no preliminary or final regulatory impact analysis has to be or will be prepared.

These regulations, relating to agency management and personnel, are exempt from all requirements of section 553 of the Administrative Procedure Act (5 U.S.C. 553) including a delayed effective date and therefore will be effective immediately upon publication in the **Federal Register**.

Because a notice of proposed rulemaking and an opportunity for public comments are not required to be given for these regulations by section 553 of the APA, or by any other law, no regulatory flexibility analysis has to be or will be prepared for purposes of the Regulatory Flexibility Act (5 U.S.C. 603(a) and 604(a)).

This final rule does not contain policies with Federalism implications sufficient to warrant preparation of a Federalism assessment under Executive Order 12612.

This rule does not contain collections of information for purposes of the Paperwork Reduction Act.

List of Subjects in 37 CFR Parts 15 and 15a

Attorneys, Administrative practice and procedure, Courts, Government employees.

For the reasons set forth in the preamble, 37 CFR is amended as follows:

1. Part 15 is added to read as follows:

PART 15—SERVICE OF PROCESS

Sec.
15.1 Scope and purpose.
15.2 Definitions.
15.3 Acceptance of service of process.

Authority: 5 U.S.C. 301; 15 U.S.C. 1501, 1512, 1513, 1515, and 1518; Reorganization Plan No. 5 of 1950; 44 U.S.C. 3101; 15 CFR 15.2(a).

§ 15.1 Scope and purpose.

(a) This part supplements 15 CFR Part 15 and sets forth the procedures to be followed when a summons or complaint is served on the Office or the Commissioner or an employee of the Office in his or her official capacity. This part is to be construed consistent with 15 CFR Part 15.

(b) This part is intended to ensure the orderly execution of the affairs of the Office and not to impede any legal proceedings.

(c) This part does not apply to subpoenas. The procedures to be followed with respect to subpoenas are set out in Part 15a of this Title.

(d) This part does not apply to service of process made on an Office employee personally on matters not related to official business of the Office or to the official responsibilities of the Office employee.

§ 15.2 Definitions.

For the purpose of this part:

(a) "Commissioner" means Assistant Secretary and Commissioner of Patents and Trademarks.

(b) "Legal proceeding" means a proceeding before a tribunal constituted by law, including a court, an administrative body or commission, or an administrative law judge or hearing officer.

(c) "Office" means Patent and Trademark Office.

(d) "Office employee" means any officer or employee of the Office.

(e) "Official business" means the authorized business of the Office.

(f) "Solicitor" means the chief legal officer of the Office or other Office employee to whom the Solicitor has delegated authority to act under this part.

§ 15.3 Acceptance of service of process.

(a) Any summons or complaint to be served in person or by registered or certified mail or as otherwise authorized by law on the Office or the

2-2-89 Published by THE BUREAU OF NATIONAL AFFAIRS, INC., Washington, D.C. 20037

Analyses by experts in the field explore recent developments and trends.

(Vol. 37) 305

ANALYSIS

BNA's
PATENT, TRADEMARK & COPYRIGHT JOURNAL

Copyrights

NINTH CIRCUIT DECISION MAY INHIBIT DEVELOPMENT OF ADD-ON SOFTWARE

(Ed. Note: This article examines a recent Ninth Circuit decision on copyright protection for derivative works, and its implications for the development of computer programs which are enhancements of existing software. The author is a member of the PTCJ Advisory Board.)

Framing Prints, Giving the Mona Lisa a Moustache, Speeding Up Video Games, and Marketing Add-on Software: A Comment on the Mirage Case
By Richard H. Stern

A conflict is emerging in computer software copyright law over the legality of enhancement programs, which improve the performance of spreadsheets, database managers, and other business software. On the one side, enhancers of such software desire to sell customers owning these software packages the enhancers' add-on programs that modify and improve the operation of the original software. Pitted against them are the original software sellers, who desire to control the identity of their computer programs in their customers' hands. Obviously they want to make any money to be had from selling enhancements to their programs, regardless of who conceives the enhancements.

To phrase the dispute in doctrinal terms, the original sellers may charge that the enhancers are preparing unauthorized "derivative work" versions of the original computer programs, in violation of the exclusive right of copyright owners to prepare derivative works. The enhancers respond by denying that there is any derivative work here; they also claim that the "first sale" rule immunizes their enhancements. Sorting the problem out is complicated further by the Copyright Act's failure to define key terms involved in the definition of "derivative work."

The courts have addressed this sort of product enhancement problem mainly in doctrinal terms, often without reference to the policies on which the doctrines are based and without consideration of whether those policies apply to the works before the court in the same way as they do to the works before courts in earlier cases. Nonetheless, the results reached in prior cases, which most of the time did not involve software-related copyrights, have generally been within the zone of acceptability. The cases did not really test the limits of the doctrines involved, or lead to clearly outrageous results.

The latest decision in this field, however, is that of the Ninth Circuit in *Mirage Editions, Inc. v. Albuquerque A.R.T. Co.*, 856 F.2d 1341, 8 USPQ2d 1171 (9th Cir. 1988), 36 PTCJ 639. Although *Mirage* involves still another non-software case, it is a step in a direction that runs counter to important copyright policies relating to progress in software technology. These are policies favoring maximum encouragement of publication and public availability of technological innovations in software.

The Software Enhancement Setting

Consider an applications program that converts data from spreadsheet form to bar or pie graphs, or that provides reports summarizing information selected from a data base. Consider a set of menus in an application program, that permit a user of the program to select particular options, for example, by entering different keystroke combination to invoke different choices. The programs and their associated screen displays have a characteristic user interface and "look and feel" that are suboptimal in terms of esthetic quality or user friendliness. The programs may also perform their tasks slowly, and may lack particular features or options that would make them more useful and attractive to users.

At this point an entrepreneur enters the stage who writes an "add-on" program. The add-on program cooperates with the original program, within the computer, adding an improvement or enhancement such as making the bar or pie charts take on a three-dimensional appearance or making a selected slice of the pie chart glow and appear to stand out from the screen. The format of the reports generated from the data base is made more attractive. The menus are no longer controlled by keystroke entries. Instead, successive choices are highlighted on a pull-down menu in inverse video or a movable arrow points at them; the user moves the lighted bar or arrow up or down with up-arrow and down-arrow keys until a desired selection is highlighted, and then the user taps the return key to register that choice. This is easier to understand and use, and leads to fewer mistakes. Or the add-on program speeds up the original or provides supplemental features that the original seller failed to include.

The question is whether sellers of such add-on programs directly or contributorily infringe the copyrights of the original sellers, for example, their copyrights in screen displays. Or to take the hypothetical a step farther, consider the following case: An add-on company purchases large numbers of the diskettes of the original application program "X-base," packages them (unaltered) together with diskettes for the add-on program, and markets the combination package as "Hyper-base," the hyper version of the well known database program. Is selling this package in some way a copyright infringement? Or is the "look and feel" of the modified screen displays an infringement of the old screen displays? Does the seller cause the customer to commit a copyright infringement?

2-2-89 BNA's Patent, Trademark & Copyright Journal
0148-7965/89/$0+.50

World Intellectual Property Report

World Intellectual Property Report is a monthly notification service on developments worldwide in intellectual property law. The service reports on court decisions, legislation, and regulatory actions in the patent, trademark, and copyright fields.

A global network of reporters and experts in the field files detailed articles every month on the latest developments in their countries.

The contents of the monthly, self-contained issues are organized as follows: Highlights, Topical Summary, Around The World, Briefs, Conferences and Meetings, Calendar, and Text. The issues are stored in one binder, with a cumulative index.

The monthly issues of this notification service provide an international perspective on the fields covered in *BNA's Patent, Trademark & Copyright Journal. World Intellectual Property Report* covers events in the United States as they relate to non-U.S. businesses. It also covers foreign countries' legislative and regulatory developments, court and agency decisions, relevant conferences, professional associations, and includes full text of pertinent materials.

Each issue begins with a Highlights page that briefly summarizes the most important stories reported elsewhere in the issue. The second page summarizes the issue's entire contents by topic and also provides bold-face country names as a cross-reference within the topical summary.

The major section in each week's issue is Around The World, which contains country-by-country reports, in alphabetical order by country name, on recent administrative, judicial, legislative, regulatory, and other activities. Many of these articles are authored by local experts in the field, and thus include insights to that country's unique intellectual property situation. *World Intellectual Property Report* also covers enforcement activities from country to country.

Also part of the coverage are the activities of many international organizations, including the World Intellectual Property Organization (WIPO), International Association for the Protection of Industrial Property (AIPPI), American Intellectual Property Law Association (AIPLA), General Agreement on Trade and Tariffs (GATT), European Patent Office (EPO), U.S. Patent and Trademark Office (USPTO), International Publishers Association (IPA), American Bar Association (ABA), International Bar Association (IBA), and U.S. Trademark Association (USTA).

The service takes a notification approach to international intellectual property, begining with its front page Highlights of each issue's most noteworthy contents.

WORLD

THE BUREAU OF NATIONAL AFFAIRS, INC.

Intellectual Property Report

Vol. 6, No. 10 October 1992

HIGHLIGHTS

CHINA'S REVISED PATENT LAW was unveiled in September and will take effect on January 1. Most of the revisions seem to follow those laid out in the January 17 Memorandum of Understanding between China and the United States, although doubts remain. More will be known when implementing regulations are released later this year. (Page 270)

UKRAINE NOTIFIED WIPO that it is a successor to the former Soviet Union with regard to the Paris Convention, Madrid Agreement, and Patent Cooperation Treaty. Ukraine also released transitional regulations that, among other things, provide for extension of former Soviet intellectual property rights. (Page 277)

FRANCE'S HIGHEST COURT has been asked to review a decision that the Novotel Hotel did not infringe CNN's copyrights by transmitting television programs into individual rooms of the hotel without authorization. Two lower courts decided that the hotel could retransmit the CNN signal without infringing its copyrights because a hotel room is not "a place accessible to the public" under French law. (Page 270)

A JAPANESE REPORT on the current state of Japanese patent law in the context of global harmonization urges consideration of several changes, such as elimination of the pre-grant opposition system, eventual change to post-grant opposition, and revisions to the utility model system. (Page 272)

SLOVENIA WILL APPLY six treaties that were applicable in Yugoslavia, according to an announcement filed with WIPO. The treaties are the WIPO Convention, Paris Convention, Madrid Agreement, Nice Agreement, Locarno Agreement, and Berne Convention. (Page 275)

SOUTH AFRICA'S COPYRIGHT ACT, which came into force in July, includes new *sui generis* protection for computer programs and provides a new definition of "author" of a computer program. (Page 275)

THE AUSTRALIAN GOVERNMENT is seeking comments on how to improve the efficiency of its trade mark system. A working-party review of the Trade Marks Act has suggested several changes. (Page 267)

NEW ZEALAND AND PORTUGAL have joined the Patent Cooperation Treaty, bringing the number of member countries to 52. New Zealand's Patents Act, which was amended in August, also abolished certain controversial compulsory-license provisions. (Page 273)

SWITZERLAND'S PATENT OFFICE has changed procedures on reinstatement and representation. Meanwhile, the Swiss Federal Court has upheld 50-year protection for sound recordings. (Page 276)

THE FREE TRADE AGREEMENT between Canada, Mexico, and the United States, which was released in September, contains a comprehensive chapter on intellectual property rights, which is reprinted in the **TEXT** section of this issue. (Page 284)

COMMENT AND ANALYSIS: *Infringement Under Australian and U.S. Circuit Layouts Legislation*, by David Webber, Davies Collison Cave, Melbourne, Australia, compares litigation under the U.S. Semiconductor Chip Protection Act of 1984 and the Australian Circuit Layouts Act 1989, and the results reached under each. (Page 280)

BNA International Inc., London, England
A subsidiary of The Bureau of National Affairs, Inc., Washington, D.C., U.S.A.

AROUND THE WORLD (Vol.6)267

AROUND THE WORLD

AUSTRALIA

GOVERNMENT SEEKS PUBLIC COMMENTS ON IMPROVEMENT OF TRADE MARK SYSTEM

CANBERRA—Following a working party review of the 1955 Trade Marks Act, the government is seeking comments on how to improve the overall efficiency of the trade mark system. Peter Richards, Deputy Registrar, said public comments will be accepted until January 31, 1993.

Richards said the current law was a "fairly cumbersome piece of legislation" and that Australia was conducting the same kind of trade mark reviews that were underway in New Zealand and the United Kingdom over the past several months.

Among the major changes recommended in the working party's 119-page report are the following:

- a new, broader definition of a trade mark, that is, any sign capable of distinguishing goods or services of one person from those of other persons. Such a sign must be capable of graphic representation.
- the legislation should be expressed in terms which make it clear that there is to be a presumption of registrability when examining an application for registration.
- rights given by a trade mark registration should be broader than those under the present act, with a wider test for infringement, similar to that proposed in the draft GATT TRIPs agreement.

Richards said the changes were designed to streamline existing procedures, including the introduction of multi-class applications; simplified provisions for recording the assignment of trade marks and the entering of licensing agreements on the Register; and a more streamlined method for removing unused trade marks from the Register.

During the annual Budget sittings, which begin on August 18, the government, through Sen. John Button, Minister for Industry, Trade and Commerce, also plans to introduce legislation to crack down on counterfeiting in the textile, clothing, and footwear industries, plus amendments to existing counterfeiting and forgery penalties—in line with the report's recommendations.

Copies of the report, Recommended Changes to the Australian Trade Marks Legislation, can be obtained from the Government Printing Office, Wentworth Avenue, Kingston, ACT 2604; fax (61-6) 257-1797.

(BNA's Special Correspondent in Australia prepared this report.)

BRAZIL

BRAZILIAN COURTS BLOCK GRAY MARKET GOODS IN VIDEO GAMES, SHOES CASES

RIO DE JANEIRO—In two recent cases, Brazilian courts have established that gray market or parallel goods will be blocked from entry into the country and will be confiscated when Brazilian trademark licensees have registered their exclusive-right-to-distribute agreements with the patent and trademark office (INPI).

The most recent case involves Sega Video games. Sega Company in Japan registered its mark with the INPI in 1976. In 1991, Sega assigned exclusive rights to the mark in Brazil to Tec Toy of Brazil, a manufacturer of electronic games. The agreement also was registered at the Brazilian office of patents and trademarks.

Subsequently, Tec Toy discovered that pirated copies of Sega games were being manufactured in Paraguay and were being shipped to Brazil, where they were being sold at a video games store. Additionally, Tec Toy found that games that had been legally manufactured and sold by Sega overseas were being imported into Brazil by other companies.

Tec Toy sought preliminary relief, which would permit confiscation of illegally produced pirated copies of Sega games and would also bar entry of gray goods as well as pirated games. Granting both requests, the court issued an injunction to confiscate the pirated games from the video game outlet, and additionally ordered the Brazilian department of customs (Servicio de Comercio Exterior do Banco do Brasil-SECEX) not to issue import licenses for any goods that bore the Sega mark.

Tec Toy's lawyer, Newton Silveira from the São Paulo firm of Leopoldi e Meirelles de Oliveira, said the order will bar both pirated and gray area goods. The court decision was based on Article 59 of Brazil's Industrial Property law, Law 5772 of Jan. 1, 1972, which states that exclusive use and ownership of a mark will be reserved to the registered holder, "in order to distinguish his products, goods, or services from identical or similar ones in the class corresponding to his activity."

The action was good news for foreign companies as well as Brazilian licensees, he said. "If the product can come into the country in any way, no one can know if it is a pirated good or not," he said. Tec Toy's director, Nelson Goncalves, said the company would next file an action for losses and damages against the stores that were selling the pirated goods.

The first case of this kind occurred in December, when a Brazilian shoe manufacturer, São Paulo Alpargatas, sought to enforce its rights under an exclusive license agreement with Nike sporting shoe company in Japan. The agreement had been filed with the INPI. As in the Sega case, the court ordered confiscation of shoes that bore the Nike mark that were not manufactured by Alpargatas. The

WORLD INTELLECTUAL PROPERTY REPORT
0952-7613/92/$0+.50

Articles inside are organized by country name and report in detail recent government activities.

Employee Benefits Cases

Employee Benefits Cases reports and compiles the full text of selected federal and state court opinions on employee benefits issues. Also included are selected decisions of labor arbitrators and the National Labor Relations Board.

As with other BNA decisional services, the opinions reported by this service are sent to subscribers initially in advance sheets, which are stored in a binder until republished in a bound volume. Each decision is preceded by a headnote or headnotes explaining the court's holdings, and each headnote is assigned a number that fits it into the service's Classification Guide and indexing system.

This service has been compiling court, arbitrator, and agency decisions on employee benefits since 1981. The decisions, which are headnoted and reported in full text, involve pension and other employee benefit issues, such as reporting and disclosure, collective bargaining, and fiduciary responsibility.

The decisions interpret and implement such laws as the Employee Retirement Income Security Act of 1974 (ERISA), the Multiemployer Pension Plan Amendments Act of 1980 (MPPAA), the Consolidated Omnibus Budget Reconciliation Act of 1986 (COBRA), the Age Discrimination in Employment Act, the Equal Pay Act, the Veterans Reemployment Rights Act, the Pregnancy Discrimination Act, and the Internal Revenue Code.

Decisions are issued weekly in the form of looseleaf pages, which are stored in a binder. These pages are republished periodically in a bound volume.

With each week's set of opinions comes a four-page "wrap" (it wraps around the opinions), which highlights the holdings of each opinion and lists the names of all the cases.

The service's system of classifying and cumulating the headnotes that are assigned to each reported decision is virtually identical to that used in BNA's *Labor Relations Reporter* and *Media Law Reporter* and is described fully elsewhere in this book.

Each decision reported in *Employee Benefits Cases* is fully headnoted, and each headnote is given a number that ties it into the service's CDI system.

10 EBC 2008 — In re HECI Exploration Co., Inc.

In re HECI EXPLORATION CO., INC.

U.S. Court of Appeals, Fifth Circuit

In re HECI EXPLORATION CO., INC., Successor in Interest to Holloway Exploration Co., Debtor; HECI EXPLORATION CO., EMPLOYEES' PROFIT SHARING PLAN, Appellant, v. PAT S. HOLLOWAY, Appellee, No. 87-1686, Dec. 13, 1988.

ERISA — PROTECTION OF RIGHTS

Preemption — In General (▸50.01)

[1] Parties may not stipulate that state law will govern their ERISA claim, even though, under some circumstances, parties may waive application of federal law in favor of federally preempted state law claim by failing to raise federal law in timely fashion, since ERISA preemption is designed to prevent development of competing lines of cases decided under state law.

ERISA — PROTECTION OF RIGHTS

Administration and Enforcement — Standard of Court Review — Arbitrary and Capricious Action (▸40.404)

Administration and Enforcement — Action for Benefits — Pension or Profit Sharing Benefits (▸40.503)

[2] Pension plan properly was denied right to use federal arbitrary and capricious standard of judicial review as defense to plan participant's claim that plan wrongfully denied his benefits, since, as plan failed to raise issue at trial, in briefs, or in oral argument, federal district court acting as appellate court did not abuse its discretion in finding that standard had been waived, and since, as plan's determination that participant had withdrawn as plan participant was arbitrary and capricious, plan would not have prevailed even if standard were applied.

On appeal from a decision of the U.S. District Court for the Northern District of Texas that former employee was entitled to benefits under bankrupt employer's pension plan. Affirmed.

Robert L. Yeager III, Norman Landa, and S. Reid Heller, of Dallas, Texas, attorneys for HECI Exploration Co. Employees' Profit Sharing Plan.

Pat Holloway, of Giddings, Texas, pro se.

Full Text of Opinion

Before RUBIN, KING, and WILLIAMS, Circuit Judges.

KING, Circuit Judge.

HECI Exploration Company Employees' Profit Sharing Plan appeals from the district court's affirmance of a bankruptcy court's final judgment that Pat S. Holloway, as a qualified participant in the Plan who had not waived his right to participate, was entitled to receive his interest in the Plan. Finding no reversible error in the district court's decision, we affirm.

I.

The facts and procedural background of this case are set forth in detail in the district court's opinion below. *See Holloway v. HECI Explor. Co. Employee's Profit Sharing Plan (In re HECI)*, 76 B.R. 563, 564-67 (N.D.Tex. 1987). Pat S. Holloway ("Holloway") was president, chief executive, and sole active officer of HECI Exploration Company, Inc. ("HECI")[1] from that company's inception in 1974 until Holloway was terminated by order of a Texas state

[1] HECI was originally known as Humble Exploration Company, Inc. but later changed its name, apparently as a result of a lawsuit brought by Exxon Corporation concerning the use of the name "Humble." *See Exxon Corp. v. Humble Exploration Co.*, 524 F. Supp. 450 (N.D.Tex. 1981), *aff'd in part, rev'd in part*, 695 F.2d 96 (5th Cir. 1983), *on remand*, 592 F. Supp. 1226 (N.D.Tex. 1984).

The decisions are reported in full text and are stored in a binder until republished in bound volumes.

In re HECI Exploration Co., Inc. — 10 EBC 2009

court in July, 1982.[2] HECI was formed to engage in the exploration and development of oil and gas properties. In 1978, at the suggestion of one of HECI's major investors, Holloway decided to establish the HECI Exploration Company Employees' Profit Sharing Plan ("the Plan") in order to boost employee morale. The Plan was to be funded with overriding royalty interests in four of the oil prospects that HECI was engaged in drilling and development. In 1978 and early 1979, Holloway caused assignments of those overriding royalty interests to be made to the Plan as well as to himself, his then-wife, and his children. HECI's treasurer, Dean Johnson ("Johnson"), and Holloway acted as co-trustees of the Plan. On November 19, 1979, both HECI and Holloway, individually, filed voluntary Chapter 11, bankruptcy petitions. The HECI case was later converted to Chapter 7.

Holloway and Johnson continued to serve as co-trustees of the Plan until Holloway's employment was terminated. In June 1984, Johnson proposed to make a partial distribution of plan benefits to terminated employees, subject to approval by the bankruptcy court. Holloway was not included in the list of proposed distributees. Upon receiving the list, Holloway sent a note to Johnson, asking "on what basis" he was being excluded. No further communication about Holloway's exclusion from the distribution was made, and the funds were ultimately distributed.

Holloway proceeded to file an ERISA action in Texas state court.[3] Holloway sought to recover from the Plan benefits allegedly due him as a Plan participant and to obtain a declaration that he was entitled to future Plan benefits. By the time of the suit, HECI was acting Plan administrator. Acting through Don Navarro ("Navarro"), HECI's trustee in bankruptcy — who, curiously enough, was also the trustee in bankruptcy of Holloway's estate[4] — HECI intervened in the state court action, removing it to the United States Bankruptcy Court for the Northern District of Texas for consolidation with HECI's Chapter 7 proceeding.

Before trial, a question arose concerning the bankruptcy court's jurisdiction to hear the matter. The bankruptcy court ultimately concluded that Holloway's suit was a "related" proceeding (as opposed to a "core" proceeding) and found that jurisdiction was proper. At the close of trial, the bankruptcy court announced findings of fact and conclusions of law with respect to Holloway's claim (*not*, as would have been consistent with "related to" jurisdiction, proposed findings of fact and conclusions of law). *See In re HECI*, 76 B.R.. at 566. In addition, the bankruptcy court reserved the right to change or add to its holdings and urged the parties "to submit proposed orders and proposed findings of fact and conclusions of law." The parties did so, and the bankruptcy court subsequently entered in writing amended findings and conclu-

[2] As the district court noted, a summary of the state court and related federal litigation which led to Holloway's termination may be found in *Browning v. Navarro*, 743 F.2d 1069, 1071-73 (5th Cir. 1984), *rev'g*, 37 B.R. 201 (N.D.Tex. 1983), and in the bankruptcy court's opinion in that case, 37 B.R. at 203-06.

[3] The district court noted that:

In his brief (Appellee Br. at 36-37) Holloway characterizes his lawsuit as a "simple breach of contract case." The court holds, however, that this is a federally-preempted field and that, pursuant to 29 U.S.C. §1144(a), Holloway has an exclusive federal cause of action (which, pursuant to 29 U.S.C. §1132(e)(1), may be maintained in federal or state court) to recover benefits from an ERISA-qualified plan. *See Metropolitan Life Insurance Co. v. Taylor*, 481 U.S. 58, 107 S.Ct. 1542, 1546, 95 L.Ed.2d 55 [8 EBC 1417] (1987).

In re HECI, 76 B.R. at 565 n. 3.

Although the district court was correct in noting that Holloway characterized his lawsuit as a "simple breach of contract case," Holloway also properly identified his case as arising under ERISA — in both his original state court complaint and his brief to the district court. The preemption issue is discussed in detail below.

[4] We note that Navarro's dual role creates the possibility of a conflict of interest which could cast doubt upon the legitimacy of the Plan's decision to deny Holloway's claim. However, because we uphold Holloway's claim on other grounds, we do not reach this issue.

BNA Pension Reporter

The *BNA Pension Reporter* is a weekly notification service covering the latest legislative, regulatory, and judicial developments affecting pension and other employee benefit programs such as health insurance. The service is designed to help lawyers and their business clients comply with pension reform laws, particularly the Employee Retirement Income Security Act of 1974 (ERISA) and its amendments, as well as the Internal Revenue Code.

Each weekly issue contains reports on court decisions, legislation, and agency activities that affect the way pension and employee benefit programs are planned, written, and administered. Related tax developments are another major focus of the publication. Editorial reports of the latest news are supplemented regularly by analyses of benefit provisions or of enacted laws and by reprints of the full text of important benefits-related documents.

These weekly current reports are fully indexed and stored in two binders, each covering a six-month period. A third binder contains special supplements, including forms, analyses, and textual documents.

This service's weekly reports on developments in the benefits field begin with a Highlights page summarizing the week's most important events. The second page of each issue, headed Index Summary, lists the issue's entire contents topic-by-topic, as well as the names of all the court decisions reported in the issue.

The News section that leads off each issue contains reports on all aspects of pension and benefit planning. It covers government, labor, and industry activities, including legislation and the legislative process, agency regulations and standards, and meetings and hearings, as well as other developments. A separate Legal section follows with reports on court decisions in the area.

Another regular although not weekly feature is the Taxes section, which contains reports on the activities of the Internal Revenue Service as they relate to pensions, including private letter rulings, general counsel's memoranda, and revenue rulings.

The Text section contains full text of important government documents, perhaps final or proposed regulations of the Pension Benefit Guaranty Corporation, the Labor Department, or the IRS. Analyses provide the insight of practitioners or experts on such key issues as provisions in benefit programs or pension legislation.

The final section in many issues is the Journal, which lists, in summary fashion, the current activities of the various federal and state branches of government, including congressional committee and bill action. Also listed are upcoming professional meetings and conferences and a bibliography of new publications and other resources.

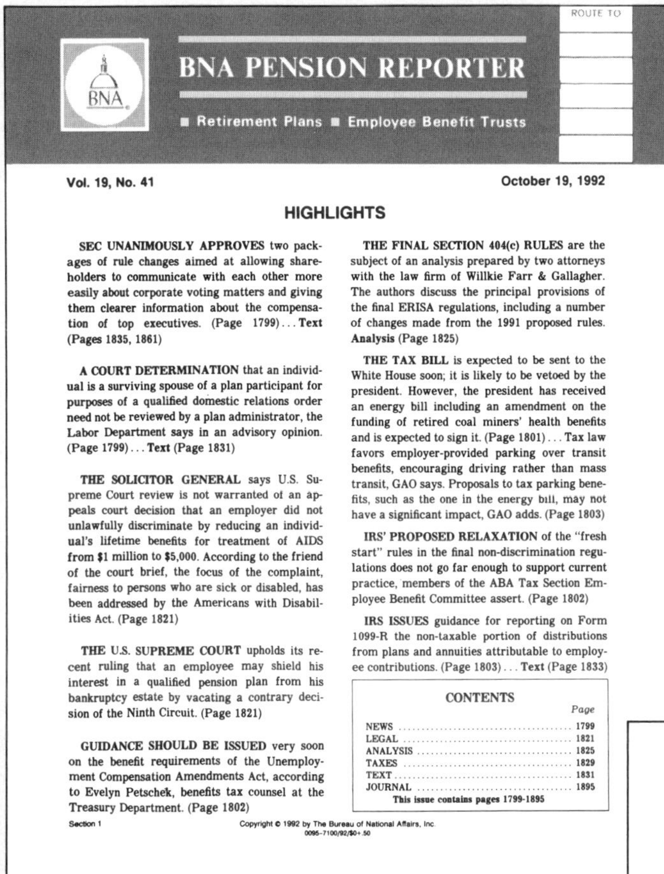

ROUTE TO

BNA

BNA PENSION REPORTER

■ Retirement Plans ■ Employee Benefit Trusts

Vol. 19, No. 41 October 19, 1992

HIGHLIGHTS

SEC UNANIMOUSLY APPROVES two packages of rule changes aimed at allowing shareholders to communicate with each other more easily about corporate voting matters and giving them clearer information about the compensation of top executives. (Page 1799) . . . **Text** (Pages 1835, 1861)

A COURT DETERMINATION that an individual is a surviving spouse of a plan participant for purposes of a qualified domestic relations order need not be reviewed by a plan administrator, the Labor Department says in an advisory opinion. (Page 1799) . . . **Text** (Page 1831)

THE SOLICITOR GENERAL says U.S. Supreme Court review is not warranted of an appeals court decision that an employer did not unlawfully discriminate by reducing an individual's lifetime benefits for treatment of AIDS from $1 million to $5,000. According to the friend of the court brief, the focus of the complaint, fairness to persons who are sick or disabled, has been addressed by the Americans with Disabilities Act. (Page 1821)

THE U.S. SUPREME COURT upholds its recent ruling that an employee may shield his interest in a qualified pension plan from his bankruptcy estate by vacating a contrary decision of the Ninth Circuit. (Page 1821)

GUIDANCE SHOULD BE ISSUED very soon on the benefit requirements of the Unemployment Compensation Amendments Act, according to Evelyn Petschek, benefits tax counsel at the Treasury Department. (Page 1802)

THE FINAL SECTION 404(c) RULES are the subject of an analysis prepared by two attorneys with the law firm of Willkie Farr & Gallagher. The authors discuss the principal provisions of the final ERISA regulations, including a number of changes made from the 1991 proposed rules. **Analysis** (Page 1825)

THE TAX BILL is expected to be sent to the White House soon; it is likely to be vetoed by the president. However, the president has received an energy bill including an amendment on the funding of retired coal miners' health benefits and is expected to sign it. (Page 1801) . . . Tax law favors employer-provided parking over transit benefits, encouraging driving rather than mass transit, GAO says. Proposals to tax parking benefits, such as the one in the energy bill, may not have a significant impact, GAO adds. (Page 1803)

IRS' PROPOSED RELAXATION of the "fresh start" rules in the final non-discrimination regulations does not go far enough to support current practice, members of the ABA Tax Section Employee Benefit Committee assert. (Page 1802)

IRS ISSUES guidance for reporting on Form 1099-R the non-taxable portion of distributions from plans and annuities attributable to employee contributions. (Page 1803) . . . **Text** (Page 1833)

CONTENTS

	Page
NEWS	1799
LEGAL	1821
ANALYSIS	1825
TAXES	1829
TEXT	1831
JOURNAL	1895

This issue contains pages 1799-1895

Section 1

0095-7100/92/$0+.50

BNA Pension Reporter provides a notification service on developments in the employee benefits field. Each week's issue begins with a Highlights page.

The Legal section in each issue contains reports on recent court decisions in the employee benefits field.

(Vol. 19) 1821

BNA

Legal

AIDS

SUPREME COURT REVIEW IN MUSIC CASE NOT WARRANTED, SOLICITOR GENERAL SAYS

U.S. Supreme Court review of a federal appellate court decision that an employer did not unlawfully discriminate by reducing an individual's lifetime benefits for treatment of acquired immune deficiency syndrome from $1 million to $5,000 is not warranted, according to the Solicitor General's friend of the court brief (*Greenberg v. H&H Music Co.*, US SupCt, No. 91-1283).

The Solicitor General maintained that the issue involved in the case—the meaning and scope of the anti-discrimination provisions of Section 510 of the Employee Retirement Income Security Act—is narrow. The court of appeals correctly held that nothing in Section 510 prohibited H&H Music Co. from adopting an amendment to its health benefits plan that disadvantaged persons with AIDS in order to reduce plan costs, according to the Solicitor General's brief.

The U.S. Court of Appeals for the Fifth Circuit upheld the employer's action Nov. 4, 1991 (18 *BPR* 2085, 14 *EBC* 1729).

Although the brief acknowledged that the case implicates health care policy issues of serious concern to the country and that the employee, John McGann—who has since died—lost insurance coverage at the time it was most needed, the brief said any other interpretation of the law cannot be reconciled with provisions of ERISA that more directly address the validity of the plan terms at issue here. Those provisions of ERISA establish that Congress decided not to prohibit plan amendments reducing existing health care benefits, the brief said.

The Fifth Circuit's decision does not conflict with the decision of any other court and the focus of the complaint, fairness to persons who are sick or disabled, is a subject that now has been addressed by the Americans with Disabilities Act, the Solicitor General continued. Thus, no further review of the case is warranted, the brief said.

The Solicitor General submitted the brief in response to a Supreme Court request for the views of the government.

Bankruptcy

SUPREME COURT VACATES DECISION INCLUDING PENSION ASSETS IN ESTATE

The U.S. Supreme Court Oct. 13 upheld its recent ruling that an employee may shield his interest in a qualified pension plan from his bankruptcy estate by vacating a contrary decision of the Ninth Circuit (*Reed v. Drummond*, US SupCt, No. 92-26, 10/13/92).

During its last term, the Supreme Court, in the case *Patterson v. Shumate*, ruled unanimously that the prohibition against the alienation of pension benefits under the Employee Retirement Income Security Act must be honored in bankruptcy proceedings (19 *BPR* 1320, 15 *EBC* 1481).

Eldon S. Reed's bankruptcy trustee contended that *Patterson* was decided incorrectly. She argued that the court's ruling that Section 541(c)(2) of the Bankruptcy Code, which excludes from the bankruptcy estate property that is subject to a restriction on transfer enforceable under "applicable nonbankruptcy law," includes ERISA renders meaningless the "plain language" of Section 522 of the code. That section, she said, exempts both Social Security and civil service retirement benefits from the bankruptcy estate.

Debtor Eldon Reed was a participant in an employer-sponsored pension plan that was covered by ERISA and the Internal Revenue Code. In his bankruptcy schedules, he claimed an exemption for all retirement benefits provided by his pension plan. The bankruptcy trustee objected and the bankruptcy court denied the exemption. The district court and the Ninth Circuit affirmed (14 *EBC* 2303).

Fiduciary Duty

SIXTH CIRCUIT RULES GM VIOLATED ERISA, MISLED WORKERS REGARDING BENEFIT BUYOUT

CINCINNATI—General Motors Corp. owes more than 270 former employees benefits that may run as high as $7 million following a decision by the U.S. Court of Appeals for the Sixth Circuit that the automaker unlawfully misled those workers about a benefit buyout plan (*Drennan v. General Motors Corp.*, CA 6, Nos. 90-3659 and 90-3660, 10/13/92).

The court found that GM breached its fiduciary duties under the Employee Retirement Income Security Act by misleading a group of workers permanently laid off from its Norwood, Ohio, assembly plant about their eligibility for benefit buyout. The court affirmed that the workers had been unfairly denied access to a more lucrative GM severance plan and ordered a recalculation of their damages award.

In an Oct. 15 interview with BNA, plaintiffs' attorney James M. Kelly called the decision a major victory for the workers. The court's ruling tells GM "it cannot play fast and loose with its responsibilities," he said.

During the period surrounding the August 1987 plant closing, managers were instructed to answer employee questions about severance plans in a way that was clearly misleading, said Kelly. After GM shut down the plant, the company notified all workers of their right to participate in a severance plan known as the Supplemental Unemployment Benefit (SUB) buyout. This plan provided employees with lump sum payments in exchange for voluntary forfeiture of their employment seniority and layoff status with GM, said Kelly.

At the time, GM had another benefit buyout plan titled Voluntary Termination of Employment Program (VTEP), which provided lump sum payments that were nearly twice that of the SUB plan. Before the worker class opted for the SUB buyout they asked Norwood plant management about their right to participate in VTEP, said Kelly, and were told "it would never, under any circumstances, be available to them."

Moreover, Kelly said workers were told the SUB plan was running out of money, so anyone seeking full participation had better sign up soon. As a result, the plaintiffs opted for the SUB buyout in September 1987. At that time, however, GM management was privately planning to allow all laid-off workers with 10 years or more seniority to participate in VTEP, including former Norwood employees, Kelly said. The workers who had already accepted the SUB buyout

10-19-92

BNA Pension Reporter
0095-7100/92/$0+.50

BNA's Americans With Disabilities Act Manual

This two-binder reference service provides practical guidance on the provisions of the Americans with Disabilities Act, including those related to employment, state and local government programs, transportation, public accommodations, and telecommunications. Like other traditional reporter services that are founded upon a major piece of federal legislation, *BNA's Americans with Disabilities Act Manual* serves as an ongoing repository of information about the ADA and how it is being interpreted by the courts and implemented by regulatory agencies.

The looseleaf reference binders, which are updated monthly, are complemented by a monthly newsletter that provides prompt notification of developments and trends. A separate, full-text decisional service, *Americans with Disabilities Cases*, is also available.

BNA's Americans with Disabilities Act Manual's two reference binders take users step-by-step through the provisions of the Americans with Disabilities Act and how they are being interpreted and implemented. Designed as a practical guide for complying with the requirements of ADA, the service also serves as a quick reference for lawyers and law students on the state of the law in this newly developing field.

The very first tab (color blue) in the first reference binder houses the monthly newsletter and is the first place to turn for the latest news and developments on disabilities law. The next tab (color red) contains the Master Index for the reference binders and is the second logical place to look in the service and the leaping off point for your research. This index is organized by topic and by case name.

The third tab, Overview, contains a brief explanation of the Americans with Disabilities Act and of the organization of the *BNA's Americans with Disabilities Act Manual*. This and subsequent tabs are all given individual numbers; each tab's number serves as the prefix for the numbers of the pages behind that tab. The next four tabs cover the provisions of the ADA and provide an editorial explanation with citations to statutes, regulations, and technical assistance from regulatory agencies. The Legal Developments tab contains summaries of major court decisions on disability, organized by type of disability.

The service also contains full text of the ADA and other relevant federal laws and regulations and, in the second binder, summaries of state disability laws, as well as technical assistance manuals, checklists, and other resource materials.

BNA's

Americans with Disabilities Act *MANUAL*

VOLUME 1, NUMBER 8 — NEWSLETTER — August 1992

Route to . . .

INSIDE

EEOC ISSUES POLICY GUIDANCE for agency staff to follow on disparate treatment as a means of proving discrimination and on compensatory and punitive damages available under the 1991 Civil Rights. (p. 44)

▪ ▪

LEGAL BRIEFS: Accommodation for depression, interpreters' duties, and obesity rulings are issued. (p. 45)

▪ ▪

PERSONAL IMPLICATIONS of ADA for attorneys is explored at annual meeting of American Bar Association. (p. 46)

▪ ▪

POLICE DEPARTMENTS may want to consider offering new training to officers to comply with ADA, police group official says. (p. 46)

▪ ▪

WORKERS' COMP POLICIES should be integrated with ADA compliance to cut compensation costs, avoid ADA litigation, consultant says. (p. 47)

▪ ▪

'CRITICAL YEAR' awaits EEOC if Congress does not appropriate sufficient operating funds, EEOC Chairman Evan Kemp warns. (p. 48)

▪ ▪

'OREGON MEDICAID WAIVER will not be approved until plan is altered to protect people with disabilities. (p. 48)

Litigation Tally: Wait And See On Title I

The U.S. Justice Department has received 375 complaints under Title II of ADA and 378 complaints under Title III since the two titles went into effect on Jan. 26, John Dunne, assistant attorney general for DOJ's Civil Rights Division, told the annual meeting of the American Bar Association Aug. 10.

The number of complaints filed under ADA's employment provision (Title I) is less certain, as that title went into effect on July 26. A number of charges have been filed with EEOC since July 26, but the agency will not release any statistics until the end of August, according to an EEOC spokesman. Under Title I rules, charges must be filed either with EEOC or a state equal employment agency before proceeding to federal court (*See Tab 70, p. 70:0502*).

DOJ's Dunne told the ABA meeting that most of the Title II (state and local governments) and Title III (public accommodations) complaints deal with accessibility issues. He added that DOJ's ADA Office currently has seven staff attorneys and two staff architects to investigate complaints, but that an additional nine attorneys should "hopefully" be on staff by the end of the next fiscal year.

Title III Lawsuits: Play Ball!

In an early case involving Title III of the ADA to reach federal court, a Little League rule banning all persons in wheelchairs from serving as on-field base coaches was thrown out by the U.S. District Court for the District of Arizona (*Anderson v. Little League Baseball Inc.*, DC Ariz, No. Civ. 92-1282 PHX EHC, 7/8/92).

Little League's policy, the court held, violates ADA because it does not provide for an individualized assessment of a person's condition and any possible accommodation of that condition.

Under the Little League rule, coaches using wheelchairs are permitted in the dugout during games, but they are prevented from being on the playing field, while their team is at bat. The policy was adopted because of safety concerns for the players.

A coach who used a wheelchair challenged the group's decision to enforce the rule during Little League's national tournament.

The ADA's requirements may be waived when a disabled individual "poses a direct threat to the health or safety of others." However, the regulations specify that an individualized assessment is required to determine the nature and probability of the risk (*See Tab 70, pp. 70:0188-0189*).

Because Little League did not conduct such an assessment, the rule falls short of ADA requirements, the court ruled in granting the plaintiff's request for a temporary restraining order.

8-92·

BNA's Americans with Disabilities Act Manual
1063-3111/92/$0+.50

The monthly newsletter provides the latest information on the enforcement and interpretation of the Americans with Disabilities Act.

EMPLOYMENT DISCUSSION

1. WHO IS COVERED UNDER TITLE I?

ADA prohibits employers from discriminating against qualified individuals with disabilities who, with or without reasonable accommodation, can perform the essential functions of a job. The Act defines the terms "disability" and "qualified individuals" in general terms, while the Equal Employment Opportunity Commission's (EEOC) regulations provide further interpretation and clarification.

42 USC §12112(a)
p. 70:0003
TAM
p. 90:0504

Under ADA, an individual is classified as disabled if he or she:
- has a physical or mental impairment, *and* the impairment substantially limits one or more of the individual's major activities in life;
- has a record or history of such an impairment; or
- is perceived as having such an impairment.

42 USC §12102(2)
p. 70:0002
TAM
p. 90:0505

In effect, the law establishes a two-step process for determining whether a worker is disabled. An impairment by itself would not be classified as a disability. It must significantly interfere with the person's ability to lead a normal life.

Obviously, the key to understanding the three classifications of disability rests in the definitions of key terms, such as "impairment," "substantial limits," "major life activities," etc. A discussion of these key terms follows:

Impairment

ADA does not define "physical or mental impairment," but EEOC adopted the same definition that it used in implementing the Rehabilitation Act of 1973:

- Any physiological disorder or condition, cosmetic disfigurement, or anatomical loss affecting one or more systems of the body (such as the nervous and musculoskeletal systems, respiratory organs, the cardiovascular system, and the glands), or

29 CFR 1630.2(h)(1)
p. 70:0101
TAM
p. 90:0508

- Any mental or psychological disorder (such as mental retardation, organic brain syndrome, emotional illnesses, and learning disabilities).

29 CFR 1630.2(h)(2)
p. 70:0102

EEOC considers an individual impaired even if he or she uses medicine or a prosthetic device to mitigate the effects of the impairment. For example:

29 CFR 1630.2(h) (Appendix)
p. 70:0108

- An individual with epilepsy would be regarded as having an impairment, even if the symptoms of the disorder were controlled by medicine.
- Hearing loss would be considered an impairment, even if the individual wore a hearing aid.

EEOC does not regard as impairments:

A typical page from the reference binders explains the coverage of the ADA, with citations on the right to statutes, regulations, and technical assistance manuals.

Environment Reporter

BNA's *Environment Reporter* is a weekly notification and multi-binder reference service that provides full coverage of current legislative, administrative, and judicial developments affecting pollution control and environmental protection. Industrial developments and new technologies also receive attention in the pages of this service.

Each weekly issue of the service's Current Developments covers the latest activities in Congress, federal agencies, state governments, courts all across the country, and private companies—activities that affect the full spectrum of environmental issues: air pollution, water pollution, solid waste management, hazardous waste, oil pollution, land use, and mining. The reports on these developments are often supplemented with the full text of related documents and with analyses from outside experts.

The service's multi-binder reference file cumulates, through looseleaf pages that are removed and replaced as needed, the full text of relevant federal laws and regulations, state laws and regulations, and both federal and state court decisions.

By combining virtually every format that reporter services have used successfully, BNA's *Environment Reporter* serves as a complete information resource on the law of environmental protection and pollution control.

Its weekly Current Developments issues serve to notify subscribers of the latest information in the field. The reference materials that are collected and continually kept up-to-date in over 30 binders provide researchers with a single source for the statutes and regulations that control the area. Finally, the full text of court decisions that are headnoted, indexed, and regularly bound into hard-cover volumes comprise a library of the important court cases on environmental law.

Each issue of Current Developments begins with a Highlights page summarizing the major events reported in the rest of the issue. On the reverse side of this page is a Table of Contents for the issue. The bulk of the rest of the issue is devoted to coverage of federal and state government activities, policies, reports, and proposals concerning, among other laws, the Clean Air Act, the Federal Water Pollution Control Act, the National Environmental Policy Act, the Resource Conservation and Recovery Act, and the Comprehensive Environmental Response, Compensation, and Liability Act (the Superfund law). Other laws covered include those relating to safe drinking water, coastal zone management, and mining.

Each weekly issue of *Environment Reporter* consists of a Current Developments report and a supplement to the multi-binder reference file.

ENVIRONMENT REPORTER

Current Developments

A weekly review of pollution control and related environmental management problems

Volume 19, Number 45 THE BUREAU OF NATIONAL AFFAIRS, INC. March 10, 1989

HIGHLIGHTS

A TOTAL BAN BY 2000 on production and consumption of five chlorofluorocarbons is agreed to by the European Community Council of Environment Ministers. President Bush and Environmental Protection Agency Administrator William K. Reilly endorse the plan to protect Earth's ozone layer (p. 2363).

AN INCINERATOR EMISSION RULE is rejected by the Office of Management and Budget, but a similar proposal on boiler and furnace emissions gets OMB approval. EPA plans to apply the incinerator standards to new permits despite OMB's action (p. 2363).

FUEL VOLATILITY LIMITS developed by New York are challenged by the American Petroleum Institute, which foresees supply problems and says pending EPA standards would pre-empt the state rule. The limits are designed to control ozone pollution (p. 2364).

INTERSTATE TRASH DISPOSAL is debated by county officials, who complain that Eastern states are overburdening landfills in rural Midwestern counties. They call for national materials use controls (p. 2365) ... A University of Arizona archaeologist says trash in landfills does not decompose, as commonly thought (p. 2368).

SENATE CLEAN AIR LEGISLATION will be introduced in three parts, Sen. Max Baucus (D-Mont) announces. Toxic air pollution will be considered first, followed by urban air quality and acid rain control, he says (p. 2366).

REILLY WILL NOT FIGHT BUSH over the budget request for sewage treatment grants, the administrator tells a Senate committee. Reilly says he will seek no changes in the White House budget (p. 2367) ... House Merchant Marine and Fisheries Committee members fault proposed cuts in coastal environmental programs (p. 2368).

CLIMATE PROGRAMS SUFFER from reduced U.S. funding, which threatens international efforts to monitor and control global climate change, the Climate Institute says. The United States should spend $350 million in 1990 on the various programs, it recommends (p. 2369)

A 10-MILLION-TON CUT in annual sulfur dioxide emissions by 2000 should be included in the Bush administration Clean Air Act proposal, the Alliance for Acid Rain Control tells Administrator Reilly. Minnesota Gov. Rudy Perpich, the chairman, says a smaller cut would hurt the proposal's credibility (p. 2370).

AN ETHANOL-GASOLINE BLEND of automobile fuel could help reduce carbon dioxide in the atmosphere and limit global warming, the Congressional Research Service says in a report. If the ethanol is made from corn, the carbon dioxide emissions would be reclaimed by the succeeding corn crop, CRS says (p. 2370).

RADIONUCLIDE STANDARDS proposed by EPA would primarily affect Nuclear Regulatory Commission licensees and coal-fired boilers, accounting for 7,500 of the 7,812 sources, EPA says (p. 2371) ... Full Text (p. 2397).

THE SETTLEMENT LOGJAM in the superfund program could be broken if EPA promotes greater use of third-party mediators, two negotiation specialists contend in a BNA Analysis and Perspective. Settlements most often break down over cost allocation, and this is where third-party neutrals can play a role, they say (p. 2384).

This week's supplement to the Environment Reporter reference file binders includes EPA's new water quality standards guidance, guidelines for federal procurement of building products containing recovered materials, the removal of the Presque Isle site from the national priorities list, amended ozone rules permitting firms holding allowances on production and importation of some CFCs and halons to transfer those allowances under certain conditions, revised sole source aquifer rules pertaining to critical protection areas, changes to various state implementation plans, and revisions to the Interior Department's endangered species list.

Section 1

0013-9211/89/$0+.50

The Current Developments contain reports on the most recent government and private actions affecting environmental law and management. Key regulations and other documents are reprinted in full text as they are issued.

2363

Current Developments

Air Pollution

EC COUNCIL AGREES ON TOTAL CFC BAN BY 2000; BUSH, REILLY SAY UNITED STATES HAS SAME GOAL

BRUSSELS—(By a BNA Special Correspondent)—The European Community Council of Environment Ministers agreed March 2 to a total ban by 2000 on the production and consumption of the five ozone-depleting chlorofluorocarbons targeted for control by the Montreal Protocol.

The ministers also agreed to eliminate 85 percent of these gases as quickly as possible.

In a related move, President Bush told the National Academy of Sciences in Washington March 3 that he authorized U.S. Environmental Protection Agency Administrator William Reilly, who is headed for a CFC meeting in London, to push for international action to eliminate CFCs and halons by 2000.

Reilly, at a White House meeting of the Domestic Policy Council March 2, urged adoption of such a policy. The council did not accept the proposal immediately but sent it to Bush along with other options, an EPA spokesman told BNA March 3. "Reilly got what he wanted from the president," the spokesman said.

A statement by White House spokesman Marlin Fitzwater said President Bush had instructed Reilly to support a total elimination of CFCs by 2000, "provided that safe substitutes are available."

The proposal considered by the ministers meeting in Brussels March 2, which was put forward by the British government, called for eliminating only 85 percent of CFCs by 2000. The Montreal Protocol itself, which came into force on Jan. 1, seeks to eliminate 50 percent of the five CFCs by 1998. In both cases, the base year used for calculating the proposed reductions is 1986.

According to the European Community Commission, 40 countries have now signed the Montreal Protocol, and 32 have ratified it, including 11 countries that represented two-thirds of world CFC production in 1986. A commission spokesman said that 1 million tons of CFCs are produced worldwide every year, with the European Community countries responsible for about 440,000 tons.

85 Percent Reduction Proposed

Lord Caithness, Britain's environment minister, said the United Kingdom proposed only an 85 percent reduction because, following opinions expressed at the meeting of the Council in November 1988, it did not believe other European Community countries would agree to go any further.

However, led by the French and the Dutch, a majority of member states reached agreement on a total elimination by 2000, or as close to that as possible. This allows for the continued use of a limited amount of CFCs for vital medical applications and in the cleaning of microchips until chemical substitutes are found. These exceptions to the ban, which were included at the insistence of the Germans, Dutch, and Belgians, will be set out more precisely in the future.

The EC environment ministers also agreed to an official mandate for the European Commission to negotiate with the other Montreal Protocol signatory countries aimed at worldwide agreement on the new European Community initiative. This will be raised formally at the Helsinki review meeting to be held May 2-5, but was expected to come up in less formal discussions at the ozone conferences to be held in London March 5-7 and The Hague later in March.

Negotiations With Industry

The EC Commission also said it has started negotiating with industry to eliminate production as quickly as possible. The commission stressed that these voluntary agreements would be non-enforceable; such agreements already have been negotiated in certain EC countries, including Belgium, Denmark, France, and West Germany. Most of these voluntary agreements call for a much more rapid reduction than what is called for in the Montreal Protocol. In West Germany, for example, an agreement reached last year will lead to the total elimination of aerosol products by 1990.

An EC Commission spokesman said it is vital that other countries agree to implement the same standards, as the EC alone cannot possibly combat this problem. In this connection, Canadian Environment Minister Lucien Bouchard said Feb. 20 that Canada has targeted CFCs for complete elimination by 1999. He said draft regulations would be issued under the Canadian Environmental Protection Act to curb the use of CFCs by more than 85 percent.

'Very Encouraging News'

In the United States, Environmental Protection Agency Administrator William K. Reilly, in a statement released before his departure March 3 for the CFC meeting in London, said the EC action is "very encouraging news for the world's environment." He added, however, "We need to be sure that any CFC substitutes do not pose new and unforeseen environmental risks such as exacerbating global warming." Reilly said he hoped that the London meeting March 5-7 "will put the nations of the world on the best possible course for meeting the goal of a safe and efficient elimination of these chemicals."

Although the European Community's agreement only relates to those CFCs covered by the Montreal Protocol, the ministers also announced they would be examining the elimination of the remaining CFCs, such as CFC-22, at a future date.

The Brussels-based European Environment Bureau, which represents national environmental groups in EC countries, said it wants even stricter action, with an agreement to ban production and consumption of all CFCs and halons by 1995. The EEB said a list of exceptions to the ban could be set up that would be controlled at the international level to regulate supply for absolutely basic needs.

Hazardous Waste

OMB REJECTS INCINERATOR EMISSION PROPOSAL, APPROVES SIMILAR BOILER, FURNACE RULE FOR NOW

Conflicting opinions by the Office of Management and Budget on proposed emission standards for different hazardous waste burning facilities have presented the Environmen-

3-10-89

Environment Reporter
0013-9211/89/$0+.50

A Text section in Current Developments supplements the notification-type coverage with full text of proposed regulations and other important documents. An occasional Analysis and Perspective provides a forum for the views of outside experts. Finally, a Journal section lists all relevant actions taken by Congress, by the Executive Branch, and by state and local governments, as well as meetings scheduled in the environmental field.

The service's reference material, consisting of full text of current laws and regulations, is collected in 36 binders: Federal Laws (2 binders), Federal Regulations (7 binders), State Air Laws (6 binders), State Water Laws (6 binders), State Solid Waste-Land Use (12 binders), and Mining Laws (3 binders). This material is all fully indexed in three separate indexes covering the federal, state, and mining materials respectively.

The full text of the major court decisions in the environmental field is issued initially in looseleaf pages and housed in a binder. Each decision is preceded by one or more headnotes summarizing the holding or holdings of that decision. Each headnote is assigned one or more numbers showing where the legal point fits into the indexing system for this part of the service. (This indexing system is similar to that for other BNA decisional services and is described elsewhere in the book.) The looseleaf pages are regularly bound into volumes, which are supplemented by cumulative indexes covering several volumes.

The service's multiple binders house:

- ▶ *Current Developments*
- ▶ *Reference Files*
- ▶ *Decisions*

The decisional part of the service uses the CDI format common to other BNA decisional services.

ENVIRONMENT REPORTER FEDERAL

Supplement No. 830 THE BUREAU OF NATIONAL AFFAIRS, INC. March 24, 1989

FILING INSTRUCTIONS

NOTE: The instructions below should be followed carefully. The boldface headings on the left correspond to the colored tab sections in the Environment Reporter binders. Obsolete pages in your service are listed in the column headed "Take Out Pages." New and replacement pages in this supplement are listed in the column headed "Put In Pages." It is important to follow instructions in both columns.

Retain the instructions sheet for this supplement in the front of the Federal Laws binder. Discard the instructions sheet for the prior supplement; it is not required. Supplements amending old material or supplying new material are numbered consecutively. Check the issue number at the top of this supplement against the number on the sheet not required to be certain your service is complete.

CUSTOMER ASSISTANCE: If you have any problems with missing pages or other questions regarding the filing of these binders, please call toll-free 1-800-372-1033.

	Take Out Pages	Put In Pages
FEDERAL REGULATIONS—1		
91—CONTENTS, PREFACE, FILING INSTRUCTIONS		
Environment Reporter Status Chart On Environmental Regulatory Actions (Material obsolete)	91:0061-91.0071	.....
101—GENERAL		
EPA Regulations on Procedures for Decisionmaking (40 CFR 124)		
(Amends citation, authority cite, 124.1(a))	101:0801, 101:0802	101:0801, 101:0802
(Amends 124.15(a), (b) introductory text)	101:0809-101:0812	101:0809-101:0812
Fish and Wildlife Service List of Endangered and Threatened Wildlife and Plants (50 CFR 17.11, 17.12)		
(Amends citation, authority cite)	101:1501, 101:1502	101:1501, 101:1502
(Amends Clams table)	101:1517, 101:1518	101:1517, 101:1518
111—GRANTS		
Tab Section Contents (Revision)	111:0001	111:0001
120—AIR STANDARDS		
EPA Regulations on National Emission Standards for Hazardous Air Pollutants (40 CFR 61: Corrects 61.04(b)(HH) address)	120:1007, 120:1008	120:1007, 120:1008

Section 3
0013-9211/89/$0+ 50

As with all BNA reference services, *Environment Reporter* issues filing instructions with each new supplement. This ensures that the correct pages are taken out of the binders, and the correct ones put in, to keep the binders up-to-date.

The reference binders pull together into one place the full current text of relevant federal and state laws and regulations, and, in the decisional part of the service, the full text of federal and state court decisions.

S-830
101:0801

ENVIRONMENTAL PROTECTION AGENCY REGULATIONS ON PROCEDURES FOR DECISIONMAKING

(40 CFR 124; 45 FR 33484, May 19, 1980, Effective July 18, 1980; Amended by 45 FR 52748, August 7, 1980; 45 FR 68391, October 15, 1980; 46 FR 22584, April 20, 1981; 46 FR 36706, July 15, 1981; 47 FR 15306, April 8, 1982; 47 FR 53675, November 26, 1982; Revised by 48 FR 14153, April 1, 1983; Amended by 48 FR 30115, June 30, 1983; 48 FR 39619, September 1, 1983; 49 FR 17718, April 24, 1984; 49 FR 25981, June 25, 1984; 49 FR 38046, September 26, 1984; Corrected by 50 FR 6940, February 19, 1985; Amended by 51 FR 16030, April 30, 1986; 53 FR 28147, July 26, 1988; 53 FR 37408, September 26, 1988; 53 FR 37934, September 28, 1988; 54 FR 254, January 4, 1989; 54 FR 9606, March 7, 1989)

[*Editor's note*: The modified information requirements contained in §124.5 have not been approved by the Office of Management and Budget (OMB) and they are not effective until OMB has approved them.]

PART 124—PROCEDURES FOR DECISIONMAKING

Subpart A—General Program Requirements

Sec.
124.1 Purpose and scope.
124.2 Definitions.
124.3 Application for a permit.
124.4 Consolidation of permit processing.
124.5 Modification, revocation and reissuance, or termination of permits.
124.6 Draft permits.
124.7 Statement of basis.
124.8 Fact sheet.
124.9 Administrative record for draft permits when EPA is the permitting authority.
124.10 Public notice of permit actions and public comment period.
124.11 Public comments and requests for public hearings.
124.12 Public hearings.
124.13 Obligation to raise issues and provide information during the public comment period.
124.14 Reopening of the public comment period.
124.15 Issuance and effective date of permit.
124.16 Stays of contested permit conditions.
124.17 Response to comments.
124.18 Administrative record for final permit when EPA is the permitting authority.
124.19 Appeal of RCRA, UIC and PSD permits.
124.20 Computation of time.
124.21 Effective date of Part 124.

Subpart B—Specific Procedures Applicable to RCRA Permits [Reserved]

Subpart C—Specific Procedures Applicable to PSD Permits

124.41 Definitions applicable to PSD permits.
124.42 Additional procedures for PSD permits affecting Class I areas.

Subpart D—Specific Procedures Applicable to NPDES Permits

124.51 Purpose and scope.
124.52 Permits required on a case-by-case basis.
124.53 State certification.
124.54 Special provisions for State certification and concurrence on applications for section 301(h) variances.
124.55 Effect of State certification.
124.56 Fact sheets.
124.57 Public notice.
124.58 Special procedures for EPA-issued general permits for point sources other than separate storm sewers.
124.59 Conditions requested by the Corps of Engineers and other government agencies.
124.60 Issuance and effective date and stays of NPDES permits.
124.61 Final environmental impact statement.
124.62 Decision on variances.
124.63 Procedures for variances when EPA is the permitting authority.
124.64 Appeals of variances.
124.65 Special procedures for discharge into marine waters under section 301(h).
124.66 Special procedures for decisions on thermal variances under section 316(a).

Subpart E—Evidentiary Hearing for EPA-Issued NPDES Permits and EPA-Terminated RCRA Permits

124.71 Applicability.
124.72 Definitions.
124.73 Filing and submission of documents.
124.74 Requests for evidentiary hearing.
124.75 Decision on request for a hearing.
124.76 Obligation to submit evidence and raise issues before a final permit is issued.
124.77 Notice of hearing.
124.78 *Ex parte* communications.
124.79 Additional parties and issues.
124.80 Filing and service.
124.81 Assignment of Administrative Law Judge.
124.82 Consolidation and severance.
124.83 Prehearing conferences.
124.84 Summary determination.
124.85 Hearing procedure.
124.86 Motions.
124.87 Record of hearings.
124.88 Proposed findings of fact and conclusions; brief.
124.89 Decisions.
124.90 Interlocutory appeal.
124.91 Appeal to the Administrator.

Subpart F—Non-Adversary Panel Procedures

124.111 Applicability.
124.112 Relation to other subparts.
124.113 Public notice of draft permits and public comment period.
124.114 Request for hearing.
124.115 Effect of denial of or absence of request for hearing.
124.116 Notice of hearing.
124.117 Request to participate in hearing.
124.118 Submission of written comments on draft permit.
124.119 Presiding Officer.
124.120 Panel hearing.
124.121 Opportunity for cross-examination.
124.122 Record for final permit.
124.123 Filing of brief, proposed findings of fact and conclusions of law and proposed modified permit.
124.124 Recommended decision.
124.125 Appeal from or review of recommended decision.
124.126 Final decision.
124.127 Final decision if there is no review.
124.128 Delegation of authority; time limitations.

APPENDIX A TO PART 124—GUIDE TO DECISIONMAKING UNDER PART 124

Authority: Resource, Conservation, and Recovery Act, 42 U.S.C. 6901 *et seq.*; Safe Drinking Water Act, 42 U.S.C. 300(f) *et seq.*; Clean Water Act, 33 U.S.C. 1251 *et. seq.*; and Clean Air Act, 42 U.S.C. 1857 *et seq.*

[Amended by 48 FR 30115, June 30, 1983; 49 FR 17718, April 24, 1984; 51 FR 16030, April 30, 1986; 54 FR 254, January 4, 1989; 54 FR 9606, March 7, 1989].

3-24-89 Published by THE BUREAU OF NATIONAL AFFAIRS, INC., Washington, D.C. 20037 3

Occupational Safety & Health Reporter

The *Occupational Safety & Health Reporter* is a weekly notification and reference service covering the ever changing federal and state requirements that employers must follow to protect the safety and health of their employees. Like BNA's *Environment Reporter*, this service is organized into separate notification, reference, and decisional components, and is housed in multiple binders.

The service's Current Reports provide weekly coverage of the Occupational Safety and Health Administration's regulatory and enforcement activities and of legislation, litigation, and research in the field of occupational safety and health. The Decisions binder and bound volumes contain full text of significant court decisions from all across the country, as well as the decisions of the Occupational Safety and Health Review Commission. All decisions are headnoted and tied into the service's Classification Outline. The Reference File binders contain material of permanent reference value, such as government standards and regulations, that is continually kept current through its looseleaf-page format.

Through its notification, reference, and decisional components, BNA's *Occupational Safety & Health Reporter* serves as a single source for the information lawyers and their corporate and business clients need to know in order to comply with federal and state regulation of occupational safety and health.

The weekly Current Reports, which alert subscribers to the most recent events in the field, begin with a front Highlights page briefly summarizing the most important contents of the issue. This is followed by a second, Topical Summary page, which lists, in index fashion, the issue's entire contents. Inside are in-depth reports of the latest developments, activities of the Occupational Safety and Health Review Commission (OSHRC), full text of important documents, and a calendar of key meetings and events. The Current Reports are stored in two binders, each covering a six-month period and each separately indexed.

The Reference File binders contain textual materials on policies and programs, standards, regulations, compliance, enforcement, directories, statutes and orders, and state plans. The binders are divided into tabbed sections and are fully indexed.

The Decisions binder contains full text of recent court and OSHRC decisions and digests of Review Commission judges' decisions. Both the full text decisions and the digests are headnoted and assigned numbers that tie them into the service's indexing system. This system is similar to that used in BNA's *Labor Relations Reporter*. Reported decisions periodically are cumulated in bound volumes. The current Decisions binder and the bound volumes are separately indexed.

The weekly Current Report notifies readers of recent developments in occupational safety and health.

OCCUPATIONAL SAFETY & HEALTH REPORTER

A weekly review of occupational safety and health developments

Volume 18, Number 43 THE BUREAU OF NATIONAL AFFAIRS, INC. **March 29, 1989**

HIGHLIGHTS OF CURRENT REPORT

ALAN C. MCMILLAN has been named deputy assistant secretary and acting administrator for the Occupational Safety and Health Administration. He has been serving as acting assistant secretary of the Employment Standards Administration and has 13 years' experience at OSHA, including stints as regional administrator in Chicago and Atlanta (p. 1795).

LOCKHEED AERONAUTICAL SYSTEMS has been cited by OSHA with penalties totaling nearly $1.5 million for numerous alleged willful violations of agency recordkeeping and job safety and health standards at the company's Burbank, Calif., plant (p. 1795).

LEGISLATIVE REFORM of the Occupational Safety and Health Act would be more effective and appropriate for congressional attention in the 101st Congress than would high-risk notification measures, according to Rep. Henry (p. 1796).

THE NEW EXPOSURE LIMIT for styrene will not be reinterpreted, OSHA Administrator John Pendergrass tells the Styrene Information and Research Center, reiterating the agency's finding that the new exposure limit is generally feasible for operations in Standard Industrial Classification 30 (p. 1796).

THE AIR CONTAMINANTS STANDARD issued by OSHA now has an index, a table of contents, and a bibliography to aid readers of the 650-page document that addresses nearly 400 substances (p. 1797; text of the index, p. 1815).

AN INDOOR AIR BILL introduced by Rep. Kennedy is designed to reduce risks posed by exposure to indoor air contaminants in workplaces, schools, and other buildings. He calls the bill "much improved" from one he introduced in the 100th Congress because it addresses the needs of the 15 percent of Americans who are particularly sensitive to certain toxins in building materials or other air contaminants (p. 1797).

WORKING CONDITIONS at government-owned nuclear weapons plants would be safeguarded by a separate and independent agency under a bill introduced by Rep. Skaggs (p. 1798) . . . The secretary-treasurer of the Industrial Union Department, AFL-CIO, tells union delegates that worker safety in such weapons plants is an important item to add to unions' legislative agendas (p. 1798).

THE BOEING CO. has recommended that the Washington Department of Labor and Industries accept portions of industrial insurance claims filed by 37 employees who blame a variety of illnesses on workplace exposure to phenol formaldehyde (p. 1798).

DESPITE CHANGES made during floor debate to the High Risk Occupational Disease Notification Act, a critic of the bill says he is still concerned that it would notify workers even in cases where no effective form of therapy is known (p. 1799).

A CONSTRUCTION ACCIDENT in Virginia that resulted in a fatality prompts a debate between an OSHA official and a congressional staff person concerning the agency's safety policies on construction sites (p. 1800).

MUSCULO-SKELETAL INJURIES can be minimized by training inspectors in the broad aspects of ergonomics, according to recommendations from a committee of state and federal government occupational safety and health officials (p. 1800).

TEMPORARY VARIANCES are granted by OSHA to Broad, Vogt & Conant Inc. regarding installation of anti-two-blocking devices used on cranes and to the Hoechst Celanese Corp. regarding the use of engineering controls to reduce employee exposure to formaldehyde (pp. 1802, 1803; text of the notices of the application and grant of interim order, p. 1812).

Section 1

SECRETARY OF LABOR v. UNION OIL OF CALIFORNIA

U.S. Court of Appeals for the Seventh Circuit

Decision granting OSHA's petition for review of hearing judge's decision [13 OSHC 1673], and granting in part and denying in part employer's petition for review, and remanding matter to Occupational Safety and Health Review Commission for reconsideration of penalties.

SECRETARY OF LABOR, Petitioner, v. UNION OIL OF CALIFORNIA and OCCUPATIONAL SAFETY AND HEALTH REVIEW COMMISSION, Respondent, Nos. 88-1374 and 88-1832, Feb. 24, 1989.

Barbara Kahl, U.S. Department of Labor, Washington, D.C. for petitioner.

Mark Lies, II, Chicago, Ill., for respondent Union Oil of California.

Before Cummings, Posner, and Flaum, Circuit Judges.

JUDICIAL REVIEW

1. Review Commission Rulings — Finality Of Judge's Decision — Reasons Review Not Directed Irrelevant ▸85.01

Hearing judge's decision becomes final, and appealable by court, when no member of Occupational Safety and Health Review Commission directs review within 30 days, and fact that commission lacked quorum necessary to review judge's decision is irrelevant since nothing in statute addresses reasons review is not directed.

GENERAL DUTY CLAUSE

2. Recognized Hazard — Likelihood Of Physical Harm ▸118.101 ▸118.08

Evidence supported hearing judge's decision that employer's failure to discover hydrogen stress corrosion cracking in vessel containing liquid petroleum products, resulting in explosion and fire that led to death of 17 workers, violated general duty of employer to furnish place of employment free from recognized hazards likely to cause death or serious physical harm to employees, despite fact that no such explosion had ever taken place before; accordingly, citation for violation of Section 5(a)(1) is affirmed.

FIRE PROTECTION

3. Failure To Train Operational Employees ▸215.01 ▸200.02

Operating employees of company who were instructed to remain at their posts in case of fire to contain emergency until fire crew arrived had duties to perform in fire, and given extraordinary hazards posed by fire in oil refinery, they ought to be trained in how to contain refinery fire; accordingly, hearing judge's finding that operating employees were not part of fire brigade is vacated, and citation for violation of 29 CFR 1910.156(c)(1), for failure to adequately train and protect operational employees, is affirmed.

4. Personal Protective Equipment — Applicability Of General Standard — Failure To Equip Fire Brigade Members ▸215.01 ▸250.01

Even though personal protective equipment provisions of fire brigade standard apply only to indoor firefighters, it would be unreasonable to infer that in prescribing personal protective equipment suitable for fighting interior structural fires, Occupational Safety and Health Administration intended to preclude application of general regulation on personal protective equipment to members of fire brigades engaged in fighting other types of fires; accordingly, citation for violation of 29 CFR 1910.132(a) is affirmed.

Full Text Of Decision

Posner, *Circuit Judge*.

This case arises out of the explosion of a pressure vessel at Union Oil Company's Chicago refinery in 1984 that killed seventeen workers. OSHA conducted an investigation, and, on January 11, 1985, cited Union Oil for three "willful" violations of the Occupational Safety and Health Act of 1970, 29 U.S.C. §§ 651 *et seq.*, and one "serious" one. On the basis of these citations, OSHA assessed penalties against the company totaling $31,000, the maximum possible given the violations. See 29 U.S.C. §§ 666(a), (b). Union Oil contested the assessment and the matter was referred to the Occupational Safety and Health Review Commission, which adjudicates disputes concerning the application of the Occupational Safety and Health Act. After a hearing which lasted twenty-seven days, the administrative law judge upheld most of OSHA's citations but reduced parts of two of them (they were composite citations) from willful (maximum penalty $10,000) to

The service also reports full text of court decisions on the subject. This part of the service follows the format and CDI system of other BNA decisional services. The service also has a reference file of statutes, regulations, and other documents.

International Trade Reporter

This notification and reference service covers legislative, regulatory, judicial, and policy developments affecting both the import and export aspects of international trade.

Among the service's many features is its compilation of court decisions on international trade, as well as those of the International Trade Commission and the Commerce Department. The decisions are reported in full text and are headnoted and provided with classification numbers in order to fit them into the service's indexing scheme.

Another significant element of the service is its Reference Manual, which not only analyzes the entire import process but also contains full text of relevant statutes, regulations, and executive orders.

The *International Trade Reporter*, as with almost all reporter services, also has its current notification aspects, namely, a weekly Current Reports, which reports and analyzes legislative and regulatory developments as well as private sector activities affecting international trade.

The *International Trade Reporter* combines the notification, reference, and decisional formats of reporter services in its coverage of the law and the policy implications of international trade.

The weekly Current Reports provide notification and analysis of recent legislative, regulatory, judicial, and private-sector developments in the field of international trade. Also, BNA's staff of foreign correspondents report on actions of the United States' major trading partners. These Current Reports are fully indexed and stored in two binders, each covering a six-month time period.

Probably of more interest to law students are the service's reference and decisional components. The Import Reference Manual contains full text of import statutes, regulations, and executive orders, plus forms, lists, and analyses of such subjects as quotas, dumping, countervailing duties, and presidential retaliation. A separate Export Reference Manual compiles information on foreign import regulations and U.S. export controls. It also includes guidelines on boycott reporting requirements, export licenses, shippers' export declarations, and currency restrictions.

Court decisions on international trade are issued to subscribers biweekly in the form of looseleaf pages. Each decision is preceded by a headnote, which explains the court's essential holding, and by a Classification Guide number, which ties the opinion into the service's indexing system. This system is similar to those of BNA's *Labor Relations Reporter* and its *Media Law Reporter*, which are described elsewhere in this book. The decisions of the International Trade Commission and of the Commerce Department's International Trade Administration are reported in the same way. The looseleaf pages are stored in a binder until they are republished in bound volumes.

Another notification, reference, and decisional service, *International Trade Reporter* issues a weekly Current Reports on new trade developments.

INTERNATIONAL TRADE REPORTER

CURRENT REPORTS

— Incorporating U.S. Export Weekly and U.S. Import Weekly —

Vol. 6, No. 13 **March 29, 1989**

HIGHLIGHTS

GUIDELINES FOR THE MIDTERM REVIEW are set out by GATT Director General Arthur Dunkel in proposals released for discussion. The proposals, which cover three of the four areas left unresolved by GATT ministers meeting in Montreal last December—agriculture, intellectual property, and safeguards—aim to revive talks in these areas. Dunkel did not release a proposal on textiles trade, the fourth area left unfinished in Montreal. (Page 382)

CAUTIOUS OPTIMISM IS expressed by USTR General Counsel Joshua Bolten about the chances for an agriculture accord during next week's midterm review meeting at GATT. Bolten adds that any short-term measures agreed to in a farm accord will have to be negotiated with care to ensure that opposition among U.S. farm groups will not ensue. (Page 382)

'TOUGH' U.S.-JAPAN TALKS ON FSX continue in Washington, while Japanese officials in Tokyo express hope that the final pact on Japan's next generation jet fighter will be approved as close to the original agreement as possible. President Bush says the U.S. "will keep its word" on the FSX deal, but insists that the agreement, negotiated during the Reagan administration, be clarified. (Page 383)

STEEL VRA PROPONENTS WON'T WAIT for President Bush to unveil his steel policy plans to start action on legislation to renew the program if the president does not make his plans known by mid-April, Sen. Rockefeller tells reporters. Rockefeller adds that he is confident the president will sign a VRA bill that extends the program to limit steel imports for five years, regardless of growing opposition to the legislation. (Page 385)

A CAIRNS GROUP WALKOUT from GATT talks in Geneva next week is possible if "satisfactory agreement" on agricultural trade is not reached, according to Australian Foreign Affairs and Trade Minister Gareth John Evans. Evans defines a satisfactory agreement as "a real freeze" on price supports, export subsidies, restrictions to access, and production. (Page 385)

COCOM AGREEMENTS ON COMPUTERS are implemented by the Commerce Department. The new rule amends Commodity Control List entry 1565A, reducing export controls and simplifying the licensing process for some computers and equipment containing computers, generally affecting certain personal computers. (Page 386)

CLASSIFICATION OF OIL-BEARING SEED from Ethiopia as "oil-bearing nuts and seeds, not specially provided for," was proper despite the fact that the seeds are only used as bird seed in the United States, the Court of International Trade rules. The decision means that the seeds are eligible for duty-free entry. (Page 392)

THE FIRST TWO AD/CVD REVIEW requests are initiated under Chapter 19 of the U.S.-Canada free trade agreement. The cases, concerning replacement parts for asphalt pavers and red raspberries, are Canadian challenges to the findings of the Commerce Department's International Trade Administration. (Page 393)

AN 80% CONTENT RULE FOR AUTOS is likely to come out of the European Community's plans to integrate its economy by 1992, but the rule may not apply to all autos sold in the EC, MIT's John Krafcik forecasts. The local content rule is not likely to affect Ford and GM, which have plants in the EC, but may hinder plans of Japanese transplants in the U.S. to export U.S.-made autos to the EC. (Page 395)

CONTENTS

News Highlights 382
Export Policy 386
Import Policy 391
Legal Action 392
General Developments 395
Also in the News 400
Legislative Calendar 403
Text of GATT discussion paper 404

This issue contains pages 379–406.

The decisions are reported in full text, headnoted, and cumulated and indexed according to the service's CDI system, which is similar to that used in other BNA decisional services.

Algoma Steel Corp. v. U.S. 10 ITRD 2169

ALGOMA STEEL CORP. v. U.S.

Court of Appeals, Federal Circuit

THE ALGOMA STEEL CORPORATION, LIMITED, Plaintiffs-Appellants, CHRISTIANSON PIPE, LTD., IPSCO, INC., and IPSCO STEEL, INC., Plaintiffs v. UNITED STATES and U.S. INTERNATIONAL TRADE COMMISSION, Defendants-Appellees, LONE STAR STEEL COMPANY, MAVERICK TUBE CORPORATION, SAWHILL TUBE DIVISION, and CYCLOPS CORPORATION, Defendants

No. 88-1491

Jan. 4, 1989

Action contesting the ITC's affirmative injury determination in dumping investigation of oil country tubular goods from Canada, 9 ITRD 1051. Following judgment for defendants, 10 ITRD 1618, plaintiffs appeal. Affirmed.

See also 8 ITRD 2389 and 10 ITRD 1943.

DUMPING

1. **Dumping — Injury — Economic impact — Volume of imports ▸37.3063**

For purposes of ITC injury determination, sales at more than fair value need not be excluded; injury determination not confined to LTFV sales is not contrary to law.

William Silverman and Dow, Lohnes & Albertson, both of Washington, D.C. (Michael P. House, on the brief), for plaintiffs-appellants. Rufus E. Jarman and Barnes, Richardson & Colburn, both of New York, N.Y., for plaintiffs.

George Thompson, ITC (Lyn M. Schlitt and James A. Toupin, on the brief), for defendant-appellee. Michael H. Stein and Dewey, Ballantine, Bushby, Plamer & Wood, both of Washington, D.C., for defendants.

Before Mayer, Circuit Judge, Nichols, Senior Circuit Judge, and Michel, Circuit Judge.

Full Text of Opinion

Nichols, Senior Circuit Judge.

This is a proceeding under 28 U.S.C. §1295(a)(5) to review a decision of the United States Court of International Trade, 688 F.Supp. 639, 22 Cust. B. & Dec. 13 [10 ITRD 1618] (1988), which affirms a determination of the International Trade Commission (ITC) which holds that the sales at less than fair value (LTFV or "dumping") of certain steel products, oil country tubular goods (OCTG) from Canada, injure or threaten injury to an industry in the United States. In the case of appellant Algoma Steel Corporation, a Canadian producer, the Department of Commerce had previously determined that, over a six-month period studied, such sales occurred, but it is undisputed that they were slightly under 50 percent of all United States sales Algoma made. Algoma had a printout made of the data establishing this, but the ITC refused to receive or consider it, holding that for purposes of its injury determination, sales at more than fair value (MTFV) were not to be excluded. The Court of International Trade rejected Algoma's assertion that this was legal error, as do we. That is the sole issue in the appeal, and our view of its requires that we affirm.

I

In the intricate administrative machinery Congress has erected over the years for dumping and countervailing duty cases, one unique feature is the allocation of responsibility to two agencies otherwise independent of one another, the Commerce Department and the ITC, the requisite injury determination for the latter, and everything else for the former. Naturally the specifics as to who does what is for dispute and discussion. Commerce, determining that sales at LTFV have occurred, normally makes no finding as to what percentage of all sales they are, but rather and in lieu thereof, states a "dumping margin" which is a weighted average adjusting appropriately for the MTFV sales. The ITC says it is not told how many or which the MTFV sales were and the raw data that was before the Commerce Department is of no use to it because its injury determination covers a different time frame. This kind of issue should be one for the agencies to resolve between themselves, and not for the courts. We think we should confine our consideration to the ultimate product: is an injury determination, not confined to the LTFV sales alone, arbitrary, capricious, or otherwise contrary to the law? We hold it is not.

Antitrust & Trade Regulation Report

The *Antitrust & Trade Regulation Report* is one of several weekly BNA services covering the regulation of business. The others are *Securities Regulation & Law Report*, *Federal Contracts Report*, and *BNA's Banking Report*. All these services share a similar format, which is primarily designed for high-speed notification purposes. Each service consists of two binders, each holding a half-year's worth of weekly issues and cumulative indexes. Yearly or half-yearly volumes with final indexes may be kept in storage binders.

The *Antitrust & Trade Regulation Report* covers federal, state, and international competition and deceptive trade practice law enforcement. It reports the latest legislative, regulatory, and judicial developments.

Each weekly, self-contained issue highlights the week's most important developments on the front page. Inside are detailed reports on these and other events. The service also contains occasional analysis pieces on specific antitrust and trade regulation developments. Selected judicial, administrative, and legislative materials are reprinted in full text.

The service provides weekly notification of all significant competiton and deceptive trade practice developments on the federal, state, and international levels. The important activities of the Antitrust Division of the Justice Department are reported, including investigations, complaints, indictments, negotiations of consent decrees, trials, appeals, and policy statements. The Federal Trade Commission, which shares federal civil antitrust enforcement with the Justice Department, is also covered in depth.

The course of litigation involving both public and private enforcement of competition laws is followed, culminating in full reports on the decisions of federal, state, and foreign courts. All significant federal legislative developments are noted, beginning with the introduction of all relevant bills and following up with reports on relevant congressional committee hearings, committee reports, Senate and House debates, congressional action, and presidential assent or veto.

The publication also covers developments in the franchising of businesses and trade regulation activities in the international arena. Included in this latter category are actions of the Commission of European Communities, the European Court of Justice, the United Kingdom's Office of Fair Trading, the German Cartel Office, and the Japanese Fair Trade Commission.

Each weekly issue, although bound by staples into a self-contained entity, is divided into several sections. The News and Comment section, which appears every week and is usually the longest section, contains reports on federal court, legislative, and agency action affecting the field of antitrust and trade regulation. Each such report covers the action in question in great detail. A report on a court decision, for instance, takes the reader step-by-step through the court's opinion, describing the specifics of the court's holding and rationale.

ROUTE TO

Antitrust & Trade Regulation Report

BNA

Vol. 56, No. 1400

HIGHLIGHTS

January 26, 1989

Manufacturer May Challenge Acquisition Of Competitor: As it concludes that *Cargill* has made competitor efforts to enjoin mergers more difficult but not impossible, the U.S. Court of Appeals for the Second Circuit rules that an herbal tea manufacturer's Clayton Act §7 challenge to the aborted purchase of a rival, which may have been "timed to head off an adverse determination on the merits," is not moot and that the purchaser's alleged post-acquisition market share of 84% constitutes sufficient evidence of antitrust injury to create a genuine issue for trial. . . . pages 118, 160

Guilty Plea Bars Double Jeopardy Attack On Sentence: The U.S. Supreme Court decides, 6-3, that antitrust defendants who entered guilty pleas to two separate indictments may not challenge the sentence imposed in the second case for infringement of the Double Jeopardy Clause because the defendants' guilty pleas and convictions foreclose the collateral attack. . . . pages 117, 152

Special Report Traces Federal, State, Foreign Enforcement Trends: Corporate counsel advising their clients on antitrust compliance for their acquisition and distribution programs will have to sift conflicting enforcement patterns from the federal agencies, state attorneys general, and foreign governments of our trading partners so as to chart a prudent course, according to a BNA Special Report. . . . page 127

Health Care Equipment Supplier Loses Treble Damage Award: Overturning a $2.3 million treble damage award, the U.S. District Court for the Middle District of Florida determines, as a matter of law, that the behavior of a joint venture, created to supply durable medical equipment, and its two venturers was not unlawfully coercive and did not violate Sherman Act §§1 and 2. . . . page 119

Canadian Bureau Starts To Ride Newest Merger Wave: Amid calls from opposition politicians and unions for the Canadian Parliament to strengthen the Competition Act to combat increased corporate concentration in the wake of contemplated acquisitions in the petroleum, brewing, and airline markets, the Bureau of Competition Policy's Director of Investigation and Research warns the participants in all three mergers that it would be a mistake to proceed with the transactions before the competitive impact of each deal is evaluated. . . . page 146

Labor Exemption Protects Conduct Until Parties Reach Impasse: The nonstatutory labor exemption cloaks the National Football League and its member clubs from players' antitrust claims based on the college draft provision of their collective bargaining agreement after expiration of the agreement and until the parties reach an impasse on this provision, the U.S. District Court for the District of Minnesota rules. . . . page 120

The Highlights page summarizes the most important court decisions and other events reported in that week's issue.

IN THIS REPORT

CALENDAR OF EVENTS 167
CONSUMER CREDIT
Equal Credit Opportunity Act: ECOA doesn't bar discrimination based on status as civil servant .. 124
Truth in Lending Act: Settlement of TILA claims is not invalid for mistake 126
DECEPTIVE PRACTICES
Credit Repair: FTC accuses clinic of making false claims about its services 123
Mail Order Sales: Jewelart patrons may be eligible for refunds 125
Used Cars: FTC wins injunction, civil penalty from independent dealer 121
ENFORCEMENT
Outlook: Practitioners must evaluate conflicting trends in federal, state, foreign enforcement to develop useful compliance programs 127
EXEMPTIONS
Labor: NFL is shielded from §1 claims until parties reach impasse 120
FRANCHISING
Automobiles: Disqualification of auto board member didn't nullify commissioner's decision .. 144
Gasoline: Failure to pay rent on time justifies termination of service station franchise 144
Trucks: Partial discontinuation of product line may have constituted dealer termination 143
Wine: Virginia Wine Franchise Act offends federal, state constitutions 142
INTERNATIONAL DEVELOPMENTS
Mergers and Acquisitions: Canadian bureau begins study of major wave of acquisitions 146
Mergers and Acquisitions: Report finds UK firms spent $32.5 billion on U.S. corporate acquisitions during 1988 149
Mergers and Acquisitions: UK agency clears merger in tour and travel sector 147
Mergers and Acquisitions: UK government imposes special regime to control water company acquisitions 149
Trade: Japanese diplomat finds no threat of discrimination flowing from FTA 148
Trade: Timely handling of protests is critical in resolving procurement disputes under FTA 150
Unfair Competition: ITC reviews chemiluminescent compositions determination 151
Unfair Competition: Skirmishes continue in litigation over distribution of infant formula 148
Unfair Competition: UK agency criticizes low disclosures, price levels in funeral service sector .. 150
MERGERS AND ACQUISITIONS
Tea: Herbal tea maker may attack attempted purchase of competitor 118
Text of opinion 160
OFFICIAL ACTIONS 166
PRICE FIXING
Airline Tickets: Travel agent's RPM claim founders on agency relationship 123
PRICE FIXING (cont'd)
Building Supplies: Concrete block supply firm faces Division charges of fixing prices 125
Moving Services: Mover must defend Division allegations of fixing Defense Department contracts 124
Trash Hauling: Waste disposal company faces charges of allocating customers, price fixing 122
RESTRAINTS OF TRADE
Health Care: Supplier of health care equipment suffers loss of $2.3 million award 119
STATE DEVELOPMENTS
Price Fixing: Last ready-mix concrete defendants settle Colorado's overcharge claims 139
Regulated Industries: FTC staff advises state to rethink restrictions on licensed professionals 140
Unfair Practices: Foreclosure without prior notice is unfair practice in Pennsylvania 138
Unfair Practices: Lumber firms resolve Maine's concerns over joint notices on holiday hours 140
UNFAIR COMPETITION
Watches: FTC declines to modify Bulova order on terminating discounters 126
U.S. SUPREME COURT
Jurisdiction and Procedure: Guilty plea bars attack on sentence for infringing Double Jeopardy Clause 117
Text of opinions 152
Orders: FTC's unfairness finding in *Orkin* case won't be reviewed 120

TABLE OF CASES

Arthur Glick Truck Sales, Inc. v. General Motors Corp. 143
Certain Chemiluminescent Compositions and Components Thereof and Methods of Using the Same, In re 151
Colorado v. Cowan 139
Douglas v. Chevron USA, Inc. 144
Ford Motor Co. v. Courtesy Motors, Inc. 144
FTC v. Credit Repair, Inc. 123
FTC v. Plaza Motors, Inc. 121
Gaines v. Continental Mortgage and Investment Corp. 126
Healy v. Beer Institute, Inc. 120
Heublein, Inc. v. Dep't of Alcoholic Beverage Control of the Commonwealth of Virginia 142
Illinois Corporate Travel, Inc. v. American Airlines . 123
Key Enterprises of Delaware, Inc. v. Venice Hospital 119
Orkin Exterminating Co. v. FTC 120
Powell v. Nat'l Football League 120
R.C. Bigelow, Inc. v. Unilever N.V. 118
Smith v. Commercial Banking Corp. 138
U.S. v. Broce 117
U.S. v. GSX 122
U.S. v. Pensacola Builders Supply Co., Inc. 125
U.S. v. Ryans 124
Williams v. Amity Bank 124
Wine and Spirits Wholesalers v. Beer Institute, Inc. .. 120

ANTITRUST & TRADE REGULATION REPORT, (ISSN: 0003-6021) published every Thursday, except the Thursday following Labor Day and the last Thursday in December, by The Bureau of National Affairs, Inc., 1231 25th Street, N.W., Washington, D.C. 20037. Subscription price $696.00 per year, $668.00 for renewal. Second Class postage paid at Washington, D.C., and at additional mailing offices. Postmaster: Send address changes to Antitrust & Trade Regulation Report, The Bureau of National Affairs, Inc., P.O. Box 40949, Washington, D.C. 20016-0949.

The second page lists the issue's entire contents.

Reports in most of the service's other sections follow the same format. The State Developments section covers the enforcement of both state and federal competition law by the state attorneys general, and also reports federal and state court decisions affecting state antitrust and trade regulation laws. Legislative, regulatory, and decisional developments in the areas of Franchising and International Developments are reported in sections by those names.

A section entitled Official Actions lists and briefly summarizes relevant bills introduced in Congress and subsequent House and Senate actions; the filing of Supreme Court cases; and FTC and Justice Department actions.

A regular, although not weekly, feature is the Text section, in which is reprinted the full text of the most significant court decisions, legislation, and other documents reported on elsewhere in the issue. An occasional Special Reports section analyzes long-term trends affecting competition law or deceptive trade practice law enforcement.

These self-contained weekly issues on antitrust and trade regulation usually include the following sections:

- *News and Comment*
- *State Developments*
- *Franchising*
- *International Developments*
- *Text*
- *Official Actions*
- *Calendar of Events*

Court decisions and legislative and regulatory actions, both federal and state, are reported in detail in the *Antitrust & Trade Regulation Report*.

(Vol. 56) 117

News & Comment

GUILTY PLEA BARS ATTACK ON SENTENCE FOR INFRINGING DOUBLE JEOPARDY CLAUSE

Antitrust defendants who entered guilty pleas to two separate indictments may not challenge the sentence imposed in the second case on double jeopardy grounds, the U.S. Supreme Court decides, 6-3, because the defendants' guilty pleas and convictions foreclose the collateral attack. (*U.S. v. Broce*, No. 87-1190, US SupCt, 1/23/89) [Text of opinions appears in Text Section]

Background

In November 1981, Broce Construction Co. and its president, Ray C. Broce, were indicted for violating Sherman Act §1 and the mail fraud statute, 18 USC 1341, in connection with a conspiracy to rig bids on a particular Kansas highway construction project.

The same grand jury in February 1982 returned a second indictment against the defendants for violating §1 in connection with a conspiracy to rig bids on another Kansas highway construction project. Pursuant to a plea bargaining agreement, the defendants entered guilty pleas to both pending indictments at the same proceeding, which was held on Feb. 9, 1982.

The district court, after entering convictions on the guilty pleas, sentenced Broce to two years' imprisonment on each antitrust count, the terms to run concurrently, and imposed a fine of $50,000 on each count. The corporation was fined $750,000 on each count for a total of $1.5 million.

Meanwhile, another set of antitrust defendants was following a different course of action. Robert T. Beachner and Beachner Construction Co. stood trial on charges of rigging bids in connection with a Kansas highway construction project and were acquitted. They then were indicted a second time on bid rigging charges with respect to three other Kansas highway projects. The second indictment was dismissed on double jeopardy grounds because there had been a pervasive conspiracy to rig bids on such projects for more than 25 years. See *U.S. v. Beachner Construction Co., Inc.*, 555 FSupp 1273 (DC Kan 1983), *aff'd*, 729 F2d 1278 (CA 10 1984).

Following the district court's decision in *Beachner*, the *Broce* defendants moved to vacate their sentences on the Sherman Act charge contained in the second indictment. They argued that the bid rigging schemes alleged in both indictments constituted a single conspiracy.

The district court denied the motion on the ground that the defendants' guilty pleas constituted an admission of the government's allegations of two conspiracies, an admission that foreclosed an attack on the sentence imposed after conviction on the second indictment.

A Tenth Circuit panel ruled that the defendants suffered entry of an illegal judgment and sentence in the second case because the defendants did not knowingly and voluntarily waive their double jeopardy rights and were punished twice for participating in a "single continuing conspiracy." See 753 F2d 811 (CA 10 1985).

The Tenth Circuit *en banc* ruled, 4-3, that a guilty plea to a "constitutionally duplicitous charge" does not waive a defendant's right to assert a double jeopardy claim. See 50 ATRR 102.

On remand, the district court vacated the sentences entered on the second indictment on the ground that the two indictments challenged different aspects of the same conspiracy. The Tenth Circuit affirmed but acknowledged that *Ricketts v. Adamson*, 483 US 1 (1987), made clear that the protection against double jeopardy is subject to waiver. While there was no such waiver here, the court of appeals found, the trial court's finding of a single conspiracy was not clearly erroneous.

General Rule

Justice Anthony M. Kennedy, reversing, initially notes a general rule: collateral attacks on sentences imposed pursuant to guilty pleas ordinarily are foreclosed whenever the defendant was advised by competent counsel and the plea was voluntary. There are exceptions to this rule, but none are applicable here.

The Court faults the Tenth Circuit for misapprehending the nature and effect of a guilty plea. A defendant who enters a guilty plea admits guilt of a substantive crime. When the *Broce* defendants entered guilty pleas to two separate indictments alleging conspiracies starting at different times and embracing separate objectives, they admitted guilt to two separate crimes.

The defendants had the right to challenge the theory of the indictment and attempt to show that there was only a single conspiracy. They chose, instead, to enter guilty pleas to two indictments alleging two conspiracies and thus lost their right to attack the theory of the indictment.

It does not matter, the Court continues, that the defendants' attorney did not discuss double jeopardy issues with them prior to their guilty pleas. Conscious waiver is not necessary with respect to each potential defense relinquished by a plea of guilty.

The exception to the rule barring collateral attack on a guilty plea set forth in *Blackledge v. Perry*, 417 US 21 (1974), and *Menna v. New York*, 423 US 504 61 (1975), is inapplicable here, the Court finds. In those cases, convictions under second indictments were set aside because the courts should not have allowed the indictments to go forward. There was no need for a reviewing court to look beyond the indictments and the original record. Here, in contrast, the defendants could not prove their double jeopardy claim without introducing new evidence.

Concurrence

Justice John Paul Stevens, concurring, writes separately to stress that this case does not resolve the question whether separate bid rigging arrangements carried

1-26-89 Antitrust & Trade Regulation Report
0003-6021/89/$00.50

Full text of the most significant court decisions and other documents discussed in the issue is also provided.

152 (Vol. 56)

Text

SUPREME COURT'S OPINIONS IN U.S. v. BROCE

SUPREME COURT OF THE UNITED STATES

Syllabus

UNITED STATES *v.* BROCE ET AL.

CERTIORARI TO THE UNITED STATES COURT OF APPEALS FOR THE TENTH CIRCUIT

No. 87-1190. Argued October 4, 1988—Decided January 23, 1989

Respondents pleaded guilty to two separate conspiracy indictments in a single proceeding in District Court. One indictment charged respondents with entering into an agreement to rig bids on a certain highway project in violation of the Sherman Act, and the other made similar charges with respect to a different project. After the District Court conducted a hearing, at which respondents were represented by counsel, and found the guilty pleas free and voluntary and made with an understanding of their consequences and of the nature of the charges, convictions were entered on the pleas and sentences were imposed. Respondents subsequently filed a motion to vacate the convictions and sentences under the second indictment, contending, in reliance on the District Court's holding in another case involving the same bid-rigging conspiracy, that only one conspiracy existed and that double jeopardy principles required their convictions and sentences to be set aside. The District Court denied the motion, but the Court of Appeals reversed, holding that notwithstanding their guilty pleas, respondents were entitled to introduce evidence outside the original record to support their one-conspiracy claim, since in pleading guilty they admitted only the acts described in the indictments, not their legal consequences, and that moreover, since the indictments did not expressly state that the two conspiracies were separate, no such concessions could be inferred from the pleas. On remand, the District Court granted the motion, finding that there was only a single conspiracy, and the Court of Appeals affirmed.

Held: Respondents' double jeopardy challenge is foreclosed by their guilty pleas and convictions.

(a) In holding that the admissions inherent in a guilty plea "go only to the acts constituting the conspiracy," the Court of Appeals misapprehended the nature and effect of the plea. By entering a guilty plea, the accused does not simply state that he did the discrete acts described in the indictment; he admits guilt of a substantive crime. Here, the indictments alleged two distinct agreements, and the Court of Appeals erred in concluding that because the indictments did not explicitly state that the conspiracies were separate, respondents did not concede their separate nature by pleading guilty to both. When respondents pleaded guilty to both indictments, they conceded guilt to two separate offenses.

(b) By pleading guilty, respondents relinquished the opportunity to receive a factual hearing on their double jeopardy claim. That their attorney did not discuss double jeopardy issues with them prior to their pleas, and that they had not considered the possibility of raising a double jeopardy defense before pleading, did not entitle respondents to claim that they had not waived their right to raise a double jeopardy defense. Conscious waiver is not necessary with respect to each potential defense relinquished by a guilty plea.

(c) Under the well-settled principle that a voluntary and intelligent guilty plea by an accused who has been advised by competent counsel may not be collaterally attacked, respondents, who have not called into question the voluntary and intelligent character of their pleas, were not entitled to the collateral relief they sought.

(d) The exception to the rule barring collateral attack on a guilty plea established by *Blackledge* v. *Perry*, 417 U. S. 21, and *Menna* v. *New York*, 423 U. S. 61, in cases where a conviction under a second indictment must be set aside because the defendant's right not to be haled into court was violated, has no application in this case. Here, in contrast to those cases which were resolved without any need to go beyond the indictments and the original record, respondents could not prove their double jeopardy claim without introducing new evidence into the record.

Reversed.

KENNEDY, J., delivered the opinion of the Court, in which REHNQUIST, C. J., and WHITE, STEVENS, O'CONNOR, and SCALIA, JJ., joined. STEVENS, J., filed a concurring opinion. BLACKMUN, J., filed a dissenting opinion, in which BRENNAN and MARSHALL, JJ., joined.

SUPREME COURT OF THE UNITED STATES

No. 87-1190

UNITED STATES, PETITIONER *v.* RAY C. BROCE AND BROCE CONSTRUCTION CO., INC.

ON WRIT OF CERTIORARI TO THE UNITED STATES COURT OF APPEALS FOR THE TENTH CIRCUIT

[January 23, 1989]

JUSTICE KENNEDY delivered the opinion of the Court.

We consider here the circumstances under which a defendant who has entered a plea of guilty to a criminal charge may assert a double jeopardy claim in a collateral attack upon the sentence. The respondents, upon entering guilty pleas, were convicted of two separate counts of conspiracy, but contend now that only one conspiracy existed and that double jeopardy principles require the conviction and sentence on the second count to be set aside. The United States Court of Appeals for the Tenth Circuit held that respondents were entitled to introduce evidence outside the original record supporting their claim and directed further proceedings in the District Court. We hold that the double jeopardy challenge is foreclosed by the guilty pleas and the judgments of conviction.

I

A

The respondents, Ray C. Broce and Broce Construction Co., Inc., bid for work on highway projects in Kansas. Two

NOTICE: These opinions are subject to formal revision before publication in the preliminary print of the United States Reports. Readers are requested to notify the Reporter of Decisions, Supreme Court of the United States, Washington, D.C. 20543, of any typographical or other formal errors, in order that corrections may be made before the preliminary print goes to press.

NOTE: Where it is deemed desirable, a syllabus (headnote) will be released * * * at the time the opinion is issued. The syllabus constitutes no part of the opinion of the Court but has been prepared by the Reporter of Decisions for the convenience of the reader. See *United States v. Detroit Lumber Co.*, 200 U. S. 321, 337.

1-26-89 Published by THE BUREAU OF NATIONAL AFFAIRS, INC., Washington, D.C. 20037

Securities Regulation & Law Report

Securities Regulation & Law Report is a notification service covering one of today's most dynamic fields of business law. It gives prompt coverage of Securities and Exchange Commission activities, including regulations and rule proposals, enforcement actions, and no-action letters, and publishes full text of many of them. Judicial decisions affecting securities law, both from state and from federal courts, also are reported, with U.S. Supreme Court decisions reprinted in full text.

The service also covers the regulation of commodities futures trading by the Commodity Futures Trading Commission, as well as aspects of accounting and auditing.

Organized along the same lines as BNA's *Antitrust & Trade Regulation Report*, this service consists of weekly, self-contained issues that are filed in one of two binders, each covering a six-month period. Each issue contains several sections encompassing different types of information. For example, a typical issue includes sections entitled Federal Securities & Corporate Developments, State Developments, Commodities Regulation, Accounting and Disclosure, and No Action Letters.

The subject area of *Securities Regulation & Law Report* affects the activities of a diverse group of subscribers. Developments in the securities field are of interest not only to lawyers who advise corporate clients on compliance with complex and ever-changing securities regulation, but also to brokers and dealers, commodities lawyers, accountants, and corporate management.

Each weekly issue of the publication begins with a Summary page that briefly describes the most important developments reported in that issue. The issue's second page serves essentially as a table of contents.

The first major part or section of the service, entitled Federal Securities & Corporate Developments, reports on developments in the federal courts, the SEC, and Congress that affect the issuance and trading of securities and certain corporate governance matters. Many of the court decisions and SEC regulatory actions are based on two main securities regulation statutes: the Securities Act of 1933 and the Securities Exchange Act of 1934. Other statutes that fall within the publication's coverage are the Racketeer Influenced and Corrupt Organizations Act (RICO), the Investment Company Act, the Investment Advisers Act, the Insider Trading Sanctions Act, the Public Utility Holding Company Act, the Trust Indenture Act, and the Glass-Steagall Act. U.S. Supreme Court decisions affecting securities law are reported in full text; the decisions of other courts are described in detail, with readers taken step-by-step through each court's holding and rationale.

The activities of the SEC are covered thoroughly, including the commission's open meetings, its rule proposals, and its enforcement actions. Legislation is tracked through Congress, from initial hearings and markup through debate and enactment. Particularly important SEC actions and congressional legislation are reprinted in full text.

ROUTE TO

Securities Regulation & Law Report®

Vol. 21, No. 1, Pages 1–60 January 6, 1989

SUMMARY

SEC TO REVIEW DECISION TO END PROCEEDINGS AGAINST ATTORNEY KERN: The Securities and Exchange Commission decides to review an administrative law judge's decision that proceedings against attorney George Kern Jr. should be discontinued, despite the ALJ's finding that Kern "caused" a client to violate disclosure requirements in connection with a tender offer (*In re Kern*) (Page 3).

CFTC TO SEEK MORE INVESTIGATORY POWERS, GRAMM TELLS BNA: The Commodity Futures Trading Commission plans to seek legislation allowing it to investigate traders and other individuals at the request of a foreign government, CFTC Chairman Wendy Gramm tells BNA editors in a recent interview. Gramm also discloses plans to establish a "regulatory coordination advisory" committee (Page 30).

DREXEL AGREES TO PLEAD GUILTY, PAY $650 MILLION FINE: Drexel Burnham Lambert Inc.—already facing a massive civil fraud suit by the Securities and Exchange Commission—agrees to plead guilty in the U.S. District Court for Southern New York to six counts of mail, wire, and securities fraud, and to pay $650 million in fines and penalties. The "agreement in principle" is contingent upon a settlement of the civil matter (Page 4).

MORE DISCLOSURE NEEDED IN MAI BID REGARDING DREXEL FINANCING ABILITY: MAI Basic Four Inc. may not proceed with its tender offer for Prime Computer Inc. without further disclosure regarding Drexel Burnham Lambert Inc.'s ability to provide adequate financing for the offer, the U.S. District Court for Massachusetts rules (*MAI Basic Inc. v. Prime Computer Inc.*) (Page 5).

FOURTH CIRCUIT SAYS §17(a) DOES NOT IMPLY PRIVATE REMEDY: Section 17(a) of the 1933 Securities Act, the statute's general antifraud prohibition, "implies no private cause of action," the U.S. Court of Appeals for the Fourth Circuit, sitting en banc, determines (*Newcome v. Esrey*) (Page 3).

MERGER CONTRACT FATALLY FLAWED, DELAWARE COURT FINDS: ConAgra Inc. is handed a setback in its quest to acquire control of Holly Farms Corp., as the Delaware Chancery Court concludes that negotiation of a merger agreement between the two entities was "fatally flawed" by the target board's failure to advise rival suitor Tyson Food Inc. that the company was for sale (*In re Holly Farms Corp. Shareholders Litigation*) (Page 38).

WORLD BODY PROPOSES HARMONIZATION OF ACCOUNTING RULES: In a major step toward the international harmonization of accounting standards, the International Accounting Standards Committee issues a series of proposals that would eliminate most of the accounting choices currently permitted under international standards for the preparation of financial statements (Page 46).

CFTC ISSUES PROPOSAL TO EXEMPT CERTAIN HYBRID INSTRUMENTS: The Commodity Futures Trading Commission unanimously agrees to issue a proposed rule that would provide an exemption from CFTC regulations for certain hybrid instruments that have option components and are subject to other regulatory oversight. The CFTC also votes to issue an interpretation recognizing an exclusion for certain hybrid instruments that combine futures characteristics with debt or depository interests (Page 6).

As with many BNA notification services, this one has a first-page summary of the week's most significant events, with references to the pages in the issue where expanded coverage is provided.

The service follows the activities of the Securities and Exchange Commission and other federal agencies, and reports decisions of the federal courts affecting securities law.

Federal Securities & Corporate Developments

SEC TO REVIEW DECISION TO END PROCEEDINGS AGAINST ATTORNEY KERN

The Securities and Exchange Commission has determined, on its own initiative, to review an administrative law judge's initial decision that proceedings against attorney George Kern Jr. should be discontinued despite the ALJ's finding that Kern "caused" a client to violate disclosure requirements (*In re Kern*, Administrative Proceeding File No. 3-6869, SEC, 1/4/89).

The initial decision by Chief ALJ Warren Blair, issued last November (20 SRLR 1747), has prompted strong, but divided reaction from the securities bar. In its Jan. 4 order, the SEC said it would review, without limitation, all issues of fact and law that were raised in the decision.

In his initial decision, Blair said the SEC does not have authority under Section 15(c)(4) of the 1934 Securities Exchange Act to issue an order requiring a lawyer to take steps to effect compliance with '34 Act provisions by an issuer the attorney does not currently represent. Since Kern no longer represents Allied, Blair declared, proceedings involving Kern, of Sullivan & Cromwell, New York, should be discontinued because Kern does not have the power or authority to require Allied to take corrective action.

However, the law judge ruled that Kern did "cause" Allied—no longer a public corporation—to violate Exchange Act disclosure requirements during its 1986 takeover fight with Campeau Corp.

Unusual Proceeding

The *Kern* decision was the first Section 15(c)(4) proceeding to be adjudicated since it was amended by Congress in 1984 to allow the SEC to bring proceedings against individuals under certain circumstances relating to proxy and tender offer requirements (16 SRLR 1383).

Allied consented in July 1987 to the entry of findings that it should have disclosed its talks with Edward J. DeBartolo Corp., a private concern, to settle related SEC proceedings (19 SRLR 1087).

The *Kern* proceeding also was unique in that Kern served both as counsel and as the corporate officer responsible for deciding whether the disclosure at issue was required. Allied had instructed Kern to make all decisions regarding disclosure.

Securities attorneys have been divided over whether the SEC should review the ALJ's initial decision because of the potential effect on the applicability of Section 15(c)(4). If Blair's position is maintained, some attorneys have argued, then the section could become useless as an enforcement tool.

FOURTH CIRCUIT SAYS §17(a) DOES NOT IMPLY PRIVATE REMEDY

Section 17(a) of the 1933 Securities Act, the statute's general antifraud prohibition, "implies no private cause of action," the U.S. Court of Appeals for the Fourth Circuit, sitting en banc, determined (*Newcome v. Esrey*, No. 87-1603, CA 4, 12/16/88).

Citing other '33 Act sections that specifically provide for private civil liability, the court decided that Congress did not intend to provide a cause of action under Section 17(a). In so concluding, the court overruled its contrary 1975 decision in *Newman v. Prior*, 518 F2d 97 (308 SRLR A-16), explaining that the criteria for deciding whether a federal statute impliedly creates a private remedy have been defined more stringently since *Newman* was decided.

Arbitration Agreement

According to Judge James Sprouse, the plaintiff sued her brokerage and an individual broker under both Section 17(a) of the '33 Act and Section 10(b) of the 1934 Securities Exchange Act. She claimed they churned her account "in a manner calculated only to generate excessive commissions." The brokers countered with a motion to dismiss on alternative grounds—that there is no private remedy under Section 17(a), and that even if there were, both the '33 and the '34 Act claims were required to be arbitrated pursuant to the agreement between the parties.

Last year (19 SRLR 677), the district court decided in reliance on *Newman* that Section 17(a) did imply a private remedy. Nonetheless, it dismissed the entire action on the ground that both the '33 and '34 Act claims were subject to arbitration. In reaching that conclusion, the district court decided that the U.S. Supreme Court's 1953 decision in *Wilko v. Swan*, 346 US 427, did not apply to antifraud claims under either statute. The *Wilko* court concluded that enforcement of an agreement to arbitrate a '33 Act claim was inconsistent with the statute's non-waiver provision.

Here, Sprouse continued, the investor challenged the lower court's holding that her Section 10(b) claim was subject to arbitration pursuant to the customer agreement. However, he noted, shortly after the lower court's decision, the high court decided in *Shearson/American Express Inc. v. McMahon*, 55 LW 4757 (19 SRLR 882), that agreements to arbitrate Section 10(b) claims are valid and enforceable. "Suffice it to say that *McMahon* requires our affirmance of the district court's action dismissing the section 10(b) claim."

Initial Determination

Next, the appeals court observed, the lower court's conclusion that an action under Section 17(a) may be waived by an arbitration agreement "necessarily was

The State Developments section covers the activities and decisions of state courts, state securities regulators, and state legislatures.

The Commodities Regulation section contains reports on developments in Congress, the courts, and the Commodity Futures Trading Commission that have a direct impact on the creation and trading of commodity futures. Among the CFTC activities covered are administrative hearings, open meetings, and advisory committee meetings.

The service covers accounting and auditing issues not related to tax in its Accounting & Disclosure section. Among the areas the publication follows are the SEC's rulemaking and enforcement actions that affect accountants, its regulation of how financial statements must be prepared, legislation and litigation affecting accountants, and the regulation of accountants by such private groups as the American Institute of Certified Public Accountants.

In its No Action Letters section, the service reports on SEC staff responses to requests for guidance from the private sector. Lawyers for private clients write the SEC, informing it of their proposed course of action and their interpretation of the relevant statutes. The SEC staff then responds with its own interpretation or request for further details. The *Securities Regulation & Law Report* also lists all the no action letters the SEC releases each week.

This service, like all BNA notification services, periodically publishes a separate index covering all the issues in the current volume that have been published up to that point in time. The index contains both a topical index and a table of cases. A final index, covering all the issues in a six-month binder, is published every six months.

Securities Regulation & Law Report also regularly has sections on State Developments, Commodities Regulation, and Accounting and Disclosure.

(Vol. 21) 37

BNA

State Developments

DELAWARE COURT REJECTS EFFORTS TO BAR USE OF TAKEOVER DEFENSES

The record "does not sustain [the] broad brush hyperbole" employed by plaintiff MAI Basic Four Inc. in its bid to enjoin Prime Computer Inc., the subject of its Nov. 15 all cash tender, from implementing certain defensive devices adopted by the Prime board of directors after MAI expressed interest in acquiring the company, the Delaware Chancery Court determined (*MAI Basic Four Inc. v. Prime Computer Inc.*, Civil Action No. 10428, DelChCt, 12/20/88).

"I find that the plaintiff is not entitled to a preliminary injunction because it has not borne its burden of showing that the directors of Prime have thus far acted unreasonably," Vice Chancellor Maurice Hartnett said.

Entrenchment Devices

According to Hartnett, on Nov. 15, plaintiff MAI commenced an all cash tender offer for the shares of defendant Prime Computer. In the action here, it asked the court to set aside a "vast array" of takeover defenses adopted by Prime after MAI expressed its acquisition interest. According to MAI, these defenses are "entrenchment devices" serving only to prevent Prime shareholders from considering on its merits the MAI offer. These defenses include a shareholder rights plan, an employee severance bonus plan, an employee pension plan where none previously existed, an employee retention plan, a stock appreciation rights plan, and stock options that accelerate upon a change of control.

All the devices may be rescinded without penalty by the Prime board, Hartnett noted. "The total economic impact of the devices makes it unlikely that any tender offer could be completed while they remain in place."

Rejecting MAI's challenge, the court first said that while the Prime directors "could have been better informed" regarding whether such takeover defenses were necessary, the record shows they had enough information "to have reasonably perceived that the plaintiff intended to acquire the shares of Prime for the lowest price possible." In Hartnett's view, the only "real basis" for MAI's challenge "is the undisputed fact that defendants have not responded to the tender offer in a way which plaintiff desires."

Reasonable Response

To obtain a preliminary injunction, the court explained, a plaintiff must show that it has a reasonable probability of success on the merits, and that it will suffer irreparable harm if relief is not granted. Moreover, in deciding whether the plaintiff has shown such reasonable probability, the court said it must consider that the ultimate responsibility for managing the corporation's affairs falls on the board of directors.

In this connection, Hartnett said that under the business judgment rule, there is a presumption that the board acted "in informed good faith and in the honest belief" that its action was in the corporation's best interest. However, the board is under a higher duty in connection with the adoption of takeover defenses. For example, antitakeover devices may not be used "merely to defeat a hostile tender offer which is neither coercive, inadequate, nor a threat to the corporation."

"The unanswered issue, therefore, is whether the failure of Prime's board to thus far do more in response to plaintiff's tender offer has been a reasonable response," the court declared. "A reasonable response," it continued, "must be one which is fair, just, equitable and appropriate, considering all the facts and circumstances."

Pertinent Factors

Reviewing the factors pertinent to deciding whether the response was reasonable, Hartnett first observed that six of the seven Prime directors undisputedly were disinterested. In addition, on being advised of the tender offer the board retained two outside financial advisors who opined that the $20 per share price was inadequate. Moreover, Prime management's projections for the future are optimistic, and two outside investment bankers independent of Prime "have publicly expressed their opinion that the value of Prime's shares is in the $23 to $28 per share range."

Further, the offer has been pending only since Nov. 15, less than 1 percent of the shareholders have tendered, and "numerous contingencies" contained in the offer have not been fulfilled. "It also appears that plaintiff is prepared, and is in a position, to offer more than $20 per share but only the existence of the antitakeover devices will compel it to do so."

On the other hand, Hartnett observed, the tender offer is for cash and there is nothing to indicate that it is coercive to shareholders. "It appears to be bona fide and represents a premium over current market value." Although Prime's directors acted on the basis of adequate information in finding the tender offer a threat and the price inadequate, "the data relied upon could have been more comprehensive," according to Hartnett.

Moreover, the Prime directors have not arrived at a value for the corporation, have not made a counter offer to the plaintiff, and have not apparently sought another suitor. The court also said that if the current "stalemate" continues, Prime shareholders will not be able to make their own investment judgment because the takeover devices are so burdensome "that no prospective tender offeror could afford to buy the shares as long as they are in place."

However, on balance, the court decided that MAI did not meet its burden of showing that the Prime directors acted unreasonably. "Of particular signifi-

1-6-89 Securities Regulation & Law Report
0037-0665/89/$0 - 50

The No Action Letters section reports on SEC staff responses to private requests for guidance.

50 (Vol. 21)

BNA

No Action Letters

STAFF SAYS INDIRECT U.S. OBLIGATIONS NOT EXEMPTED FROM '40 ACT REPORTING RULE

The staff of the Division of Investment Management refused relief from the reporting provisions of Rule 17j-1(c)(1) under the 1940 Investment Company Act to certain closed-end investment companies investing in long-term government securities, saying it does not agree that "indirect" obligations are covered by the exemption provided by Section 2(a)(16) of the act (*ACM Government Spectrum Fund Inc., ACM Government Income Fund Inc., ACM Government Securities Fund Inc., ACM Government Opportunity Fund Inc.*, avail. 12/25/88).

However, the staff concurred in counsel's view that direct obligations, such as Treasury Bills, Notes, and Bonds, whether short, intermediate, or long-term, are government securities within the meaning of the rule.

Long-Term Obligations

According to counsel, each of the funds invests in obligations of greater than one-year's maturity that are issued or guaranteed by the U.S. government or its agencies or instrumentalities. In seeking no-action relief, he noted that Rule 17j-1(c)(1) of the act requires every access person of a registered investment company to report personal transactions in "any security."

Under Rule 17j-1(e)(5), counsel continued, a "security" is defined as having the same meaning as that term set forth in Section 2(a)(36) of the act, "except that the term does not include, among other things, 'securities issued by the Government of the United States.'" The Securities and Exchange Commission has indicated that this phrase refers to securities that are "government securities" within the meaning of Section 2(a)(16), he noted.

Section 2(a)(16) defines a government security as any security issued or guaranteed by the United States. However, in 1980, when it adopted Rule 17j-1(e)(5) (577 SRLR I-1), the commission expanded this exception to the definition of a security to include money market instruments and shares of open-end investment companies, saying these instruments presented little opportunity for the type of abuse the rule was intended to prevent.

Length To Maturity

The attorney conceded that the release focused on the possibility for abuse rather than the instruments' length to maturity. However, he said, the staff generally has considered money market instruments to be debt securities that mature within 12 months or less and "that have the quality and trading characteristics associated with the money markets."

According to counsel, there is nothing in the definition of "government security" under Section 2(a)(16) to suggest that the definition applies only to short-term instruments. However, he said, the staff has indicated in prior no-action responses that Rule 17j-1(e)(5) excepts "short-term" government securities.

Here, however, the funds invest in government securities that often mature in more than one year. Since these securities cannot be characterized as short-term U.S. government obligations—and because the staff's prior responses could be construed as being limited to short-term government obligations—"there is doubt as to whether intermediate and long-term Government Securities are excepted by subparagraph (e)(5)," counsel wrote. "Accordingly, we are seeking the Staff's concurrence with our view that Government Securities (within the meaning of Section 2(a)(16) of the Act) are excepted from the definition of 'security' pursuant to subparagraph (e)(5) of the Rule regardless of their maturity."

In seeking no-action relief, counsel asserted that because no factors other than the prevailing interest rate affect the market price of short, intermediate, or long-term government securities, the rule's recordkeeping requirements should not be applicable to these securities because they are not subject to improper trading practices, which the rule was designed to prevent. As such, he urged, Section 2(a)(16) should be read into Rule 17j-1(e)(5) entirely, without regarding to the maturity of the instrument.

Staff Response

"We agree with your interpretation with respect to direct obligations," the staff responded. In this connection, it noted that the commission—in defining a "security" for purposes of the rule—did not refer explicitly to Section 2(a)(16). However, it did propose a definition similar to that found in Section 2(a)(16), although the rule as adopted did not include the express reference to securities issued by an instrumentality of the government. "We thus agree that all direct obligations, regardless of their maturities, are government securities within the meaning of paragraph (e)(5)."

However, the staff said it disagreed as an interpretive matter that indirect obligations—for example, securities issued by the Federal National Mortgage Association—fall within this paragraph, "and, therefore, believe that they are subject to the applicable provisions of the rule."

CLOSED-END FUND'S REAL ESTATE SPINOFF DOES NOT QUALIFY FOR '40 ACT EXEMPTIONS

A closed-end investment company's plan to spin off its real estate properties holdings to a new partnership in exchange for holdings in the partnership would not be deemed a transfer between affiliates and would not qualify for an exemption under the 1940 Investment Company Act, according to the Division of Investment Management staff. On a separate question, the staff said a proposed distribution of the partnership interests to the investment company's shareholders also does not qualify for a '40 act exemption (*Chicago Milwaukee Corp.*, avail. 12/16/88).

Chicago Milwaukee Corp. is a closed-end, non-diversified management investment company. The company and its subsidiaries intend to transfer (the "Transfer") substantially all of their real estate properties, together with certain other assets and certain liabilities, to a newly formed general partnership, to be called CMC Heartland Partners L.P., a newly formed Delaware limited partnership, its attorney explained.

In consideration for the properties and other assets and liabilities, Heartland Partners would issue units representing Class A and Class B limited partnership interests in Heartland Partners, counsel said.

1-6-89
0037-0665/89/$0+ 50

BNA's Bankruptcy Law Reporter

This notification service provides a weekly review of significant developments in bankruptcy law. *BNA's Bankruptcy Law Reporter* covers bankruptcy decisions from the various federal courts: bankruptcy courts, district courts, bankruptcy appellate panels, circuit courts, and the U.S. Supreme Court. Legislative initiatives and rule-making developments also are covered.

BNA's Bankruptcy Law Reporter follows the format of many other BNA notification services, with a front page highlighting the most significant developments reported in the rest of the issue. Inside are detailed accounts of these and other developments written by the lawyers who edit the publication. When warranted, key court decisions, legislation, and new rules are provided in full text.

Each weekly issue of *BNA's Bankruptcy Law Reporter* contains reports on the latest judicial and legislative developments in bankruptcy law. Since bankruptcy law is primarily federal in nature, most of the reported court decisions and legislative actions are also federal. Related state developments are covered when warranted.

The front page of each issue summarizes, in the left-hand column, the most significant court decisions reported in that issue, and lists, in the box on the right, other judicial, legislative, and regulatory reports of particular note. For a quick look at the entire contents of the issue, you can scan the Topical Summary on the second page, which, among other things, lists the reported court decisions by Bankruptcy Code section.

The first and major section of each issue is the News section, which begins with articles about bankruptcy developments in the U.S. Supreme Court, including petitions filed with the court, cases granted review, oral arguments, and, of course, opinions handed down. Accounts of the most significant bankruptcy decisions from all across the country follow next in the issue. The holding, factual background, and the legal reasoning of each case are spelled out in detail. Similarly detailed reports on congressional and agency actions close out the News section.

As with other BNA notification services, *BNA's Bankruptcy Law Reporter* also provides full text of key court decisions, legislation, and new bankruptcy rules, as well as periodic analyses and special reports from outside experts. A Calendar lists upcoming conferences and recent law review articles. The weekly issues are housed in two binders, each containing a half year's worth of issues, and are indexed in a separate section every two months.

The front page of each issue highlights the issue's contents. The paragraphs on the left give brief summaries of the most important court decisions reported in the issue. The box on the right describes other judicial, legislative, and regulatory actions.

BNA's Bankruptcy Law Reporter

Volume 4, Number 39 THE BUREAU OF NATIONAL AFFAIRS, INC. **October 8, 1992**

A SECURED CREDITOR ISN'T BOUND BY A CH. 13 PLAN that reduces its claim, if the debtor failed to object to the claim under Rule 3007. The right of a secured creditor who has filed a proof of claim to remain outside bankruptcy proceedings until an interested party objects would be meaningless if its claim could be compromised without further notice. (*Sun Finance Co. v. Howard*, **CA 5**, Higginbotham, J., 9/8/92) Page 1156

THE PURPORTED RECONVEYANCE TO THE DEBTOR of accounts receivable previously sold to a third party allowed the debtor to use Section 108(a) to extend the time for bringing actions to recover freight undercharges under the Interstate Commerce Act. A dissenting judge decries allowing a time-barred action to be "magically restored to life." (*Coliseum Cartage Co. v. Rubbermaid Statesville Inc.*, **CA 4**, Butzner, J., 9/16/92) Page 1157

A SETTLEMENT AGREEMENT THAT TRANSFERS a debtor's overfunded pension plan assets to another employer's plan in exchange for **$15** million violates neither **ERISA** nor the Internal Revenue Code and is thus approved. (*In re Bicoastal Corp.*, **US BankrCt MFla**, Paskay, C.J., 9/25/92) Page 1159

A CAR DEALER'S SALES AND SERVICE AGREEMENT with General Motors does not fall within the scope of a financing statement that covers "contract rights" and "accounts." The agreement is a "general intangible," as defined by the UCC, because it is not an agreement for the sale or lease of goods or the rendering of services requiring payment. (*Century National Bank v. Scheidmantel Olds-Cadillac Inc.*, **US BankrCt WPa**, Fitzgerald, J., 9/15/92) Page 1160

A DEBTOR'S NINTH BANKRUPTCY CASE IN 14 YEARS is dismissed for bad faith under Sections 1307(c) and 1325(a)(3). The debtor, likened to an addict whose "drug of choice" is Chapter 13, is barred from refiling until she can meaningfully commence a Chapter 7 case. (*In re Belden*, **US BankrCt Minn**, Kressel, J., 9/16/92) Page 1161

VA. LAW, NOT RULE 9006(a), GOVERNS CALCULATION of the five-day period within which Virginia allows a debtor to timely file for a homestead exemption. Thus, Saturdays, Sundays, and legal holidays are included within the period. (*In re Haynesworth*, **US BankrCt EVa**, Shelley, J., 9/8/92) Page 1163

Also Inside

US SupCt: In its first session of 1992–93 term, court vacates judgment in one bankruptcy-related case and denies review in 15 others. Page 1155

US BankrCt WMo: Both debtor and mortgagee had interest in post-petition rents, which were thus "cash collateral" subject to use by debtor in return for adequate protection to mortgagee. Page 1164

US BankrCt NInd: EPA, Interior Department agree to accept shares of stock in Ch. 11 debtors to settle multimillion-dollar environmental damage claims. Page 1168

Congress: House passes S 1985, but only after substituting language of HR 6020 for bankruptcy reform bill approved by Senate. Page 1166

Congress: Senate passes S 1675, which would overrule *Maislin* regarding recovery of debtor motor carrier undercharges. Page 1167

Agencies: Justice Department announces results of U.S. Trustee program implemented to close thousands of bankruptcy cases open since 1979. Page 1167

Pages 1153–1173

1044-7474/92/$0+.50

The News section begins each week with reports on U.S. Supreme Court opinions and actions. This article describes the cases in which the Supreme Court granted and denied review. Reports on cases decided by other courts follow the Supreme Court section.

BNA's
BANKRUPTCY LAW REPORTER

U.S. SUPREME COURT

Certiorari

CA 10 JUDGMENT VACATED IN ONE CASE; CERTIORARI DENIED IN 15 OTHER CASES

In its first session of the 1992–93 term, the U.S. Supreme Court Oct. 5 granted certiorari in one bankruptcy-related case, but immediately vacated the judgment and remanded the case back to the Tenth Circuit for further consideration in light of *Taylor v. Freeland & Kronz*, 60 LW 4333 (US SupCt 1992) (4 BBLR 478, 4/23/92). The Chapter 11 debtor in the present case asserted in its certiorari petition (4 BBLR 690, 6/11/92) that exemptions it claimed should be deemed allowed if no party in interest objected within 30 days after the meeting of creditors. In *Taylor*, the Supreme Court, affirming the Third Circuit, held that a trustee may not contest the validity of a claimed exemption after the Bankruptcy Rule 4003(b) 30-day period has expired, even though the debtor had no colorable basis for claiming the exemption. (*Coones v. Federal Deposit Insurance Corp.*, **US SupCt**, No. 91-1793, cert. granted, 10/5/92)

At its opening session, the Supreme Court also denied certiorari in 15 bankruptcy-related cases. The petitioners sought review of the following questions:

- *Davis v. Department of Energy (In re Transcontinental Energy Corp.)*, No. 91-1803 (4 BBLR 716, 6/18/92): Should the Energy Department's allowed claim for crude oil overcharges have been disallowed as a penalty, rather than allowed as a claim for restitution under Section 57(j) of the 1898 Bankruptcy Act?
- *Miller v. Briggs*, No. 91-1847 (4 BBLR 769, 7/2/92): Did the Ninth Circuit err in finding that an involuntary bankruptcy petition, which was filed by creditors possessing an unrecorded deed of trust on the debtor's real property, put the bankruptcy trustee on inquiry notice of the creditors' interest?
- *General Electric Capital Corp. v. North County Jeep & Renault Inc.*, No. 91-1901 (4 BBLR 770, 7/2/92): Did the Ninth Circuit err in granting standing to a third-party administrative claimant to surcharge the collateral of a secured lender under Bankruptcy Code Section 506(c)?
- *Greystone III Joint Venture v. Phoenix Mutual Life Insurance Co.*, No. 91-1902 (4 BBLR 845, 7/16/92): Did the Fifth Circuit err in ruling that a nonrecourse deficiency claim cannot be classified separately from the claims of a trade creditor class, under Bankruptcy Code Section 1122, in order to create an impaired class of claims that will accept a reorganization plan, as required by Section 1129(a)(10)?
- *Phoenix Mutual Life Insurance Co. v. Greystone III Joint Venture*, No. 92-58 (4 BBLR 953, 8/13/92): Was the Fifth Circuit's determination that the new value exception to the absolute priority rule did not survive enactment of the Bankruptcy Code clearly correct and erroneously withdrawn?
- *O'Neill Group v. Continental Airlines Corp.*, No. 91-2014 (4 BBLR 847, 7/16/92): Must a debtor's employees forgo their right to strike in order to preserve their entitlement to obtain contract rejection damages under the Bankruptcy Code?
- *Besing v. Seeligson, Douglass, Falconer & Vanden Eykel*, No. 91-2050 (4 BBLR 877, 7/23/92): Does Bankruptcy Code Section 108(a) apply to extend the limitations period governing the debtors' malpractice suit against their attorneys, even though the suit was filed after confirmation of the Chapter 11 plan?
- *Sumwalt v. Boice*, No. 91-2053 (4 BBLR 878, 7/23/92): Would a bankruptcy judge's statement in court that he did not "think a bankrupt ought to be sitting in the first row of the basketball arena ..." lead a reasonable person to anticipate that the judge's conclusions supported his personal view and that the scales of justice were tipped in favor of separating the debtor from his right to use and renew season tickets?
- *General Motors Acceptance Corp. v. Mitchell*, No. 92-9 (4 BBLR 903, 7/30/92): Should the "value" of collateral securing a claim that a debtor proposes in a reorganization plan to retain and use be its retail value or its wholesale value for purposes of Bankruptcy Code Section 506(a)?
- *Rochman v. Northeast Utilities Service Co. (In re Public Service Company of New Hampshire)*, No. 92-14 (4 BBLR 904, 7/30/92): Did the First Circuit improperly dismiss the appeal of investors who objected to plan confirmation in the bankruptcy case of a New Hampshire utility?
- *Apex Oil Co. v. Clark Oil Refining Corp. (In re Apex Oil Co.)*, No. 92-22 (4 BBLR 931, 8/6/92): Did a bankruptcy court's transformation of a preliminary hearing into a final hearing, without adequately and unambiguously notifying the parties, constitute a denial of due process?
- *Rand v. Prostko*, No. 92-85 (4 BBLR 977, 8/20/92): Was the doctrine of judicial estoppel erroneously applied by a bankruptcy court to estop a purchaser of a debtor's property from denying personal liability under an order of sale?
- *Koreag, Controle et Revision S.A. v. Refco F/X Associates Inc. (In re Koreag, Controle et Revi-*

1044-7474/92/$0+.50

BNA's Health Law Reporter

BNA's Health Law Reporter is a weekly notification service providing comprehensive coverage of federal and state health care legislation, regulation, and litigation. The service covers the full spectrum of legal areas that have an impact on health care, including antitrust, tax, professional liability, insurance, fraud and abuse, reimbursement from Medicare and Medicaid as well as private insurers, medical ethical issues, AIDS, abortion, and licensure issues.

Organized much like other BNA notification services, *BNA's Health Law Reporter* begins each issue with a front-page summary of the most significant developments reported in the rest of the issue. Inside is a Lead Report that provides an in-depth analysis of the week's most important event, and this is followed by the News and Development section, which is organized alphabetically by topic.

This weekly service provides readers with rapid notification of major federal and state court decisions across the wide spectrum of legal disciplines that have an impact on health care providers—from hospitals to health maintenance organizations. It also pays close attention to the numerous government agencies that influence the health care market. State and federal health care reform initiatives are also tracked.

By scanning the service's front Highlights page, which contains capsule descriptions of the week's most important developments, or the Table of Contents on the second page, which provides a brief description of every story in the issue, readers can turn quickly to the articles in the issue that interest them most.

In recognition of the diversity of legal problems subsumed under the rubric of health law, *BNA's Health Law Reporter* organizes its News and Development section by topic. Among the topics covered in any given issue of the service are health care reform, antitrust, drugs and devices, insurance, Medicare, and patient management. The Lead Report takes an in-depth look at the week's most important event or issue regardless of its subject matter.

Other features contained in each issue are the Congressional Calendar and the Regulatory Calendar, which summarize the past week's developments in those arenas, and the Journal, which lists relevant documents and upcoming seminars and conferences. In the service's Text section, you will find the full text of key documents, such as court decisions, proposed and final laws and regulations, policy directives, and IRS memorandums. An occasional Analysis & Perspective or Special Report provides a legal analysis of a particular problem or an interview with a key policy-making official.

The service is housed in two binders, each covering six-month periods, and is fully indexed in a separate section that is updated every six weeks.

The front page of *BNA's Health Law Reporter* provides a quick look at the most significant contents of the issue. On the second page is a Table of Contents listing the entire contents.

BNA's
HEALTH LAW
REPORTER

A Weekly Review of Legislative, Regulatory, and Legal Developments.

Vol. 1, No. 5 — October 15, 1992

PHYSICIAN RECRUITMENT AGREEMENT is ruled illegal under the anti-kickback rules by a federal magistrate in Texas. In a case of first impression, the magistrate finds the agreement clearly offers the doctor an inducement to make referrals to the hospital, and so violates antifraud rules. The court rules the hospital cannot force the doctor to repay more than $30,000 advanced under the contract. Page 123

PATIENT DUMPING CLAIM against a hospital that directed an ambulance to another facility is allowed to proceed even though the critically ill infant, who died after being admitted elsewhere, never entered the hospital's emergency room. The Seventh Circuit rules the hospital's direction to the ambulance by radio can form the basis for the COBRA claims of the infant's mother. Page 135

FEDERAL DISPROPORTIONATE SHARE funding under Medicaid will be lower than many states anticipated, according to OMB projections. Although HHS has yet to issue allotment figures for federal caps imposed by a 1991 law, an administration official says the mandatory 12 percent cap on DSH payments will result in less money than some states spent in 1992 on these programs. Page 131

HOSPITAL TOLD TO CHANGE POLICY on employment restrictions imposed on an HIV-positive, intensive-care nurse. The HHS sends a letter to St. Luke's Hospital in Kansas City saying its policy—which resulted in the nurse being transferred to a position with little patient contact—violates Section 504 of the 1973 Rehabilitation Act. Page 125

CONGRESS APPROVES HEALTH CARE measures before it leaves town, but the president is expected to veto a tax bill that includes Medicare reforms, including an exemption from HCFA's self-referral ban for shared labs. Measures approved by Congress include a bill to establish standards for mammography facilities and a bill to impose a user fee and speed FDA drug approvals. Pages 126, 127

SUPREME COURT AGREES TO REVIEW a Medicare case on whether rural hospitals are entitled to a corrective retroactive adjustment to HCFA's 1979 wage index. The court also declines to review other health care cases. Page 137

ALSO IN THE NEWS

OREGON: State officials worry a change in administrations could derail the state's Medicaid waiver (Page 130).

CAMPAIGN '92: President Bush and Gov. Clinton support health care spending caps during the first presidential debate (Page 130).

MEDICARE: HCFA proposes a rule to amend the administrative review procedure for HMOs and other prepaid health care organizations (Page 134). The agency also proposes uniform criteria to determine provider agreement effective dates (Page 134).

ANTITRUST: Blue Cross of Massachusetts agrees to conditions on its merger with a failing HMO to settle antitrust concerns (Page 126).

FRAUD: A state court upholds a dentist's conviction on theft charges for billing for work never done (Page 129).

MEDICAID: Oklahoma Human Services Commission approves funding cuts in anticipation of voter rejection of a health care provider tax (Page 133).

■ ■ ■

ANALYSIS AND PERSPECTIVE

New Merger Guidelines from FTC and DOJ suggest efficiences resulting from a hospital merger may mitigate anticompetitive effects, authors Michael Peregrine and James W. Teevans say (Page 139).

Pages 119-145

1064-2137/92/$0+.50

The first article in each issue, the Lead Report, takes a close look at the week's most important story.

Lead Report

Fraud and Abuse

FEDERAL MAGISTRATE FINDS HOSPITAL's PHYSICIAN RECRUITMENT CONTRACT ILLEGAL

Polk County Memorial Hospital's physician recruitment agreement violated the Social Security Act's antifraud provisions, a federal magistrate ruled, preventing the hospital from enforcing a physician's obligation to repay more than $30,000 advanced by it under the agreement (*Polk County, Texas v. Peters*, DC ETexas, Civil Action No. 9:92CV45, 8/28/92).

The magistrate judge of the U.S. District Court for the Eastern District of Texas called the case one of first impression on physician recruitment and patient referral issues.

Although the case does not involve a kickback, the magistrate ruled the underlying agreement violates the antifraud law. It is undisputed that the hospital compensated the physician in the form of an interest-free loan, as well as free office space, rent and utility subsidies, and malpractice insurance reimbursement, the magistrate noted.

"While the hospital may have been motivated to a greater or lesser degree by a legitimate desire to make better medical services available in the community, there can be no doubt that the benefits extended to [the physician] were, in part, an inducement for him to refer patients to the hospital. The Court must, therefore, find that the agreement made on the basis of this action violates 42 U.S.C §1395nn(b)."

> [T]here can be no doubt that the benefits extended to the [physician] were, in part, an inducement for him to refer patients to the hospital . . . .

Finding the illegal contract void and unenforceable under Texas law, the magistrate added, "Indeed, the policy against aiding in the enforcement of an illegal contract is such that a party that has inserted an illegal provision for its own benefit may nevertheless defend against a suit for breach of contract on the basis of the illegality."

One attorney noted that the magistrate relied on a fraud alert from the Health and Human Services Department's Inspector General's office in determining the contract illegal. However, the attorney pointed out that the fraud alert does not have the same legal basis as would regulations.

Suspect Practices

A May 1992 Fraud Alert from HHS outlined a number of questionable practices in the area of hospital incentives to physicians, the magistrate noted. These practices included the use of free or significantly discounted office space or equipment, income guarantees, and low- or no-interest loans that may be forgiven in exchange for some level of patient referrals. According to HHS, these financial incentives could affect a physician's judgment on appropriate patient care and could inflate Medicare and Medicaid costs through overuse of a particular hospital's services.

From 1977 to 1987, the Medicare-Medicaid Antifraud and Abuse Amendments to the Social Security Act specifically barred payment or receipt of payment for patient referrals. The amendments also barred arrangements to induce persons to obtain or to recommend that others acquire goods, services, facilities, or items payable under the law. Discounts obtained by a service provider are excepted so long as they were disclosed in reimbursement claims, as are sums paid by an employer to an employee in a good faith employment relationship. Violations are punishable by a fine of up to $25,000, imprisonment for up to five years, or both.

Modifications in the law in 1987 specifically addressed permissible conditions for physician recruitment arrangements. Among other things, physicians could not be required to refer patients to the hospital and the amount of payment could not be tied to the volume or value of referrals. The law also provided for imposition of other requirements through HHS regulations.

Recruitment Agreement

In mid-1985, Polk County Memorial Hospital arranged with Dr. Kenneth W. Peters to locate his private surgical practice in Livingston, Texas, and to use the hospital for his patients where appropriate. The hospital guaranteed Peters gross cash receipts of $8,500 per month for one year, at the end of which Peters was to repay the amounts advanced either in three equal monthly installments or by assigning his accounts receivable.

The hospital also agreed to provide Peters free office space for three months, $6,000 for rent and utilities for six months, $5,000 in moving expenses, and $7,500 for malpractice insurance premiums.

> This is the first instance where the illegality of a recruitment agreement used by the physician as a basis for avoiding obligations under the contract, one attorney notes.

The agreement stated that, on commencing private practice in Livingston, the physician "shall utilize Hospital for his patients who require hospitalization, unless, in Physician's professional judgment, the use of another medical facility is necessary or desirable in order to provide proper and appropriate treatment

BNA's Banking Report

Legal and regulatory developments in banking and in the rest of the financial services industry are the focus of *BNA's Banking Report.* This weekly notification service provides information that bankers and lawyers need to track and comply with laws and regulations affecting financial service providers.

Specifically, the service covers the federal bank and savings and loan agencies; other federal agencies that affect banking policies; congressional developments; court decisions; trend-setting state developments; banking industry activities that have public policy ramifications; significant international and economic developments; and major banking and legal conferences.

Besides editorial reports on the week's regulatory, legislative, and judicial actions, the publication regularly contains full text of important documents, plus analysis pieces, special reports, and interviews. Stored in two binders each covering a six-month period, the service is fully indexed for easy reference.

BNA's Banking Report is a weekly notification service providing detailed and timely information on federal legislation and regulation, litigation, and international legal and regulatory developments that have a direct impact on financial service providers, principally banks and savings and loan institutions.

Several federal agencies are covered in depth: the Federal Deposit Insurance Corp., the Office of Thrift Supervision, the Resolution Trust Corp., the Federal Housing Finance Board, the Federal Reserve Board, the Treasury Department, and the Office of the Comptroller of the Currency.

Each weekly issue begins with a News section, which contains detailed reports on the activities of federal banking agencies, as well as developments in the congressional arena, particularly in the Senate and House Banking Committees. The Thrift News section, which follows, contains detailed reports on regulatory and congressional developments affecting savings associations and savings banks. Next, the Legal section reports recent decisions of courts across the country that affect the banking industry. Another section covers economic developments and international finance.

The service regularly supplements its editorial reports with the full text of important court decisions, legislation, and regulations. Other sections that appear frequently in the weekly issues are Special Reports and Analysis and Perspective, which often offer the viewpoints of outside experts in the banking regulation field. The service's Journal section near the end of each weekly issue summarizes the week's actions by the various regulatory entities involved in the field.

To do research in *BNA's Banking Report*, simply go to the current binder and use the separately bound index. For the last several weekly issues that may not yet be covered in the index, the best place to start researching is on each issue's second page, which summarizes that issue's entire contents. Repeat this process for back issues stored in separate binders.

BNA's
Banking Report

Legal and Regulatory Developments in the Financial Services Industry

Vol. 52, No. 13 — March 27, 1989

THE HUDSPETH DOCTRINE is overturned by the Supreme Court, which says the FSLIC may not try claims against failed S&Ls. FSLIC may not require creditors to exhaust administrative remedies before going to court, because the absence of time limits enables the FSLIC to keep claims in the "black hole" of administrative proceedings indefinitely, the court says. In response, FHLBB sets time limits on administrative review. Pages 725, 746

A RAPID GROWTH RULE proposed by the FDIC would require banks planning to increase their assets by more than 9 percent in a given quarter to notify the FDIC in advance. The proposal also would require banks to notify the FDIC any time unplanned asset growth exceeds 9 percent in any three-month period. Page 725

CERCLA CLAIMS AGAINST a bank are left standing by a federal court in Colorado. The court says the plaintiffs may ask the bank to contribute to environmental cleanup even though the plaintiffs themselves may have been partially liable for the cleanup. The court dismisses state-law negligence and nuisance claims against the bank for lack of jurisdiction. Page 748

HEARINGS AND DEBATE on the administration's thrift rescue plan continue as the Treasury prepares technical amendments, Secretary Brady says the plan is on a fast track in Congress, Fed Chairman Greenspan recommends letting BHCs acquire healthy thrifts immediately, and some S&Ls in conservatorship verge on requiring funding through a standby lending facility set up with the Fed and the FHLBanks. Pages 730, 731

HARSH CRIMINAL PENALTIES in the administration's FSLIC rescue bill will not deter bank crime, a criminal defense lawyer tells a House Judiciary subcommittee. Witnesses from the Justice Department and the FHLBB, however, praise the bill's strong sanctions and urge Congress to allow prosecutors to share information from grand jury proceedings with other government lawyers. Pages 734, 735

CREDIT UNION COMMON BOND requirements would be stiffened under an NCUA proposal. Tougher standards under the proposal would make it more difficult for national groups—such as the American Association of Retired Persons—to set up credit unions serving their national membership. Page 728

ALSO IN THE NEWS

BANK SECRECY: Treasury proposes lowering the $10,000 reporting threshold for banks in a designated area (Page 727).

BRANCHING: OCC lets two national banks in Wisconsin branch to the same extent as state-chartered S&Ls (Page 727).

PROFITS: National bank profits top $14 billion in 1988, up significantly from the $338 million profit recorded in 1987, the OCC reports (Page 729).

TAXES: Study says loss of mortgage tax break would slow economy, make it more difficult for first-time buyers to enter market (Page 740).

SUPREME COURT: The court declines review of an appeals court decision upholding an automobile dealer's bank fraud conviction, and other cases involving tax treatment of early withdrawal penalties imposed by an S&L, shareholders' rights in bank mergers, and Texas foreclosure law (Page 749).

CALIFORNIA: Report of legislative panel recommends state funding for S&L regulator, says lack of support for regulator contributed to S&L problems (Page 742).

BHC ACT: A state court had jurisdiction to hear counterclaims on violation of the BHC Act in a bank's foreclosure action against a borrower, the Iowa Supreme Court decides (Page 750).

■ ■ ■

TEXT: Decision of Supreme Court overturning the **"Hudspeth doctrine"** in case involving FSLIC's right to try claims against a failed S&L in administrative proceedings (Page 761).

Pages 723-770

Copyright © 1989 by The Bureau of National Affairs, Inc., Washington, D.C.
0891-0634/89/$0+.50

The front page of *BNA's Banking Report* highlights the contents of the issue.

Inside are in-depth reports of court decisions, and of legislative and regulatory actions, affecting the banking and financial services industry.

746 (Vol. 52)

BNA

Legal

SUPREME COURT SAYS FSLIC MAY NOT TRY CLAIMS, OVERTURNING HUDSPETH DOCTRINE

A unanimous U.S. Supreme Court March 21 overturned the "*Hudspeth* doctrine," holding that the Federal Savings and Loan Insurance Corp. does not have the power to try claims against a failed thrift in administrative proceedings (*Coit Independence Joint Venture v. Federal Savings and Loan Insurance Corp.*, US SupCt, No. 87-996, 3/21/89).

Because the FSLIC placed no time restrictions on its administrative proceedings for reviewing creditors' claims, the Supreme Court rejected the government's argument that creditors must exhaust their administrative remedies in FSLIC proceedings before getting a federal court to review the FSLIC's decisions (*The text of the decision is in the text section*).

The Supreme Court left open the possibility, however, that the Federal Home Loan Bank Board could amend its regulations to provide "that FSLIC be given notice of creditors' claims and a reasonable period of time to decide, in the first instance, whether to pay, settle, or contest those claims in court."

"In sum, we conclude that Congress has not granted FSLIC the power to adjudicate claims against the assets of a failed savings and loan association under FSLIC receivership, and that creditors are entitled to *de novo* consideration of their claims in court," Justice Sandra Day O'Connor wrote for the Supreme Court. "Moreover, creditors are not required to exhaust the current administrative claims procedure established by the [Federal Home Loan] Bank Board because it places no reasonable time limit on FSLIC's consideration of creditor claims."

In response to the Supreme Court ruling, the Federal Home Loan Bank Board March 22 placed a six-month time limit on the resolution of creditors' claims, after which creditors would be free to sue the FSLIC (see story in the news section).

As part of its sweeping thrift reform plan, the administration has proposed legislation that would give the Federal Deposit Insurance Corp. the powers that the decision denied the FSLIC. One congressional aide said the administration's legislation could be amended to address the court's concern on notice and timing.

The court did not address several constitutional questions raised in the case.

Justices Antonin Scalia and Harry Blackmun concurred separately, agreeing with the majority's result but saying they would have used different reasoning on the "exhaustion of remedies" question. Scalia said he would have based the exhaustion of remedies ruling "on the more categorical ground that FSLIC's claim procedures cannot preempt the filing of suits under state law." Blackmun said the exhaustion of remedies ruling "seems to me to amount to only an advisory opinion on what the Bank Board may do, based on a surmise of what the Bank Board might someday conclude it *must* do in order to liquidate 'in an orderly manner.'"

The court's decision resolved a split among lower courts. Several other cases involving the same issue are awaiting Supreme Court review.

A lender liability plaintiffs' attorney praised the ruling, saying it will bar the FSLIC from tying up debtors' legitimate counterclaims in administrative proceedings.

1985 Hudspeth Ruling

The March 21 ruling expressly rejected the reasoning of a 1985 U.S. Court of Appeals for the Fifth Circuit's decision, *North Mississippi Savings & Loan Association v. Hudspeth*, 756 F2d 1096. In *Hudspeth*, the Fifth Circuit held that because 12 USC 1729(d) empowers the FSLIC to "settle, compromise, or release claims" against failed S&Ls, the FSLIC had the authority to try claims in administrative proceedings. Moreover, because 12 USC 1464(d)(6)(C) says that no court may "restrain or affect" the FSLIC's receivership powers, the Fifth Circuit held that federal courts lacked subject matter jurisdiction over such claims.

Other courts, citing *Hudspeth*, have dismissed creditor claims against failed thrifts, including contract, tort, antitrust, and racketeering claims. However, in *Morrison-Knudsen v. CHG International Inc.*, 811 F2d 1209 (1987), the U.S. Court of Appeals for the Ninth Circuit rejected *Hudspeth*.

Constitutional Issues Not Addressed

In its petition for certiorari, Coit Independence Joint Venture, a creditor of the failed FirstSouth F.A., argued that letting the FSLIC try claims was unconstitutional because only judges appointed under Article III of the U.S. Constitution should try such claims; because letting the FSLIC, usually a failed institution's largest creditor, try other creditors' claims constituted a conflict of interest and a denial of due process of law; and because the Seventh Amendment entitles such litigants to a jury trial.

The Supreme Court based its ruling on the statutes governing the FSLIC's receivership powers, and did not reach any of the constitutional issues. However, citing *Northern Pipeline Construction Co. v. Marathon Pipe Line Co.*, 458 US 50 (US SupCt 1982), O'Connor noted that Coit's usury and breach of fiduciary duty claims "involve 'private rights'

3-27-89 Copyright © 1989 by The Bureau of National Affairs, Inc., Washington, D.C.
0891-0634/89/$0+.50

Federal Contracts Report

Federal Contracts Report is a weekly notification service that reports legislative, regulatory, and judicial actions affecting the federal government's purchase of goods and services from the private sector. Legal decisions on the subject, particularly from the U.S. Claims Court, the U.S. Court of Appeals for the Federal Circuit, agency boards of contract appeals, and the Comptroller General, are an important part of the service's coverage, as are the acquisition policies, guidance, and regulations of several federal agencies: the Department of Defense, the General Services Administration, the Office of Federal Procurement Policy, and NASA.

The service consists of weekly issues, which are housed in a set of two binders, each covering a six-month period. The front page of each issue highlights the major stories appearing in that issue. Inside are reports on the week's significant regulatory, legislative, and judicial events. Key agency directives and memorandums, legislation, regulations, and policies are printed in full text.

Federal Contracts Report's weekly issues notify readers of recent court decisions, legislative activities, and agency rulings and policies that affect the federal government's procurement of goods and services. Each issue contains two main sections—News and Legal Developments. The News section contains stories on pending legislation, proposed and final regulations, agency policies, and industry and bar initiatives in the area of government contracting.

The Legal Developments sections features articles about decisions from courts and from the boards of contract appeals and the Government Accounting Offices, as well as about indictments and settlements.

From time to time, analyses by outside authors of a particular topic of interest are featured. A calendar lists upcoming conferences, public meetings, and comment-due dates.

To do research in *Federal Contracts Report*, simply go to the topical-word index in the current binder and look up the subject in which you are interested. There are numerous cross-references and separate headings for legislation, company names, and government agencies. The index provides brief descriptions of the relevant material covered in the service and directs you to the specific pages where this material is covered. Repeat this process for back issues stored either in the preceding six-months' binder or in storage binders. For more recent issues not yet covered in any index, researchers should refer to the topical indexes that appear on the second page of each issue.

Federal Contracts Report illustrates a three-step reporting approach common to many BNA notification services. First, a significant event, such as proposed federal legislation, is briefly summarized on the front page.

FEDERAL CONTRACTS REPORT

Vol. 58, No. 12, Pages 327-386 — **September 28, 1992**

GovOps, HASC Reach Compromise on HR 3161—The House Government Operations and Armed Services Committees appear to have reached a compromise on HR 3161, the wide-ranging procurement reform bill, and it is possible, though not certain, that the bill will be brought to the House floor late this week. Significant changes to the bill include limiting "interested party" for purposes of Brooks Act subcontractor protests to first-tier subcontractors, deleting the provision regarding the GSBCA's authority to hear protests "by or on behalf of" a federal agency, limiting the requirements to synopsize contract modifications to commercial items, and substantially revising the sections on post-award debriefings and commercial acquisitions. pp. 329, 353

GSBCA Awards Successful Protesters In-House Counsel Costs—The costs of in-house counsel may be included in the attorney fees awarded to successful protesters, the GSBCA rules in a case involving a successful protest of the Air Force's Desktop IV procurement. The board, which expressly did not address this issue in its recent *Sterling* decision, states that "an arbitrary distinction should not be drawn with respect to the roles of in-house versus retained counsel." p. 339

DOL Overtime Policy Could Cost Private Sector $39B in Back Pay—The potential back pay liability faced by the private sector as a result of the Labor Department's treatment of partial day absences under the Fair Labor Standards Act could reach nearly $39 billion, according to a recent report by an employee policy group. p. 329

Qui Tam Plaintiff Must Have Been Involved in Disclosing Allegations to Be Original Source—A qui tam plaintiff must not only have direct and independent knowledge of fraud, but also must have had a hand in disclosing allegations of fraud that are now in the public domain in order to be considered an original source eligible to maintain a lawsuit based on those allegations, the Ninth Circuit decides. "A whistleblower sounds the alarm; he does not echo it," the court says. p. 340

SBA Proposes to Revamp 8(a) Program—The Small Business Administration, in the wake of criticism of its handling of the 8(a) program, is preparing to submit to Congress proposed changes to the program that would streamline the approval process by simplifying some of the key requirements for program eligibility. Further, SBA proposes to relinquish its role as prime contractor. p. 330

Analysis

This issue contains an analysis, *Financing Environmental Remediation Under Negotiated Government Contracts: A Proposed Solution*, prepared by Peter McDonald, an attorney-C.P.A. with the Washington, D.C. office of Deloitte & Touche. p. 348

Also Inside

Claims: Finding that a certified 'claim' was in fact a request for an equitable adjustment, the ASBCA refuses to consider whether the request was converted into a claim by government inaction where the contractor did not not later certify any converted claim. p. 343

▪

Claims Certification: The fact that the major portion of work under a contract is performed by a subcontractor in the sub's plant does not make that plant the prime contractor's location of primary contract activity for purposes of claims certification. p. 343

▪

Cost Realism: A cautionary statement in an RFP that low proposed rates may result in lowered technical and management scores does not require the agency to downgrade an offeror for proposing labor rates which were lower than the agency's cost estimate, GAO decides. p. 346

▪

False Claims Act: The provisions of the 1986 FCA Amendments which increase the damages recoverable by the government for fraud may be applied retroactively, a federal district court has ruled. p. 345

0014-9063/92/$00.50

Second is a full report of the proposal. Third is full text of the proposed legislation.

NEWS

Acquisition Policy

GovOps, HASC Reach Compromise on HR 3161; Bill Could Reach House Floor This Week

After lengthy negotiations between the House Government Operations and House Armed Services Committees, it appears that a compromise on HR 3161, the "Federal Property and Administrative Services Authorization Act of 1992," has been reached, and it is possible—although by no means certain—that the bill will be offered on the floor late this week, according to a staff aide to Government Operations Chairman John Conyers (D-Mich).

The House Rules Committee had been expected to issue a rule last week setting the parameters for floor consideration of the bill. However, the committee failed to do so. Apparently, the committee wanted time to "review the bill." Accordingly, the committee decided to postpone issuing a rule for floor debate on HR 3161 until this week. Assuming it does so and the bill is brought to the floor, Conyers will offer an amendment in the nature of a substitute to the bill that incorporates the changes agreed upon by GovOps and the HASC.

Among other things, the compromise version of HR 3161 contains a new Title III, which amends Title 10 USC, including changes to the Truth in Negotiations Act and the Competition in Contracting Act regarding source selection factors.

In addition, the compromise bill:

— substantially revises the section on commercial acquisitions. It eliminates the declaration that an acquisition is a "commercial item acquisition"; eliminates sales data restrictions; eliminates the 30 percent minimum and substitutes a direction that regulations be issued regarding price as a source selection factor.

— substantially revises the section on post-award debriefings, leaving it to regulation writers to spell out the details, taking into consideration certain factors. (The section on debriefings had been a contentious area during negotiations with the HASC, with concerns being raised that the provisions would entail a risk of divulging proprietary data.)

— substantially revises the section on synopsizing contract modifications to limit its applicability to commercial items valued at $100,000 and to provide authority to contracting officers—rather than heads of procuring activities—to grant exceptions on a case-by-case basis.

— limits "interested party" for purposes of Brooks Act subcontractor protests to first-tier subcontractors only and includes a Dec. 31, 1995 sunset provision; also deletes the provisions regarding: (1) the General Services Board of Contract Appeals' authority to hear protests "by or on behalf of" a federal agency (i.e., contracts by M&O contractors) and (2) GSBCA's authority to suspend, revoke or revise the procurement authority of the GSA administrator or the administrator's delegation of procurement authority.

The compromise version of HR 3161 appears in the text section.

The bill repeals the General Services Administration's permanent authorization and establishes a three-year authorization. An earlier version would have provided only a two-year authorization.

Title III

The new Title III amendments to 10 USC states that in prescribing evaluation factors, agencies are to:

— "clearly establish the relative importance" assigned to evaluation factors and subfactors, including the quality of the product or services to be provided (including technical capability, management capability, and prior experience of the offeror);

— include cost or price to the government as "an evaluation factor that must be considered" in evaluating proposals; and

— disclose to offerors whether all evaluation factors other than price or cost, when combined, are significantly more important than, approximately equal to, or significantly less than, price or cost.

Conyers had attempted to bring the bill to the House floor under a suspension of the rules procedure but withdrew it Aug. 4 after opposition from the HASC. During the past several weeks, the staffs of the two committees have been endeavoring to reach a workable compromise (58 FCR 183).

However, time is of the essence. Congress is expected to adjourn around Oct. 4. If HR 3161 passes the House, it will have to be approved by the Senate. It is possible that the Senate will substitute the text of its own, somewhat similar bill, S 1958, sponsored by Senate Governmental Affairs Committee Chairman John Glenn (D-Ohio) and approved by that committee June 25 (57 FCR 948, 967). If that happens, the substitute bill would be sent back to the House. The House would then have to approve that version in order to avoid having to go to conference with the Senate. A Senate Governmental Affairs Committee staffer told FCR last Friday that the two committees are discussing bill strategies.

Labor Standards

DOL Overtime Policy Could Cost Private Sector $39B in Back Pay, Employment Group Says

The potential back pay liability faced by the private sector as a result of the Labor Department's treatment of partial day absences under the Fair Labor Standards

Tax Management

The *Tax Management Portfolio Series* is a unique tax reference service consisting of a series of portfolios, each written by an experienced, practicing tax specialist. The hundreds of current portfolios are divided into three major subject areas or series: U.S. Income; Estates, Gifts, and Trusts; and Foreign Income.

Each portfolio brings together in one place the data required to solve a particular tax problem. Each contains a detailed analysis of the specific tax issue, plus the documents, checklists, and other working papers needed to solve the problem, and an exhaustive bibliography of sources and references.

New portfolios treating additional subjects and revised portfolios replacing existing ones are issued regularly for each series. In addition, each portfolio is kept up-to-date by the issuance of new pages designed to be inserted into the front of the portfolio.

Within the entire library of materials offered by *Tax Management* are other reference and current notification services.

The *Tax Management Portfolio Series* is a constantly expanding and regularly updated program of tax guides written and compiled by hundreds of respected practicing tax specialists. Although the *Tax Management Portfolio Series* borrows reference and notification elements used by other reporter services, the heart of the service is its unique system of portfolios.

Each portfolio, which resembles a spiral notebook, addresses a different specific tax topic. The tax-specialist author analyzes the issue and pulls together the law, cases, and other information needed to resolve the problem. The portfolios are also available on CD-ROM.

The portfolios are divided into three large series. The *U.S. Income Series* covers tax planning problems related to federal income taxation. It also tackles compensation planning and real estate issues. Among the over 150 portfolios in this series are ones entitled Estimated Tax, Transfers to Controlled Corporation, Uniform Capitalization Rules, and Employee Fringe Benefits.

The *Estates, Gifts, and Trusts Series* includes over 50 portfolios on such subjects as Estate Tax Deductions, Gifts to Minors, and Estate Planning.

Over 60 portfolios make up the final series, the *Foreign Income Series*, which takes up such topics as U.S. Income Taxation of Foreign Corporations. It also includes analyses of Business Operations Abroad, in such major countries as Germany, Japan, and Mexico.

The title page of a typical portfolio—this one is No. 2 in the U.S. Income Series.

TAX MANAGEMENT

Uniform Capitalization Rules

PORTFOLIO DESCRIPTION SHEET

Tax Management Portfolio, *Uniform Capitalization Rules*, No. 2, analyzes the cost capitalization rules applicable to manufactured inventories, inventories of wholesalers and retailers, self-constructed assets, real property produced for sale and long-term contracts.

The 1986 Tax Reform Act overhauled these costing rules, essentially creating a uniform set of rules for these areas. Costs related to a particular category of produced or acquired property must be associated with that property and deducted either when the property is sold or through depreciation deductions.

This Portfolio discusses §263A (relating to the capitalization rules) and §460 (relating to the costing rules) and the regulations thereunder. Further, it analyzes (1) the allocation of costs between production activities and other activities, including the various simplified methods and (2) the various rules regarding the implementation of the 1986 Act changes (including the §481(a) adjustment).

For additional relevant Tax Management Portfolios, check the "U.S. Income Portfolio Classification Guide" in the Tax Management Portfolio Index.

Latest developments will be reported on Changes and Analysis pages as conditions warrant. These pages should be filed immediately following the Table of Contents. Always check these pages and the *Tax Management Weekly Report* for current material.

This Portfolio may be cited as Garrett and Connor, 2 T.M., *Uniform Capitalization Rules*.

2 (US) 11/21/88 (iii)

3

The Detailed Analysis in this portfolio is an in-depth examination of the topic, totalling more than 120 pages written by two experienced professionals, a lawyer and an accountant. A Table of Contents in the front of the portfolio outlines the Detailed Analysis and directs the researcher to specific pages.

DETAILED ANALYSIS

DETAILED ANALYSIS

I. Introduction

A. Basic Concepts Underlying the Uniform Capitalization Rules

1. In General

The federal income tax system operates under a series of timing rules that define when income from transactions must be reported, and when the costs of earning that income may be deducted. As a general principle, there is one set of timing rules for income inclusion [1] and another for deductions.[2]

Example: Law firm X, which utilizes the cash method of accounting, spends two months preparing an opinion letter, expending $10,000 in costs. X is paid $15,000 for the opinion letter upon completion. X must apply the timing rules for income inclusion (§451) applicable to its overall method of accounting (*i.e.*, cash) to determine when the $15,000 is includible, and the timing rules for deductions (§461) to determine when the $10,000 of costs are deductible. Under these rules, X would include the $15,000 upon receipt, and would deduct the $10,000 in expenses when paid.

Comment: If X, a calendar year partnership, began the opinion letter on November 2, 1990 and finished it in January 1991, X would receive most of the deductions in 1990, but all of the income in 1991.

There is, however, a transactional linkage (*i.e.*, a matching) between income and expense items on several significant categories of transactions. It is these categories — inventories, self-constructed assets, and long-term contracts — that are affected by the uniform capitalization rules.

2. Transactions Subject to Uniform Capitalization Rules

a. Inventories

(1) General

A business must use an inventory method of accounting whenever the production, purchase or sale of goods is an income producing factor.[3] Under an inventory method, costs related to producing, acquiring, storing and handling the inventories are not deducted until the amounts earned upon sale of inventories are includible in income. The result of this is that some costs that would otherwise be deductible currently may not be recovered until the inventory items are sold.

Example: Company X, a calendar year corporation, begins business on January 1, 1991. X, which uses the specific identification method to identify goods in ending inventory, produces 10 widgets during 1991; 8 are sold during that year. Costs related to producing the inventories total $500 (each widget costs $50 to produce). X recovers, as part of the cost of goods sold, $400 of the costs of producing the widgets in 1991, determined as follows:

Opening inventory	$ 0
Costs of production	500
Costs of goods available	$500
Less ending inventory	(100)
Cost of goods sold	$400

The $100 of costs in 1991's ending inventory may not be recovered until a later year.

Comment: Inventory costs are so-called "above-the-line" deductions; they are recovered as part of cost of goods sold in determining gross income,[4] rather than as deduction items in reaching taxable income. This is illustrated by the following formulas:

Gross sales − cost of goods sold = gross income

Gross income − deductions = taxable income.[5]

Those costs determined to relate to inventory are known as "inventoriable costs" or "inventory costs."

The uniform capitalization rules (referred to throughout this portfolio as the "UCR") were enacted by the Tax Reform Act of 1986 (1986 TRA).[6] The UCR address the degree to which direct and indirect costs must be treated as inventoriable costs. These rules represent a significant expansion of the set of costs required to be inventoried.[7] That is, certain costs that were deductible for years beginning before 1987 must now be treated as inventory costs. This tends to accelerate the reporting of income.[8]

Example: X, a calendar year corporation that manufactures widgets, began business on January 1, 1990. X incurred $1,000,000 of "excess" depreciation (*i.e.*, tax depreciation in excess of financial statement depreciation) during 1990 in connection with its production operations. Eighty percent of the widgets produced in

[1] *See* §451. Unless otherwise specified, all section references are to the Internal Revenue Code, as amended, and the regulations promulgated thereunder.
[2] *See* §461.
[3] Regs. §1.471-1.
[4] Regs. §1.61-3(a).
[5] §63(a).
[6] P.L. 99-514, signed into law Oct. 22, 1986.
[7] *See* §§263A and 460(c).
[8] It is this consequence of the uniform capitalization rules that provided the revenue increase. The uniform capitalization rules were projected to raise $35 billion over five years, second only to the repeal of the investment credit ($60 billion) among corporate revenue raisers in the Tax Reform Act of 1986. It should be noted that much of the $35 billion is a one time pickup, generally spread over four years, resulting from the switch from the old costing rules to the new costing rules.

2-2nd **Changes and Analysis of New Developments appear in the front of this portfolio** A - 1

The best place to look to find a portfolio addressing any particular topic is the Portfolio Index binder. There researchers will find several indexes enabling them to get into the portfolios themselves in a variety of ways. For example, the Code Section Index takes the Internal Revenue Code section by section and lists the portfolios that address each section. For each of the three portfolio series there is a Portfolio Classification Guide, which lists the portfolios in that series both alphabetically within major subject groupings and numerically. Next is the Master Index, which, through a key-word approach, directs researchers to all portfolios covering specific topics.

Besides the portfolios, *Tax Management* offers a wealth of other reference materials, as well as several notification components. The *Estates, Gifts, and Trusts Series*, for instance, has a Reference File similar to those associated with other BNA services. There are also reference binders containing IRS tax forms and instructions, and another set, entitled *Primary Sources*, containing a continuing, section-by-section legislative history of the Internal Revenue Code. Among the several notification components offered by *Tax Management* is the *Tax Management Weekly Report*, which provides concise, comprehensive reports on recent court decisions, IRS revenue and letter rulings, and other news events, all cross-referenced to the portfolios.

Other resources from Tax Management:

▶ Tax Practice Series, *an analytical service giving fast access to guidance on day-to-day tax matters.*

▶ IRS Practice & Policy, *a single resource for resolving tax controversies more effectively and efficiently.*

▶ IRS Forms, *a comprehensive collection of Internal Revenue Service forms and instructions.*

▶ Journals *associated with the various portfolio series, and providing in-depth analysis of current tax issues in the areas of international tax, compensation planning, real estate, and estates, gifts, and trusts.*

The *Tax Management* portfolios contain full text of related documents, plus sample checklists and forms. This is a list of the ones found in the Uniform Capitalization Rules portfolio.

WORKING PAPERS

Item Description Sheet

B-1 **ITEM DESCRIPTION SHEET**

B-101 **LEGISLATIVE HISTORY**

B-101	Worksheet 1	Conference Report to Accompany H.R. 3838, H.R. Rep. No. 841, 99th Cong., 2d Sess. II-302-313 (1986) (Tax Reform Act of 1986).
B-201	Worksheet 2	General Explanation of the Tax Reform Act of 1986 (Staff of the Joint Committee on Taxation) 501-530 (May 4, 1987).
B-301	Worksheet 3	Conference Report to Accompany H.R. 3545, H.R. Rep. No. 495, 100th Cong., 1st Sess. 922-924 (1987) (Omnibus Budget Reconciliation Act of 1987).
B-401	Worksheet 4	Conference Report to Accompany H.R. 4333, H.R. Rep. No. 1104, 100th Cong. 2d Sess. 116-120 and 145-146 (1988) (Technical and Miscellaneous Revenue Act of 1988).
B-501	Worksheet 5	Conference Report to Accompany H.R. 3299, H.R. Rep. No. 386, 101st Cong., 1st Sess. 614-616 (1989) (Omnibus Budget Reconciliation Act of 1989).

WORKING PAPERS

B-601 **FILLED-IN IRS FORMS**

B-601	Worksheet 6	Form 8697 (Interest Computation Under the Look-Back Method for Completed Long-Term Contracts).
B-701	Worksheet 7	Form 3115 (Application for Change in Accounting Method).

B-801 **IRS PRONOUNCEMENTS**

B-801	Worksheet 8	Preamble to Regs. §1.263A-1T, T.D. 8131, 52 Fed. Reg. 10052 (March 30, 1987).
B-901	Worksheet 9	Preamble to Regs. §1.263A-1T, T.D. 8148, 52 Fed. Reg. 29375 (August 7, 1987).
B-1001	Worksheet 10	Preamble to Regs. §1.460-6, T.D. 8315, 55 Fed. Reg. 41665 (October 15, 1990).
B-1101	Worksheet 11	Notice 88-86, 1988-2 C.B. 401.
B-1201	Worksheet 12	Notice 88-99, 1988-2 C.B. 422.
B-1301	Worksheet 13	Notice 89-15, 1989-1 C.B. 634.
B-1401	Worksheet 14	Notice 89-67, 1989-1 C.B. 723.
B-1501	Worksheet 15	Draft Table of Contents for Revised Uniform Capitalization Rules.

B-1601 **DOCUMENTS TO BE SUBMITTED TO THE IRS**

B-1601	Worksheet 16	Sample Election Statements — Manufacturers.
B-1701	Worksheet 17	Sample Election Statements — Retailers/Wholesalers.
B-1801	Worksheet 18	Sample Election Statements — Long-Term Contractors.
B-1901	Worksheet 19	Sample Election Statements — Self-Constructed Assets.
B-2001	Worksheet 20	Sample Election Statements — Interest Capitalization.
B-2101	Worksheet 21	Sample Election Statements — Real Property Produced for Sale.
B-2201	Worksheet 22	Statutorily Mandated Inventory Change: Sample Statements.

2-2nd

This weekly report is one of several regular notification features of *Tax Management*.

BNA

TAX MANAGEMENT
WEEKLY REPORT

Volume 8, Number 15 Tax Management Inc., a subsidiary of The Bureau of National Affairs, Inc. April 10, 1989

ITEMS

§401(h) benefit contributions are subject of unnumbered PLR **460**

Form 1040 is invalid where perjury penalty was obliterated **474**

§2056(b)(7) QTIP election is unavailable for portion of property **473**

Pass-through to partners, shareholders subject of IRS rules **470**

§132 exclusion is unavailable for free counseling services **465**

Transfer of assets to §401(h) account is considered by IRS **468**

§163 deduction is allowed for interest on tax deficiency **466**

"Drug ledgers" are admissible hearsay for proving income **477**

§1031(a) treatment is accorded exchange of partnership interests **471**

Multiple testamentary trusts are not subchapter S trusts **472**

§512 income does not result from purchase of partner's interest **469**

Certified mailing form does not validate deficiency notice **475**

S corporation may pass through ITC to shareholders **464**

Refusal to concede costs is not *per se* unreasonable under §7430 **476**

§170 deduction is limited to basis of donated property **467**

Portfolios Affected	**488**
Current Developments	**459**
Focus	**462**
IR Manual Highlights	**479**
IRB Highlights	**457**
IRS Update	**482**
Technical Developments	**464**
Text	**481**

Documents Available 800-452-7773

HIGHLIGHTS

PASSIVE ACTIVITIES: Long-awaited regulations defining "passive activity" should be out by the end of April, according to IRS official Michael Grace. The rules will adopt a "building block" approach, under which certain factors must be considered in identifying discrete activities and determining the level of aggregation. Moreover, the regulations may split the definition of activity according to whether it is being disposed of or is in operation, Grace explains. **459**

FOCUS: EXEMPT ORGANIZATIONS: Complaints have been increasing from many for-profit businesses which consider the use of tax-exempt status by nonprofit companies engaged in commercial activities as promoting unfair competition. In response, Congress has begun to consider changing the unrelated business income tax to level the playing field. This week's *Focus* discusses the UBIT, businesses' opposition to it, and legislative recommendations to make it more fair. **462**

ROYALTIES: Payments labeled minimum royalties do not qualify for the minimum royalty exception under Regs. §1.612-3(b)(3) and, thus, are nondeductible advance payments, the First Circuit decides (*Fredkin v. Comr.*). The court states that the payments do not meet the requirement that minimum royalties be paid in a substantially uniform amount at least annually over the life of the lease. Here, the obligation to pay royalties could terminate before the lease expires, the court notes. **465**

LIMITATIONS PERIODS: Where the limitations period on assessment against a trust has run, the IRS is still entitled to assess a deficiency against a beneficiary arising out of the disallowance of losses claimed by the trust, the Tax Court holds (*Fendell v. Comr.*). Analogizing the situation to one involving an estate and a beneficiary, the court reasons that the filing of fiduciary returns on the trust's behalf triggers the beginning of the limitations period only against that entity, not against individual beneficiaries. **470**

NEW WEEKLY REPORT FORMAT
MAKES UPDATING YOUR RESEARCH EASIER

All developments reported in the Tax Management *Weekly Report* are now organized by Code section. Practitioners thus can update their research on a particular Code section simply by turning to a single location. Alternatively, practitioners can use the Topical Summary on the inside front cover to locate major developments on a particular subject, and can continue to use the Code Section and Tax Management Portfolio Index on the back cover.

4-10-89

0884-6057/89/$0+.50

Corporate Practice Series

The *Corporate Practice Series* borrows *Tax Management's* portfolio format to provide guidance to corporate lawyers on a wide range of legal, regulatory, and operational issues that confront their clients. The service's collection of portfolios, which is constantly being expanded and updated, addresses such specific topics as corporate financing techniques, responses to takeover bids, proxy contests, and incorporating in Delaware and selected other states.

The portfolios are written by practicing specialists in the field of corporate law. Each portfolio is divided into three distinct parts: a Detailed Analysis, which conveys the author's research, experience, and expertise on the topic; Worksheets, such as documents, forms, checklists, and other pertinent source materials; and a Bibliography of other resources.

A second, important feature of the service is its weekly newsletter: *BNA's Corporate Counsel Weekly*, which contains timely reports on legal developments affecting business entities.

Designed both for in-house corporate lawyers and for corporations' outside counsel, the *Corporate Practice Series'* library of portfolios and its weekly notification component, *BNA's Corporate Counsel Weekly*, can be used by anyone who needs to do research on corporate law or who wants to keep abreast of current developments in the area.

Several finding aids assist in locating the treatment of any given topic. The Current Portfolio Classification Guide, filed behind the cover page of the *Corporate Counsel Weekly* binder, lists all portfolios—first, according to major subject groups, and second, in numerical order. The master index, bound separately and shelved with the portfolios, breaks the coverage of the portfolio collection into major topics and subtopics, with references to page numbers in specific portfolios. Each portfolio contains both a detailed table of contents and its own index. Finally, the *Corporate Counsel Weekly* binder contains its own separate indexes for that part of the service.

Through this method, researchers can find, for example, portfolios entitled The Board of Directors, Proxy Contests, Insider Information: Prevention of Abuse, and Limited Partnerships. These and the other portfolios are kept up-to-date through the issuance of Changes and Additions pages designed to be inserted in the front of the portfolio. Also, new portfolios are added and existing ones are completely revised and reissued as the need arises.

BNA's Corporate Counsel Weekly, this service's notification component, is an eight-page roundup of the latest developments in the law affecting business entities, including coverage of the courts, federal agencies, the executive branch, state actions, and professional associations. Topics covered include not only the core areas of corporate governance, securities, and antitrust but also labor, pensions, environmental law, product liability, and occupational safety.

DETAILED ANALYSIS

DETAILED ANALYSIS

I. Interface of the Federal and State Antitrust Laws

Although this portfolio concerns state antitrust law, a necessary and threshold concern is an awareness of the federal constitutional limits on state antitrust law and the interrelationship between federal antitrust law and comparable state laws. Notwithstanding Senator Sherman's declaration[1] that the federal statute was to complement existing state laws, not to supplant state antitrust laws, federal constitutional challenges persist in actions that seek to enforce state antitrust laws. Thus, a brief review of relevant federal and state constitutional principles is necessary before discussion of the substantive state antitrust law issues.

The common federal constitutional challenges are: (1) that state antitrust laws are preempted by federal antitrust law or (2) that the application of the state antitrust laws constitutes an undue burden on interstate commerce. It is noteworthy that the constitutional presumption is that "the historic police powers of the states are not superseded by the Federal Act unless that was the clear and manifest purpose of the Congress."[2] With noted exceptions, neither the Commerce Clause nor preemption arguments have fared well in challenges to the enforcement of state antitrust laws in the state courts.

A. State Antitrust Laws as an Undue Burden on Interstate Commerce

The landmark decision on application of state antitrust laws to interstate commerce is *Standard Oil of Kentucky v. Tennessee*.[3] The Supreme Court, in an opinion by Justice Oliver Wendell Holmes, upheld a Tennessee state court's injunction against a Kentucky corporation that had been adjudged in violation of Tennessee's antitrust law. Justice Holmes found that the mere fact that interstate commerce was affected by enforcement of Tennessee's antitrust law posed no constitutional infirmity or restriction upon the state's regulatory power.

In its 1985 term, the Supreme Court restated as a two-tier test its constitutional analysis of whether state regulations unduly burden interstate commerce:

> (1) Does the state statute, on its face or in its application, directly regulate interstate commerce or clearly discriminate against out-of-state firms? If so, the state statute is unconstitutional as an undue burden on interstate commerce.
>
> (2) If the state statute is neutral on its face and as applied to out-of-state firms, are the state's legitimate interests in the matter clearly outweighed by the federal interest in an absence of undue burdens on interstate commerce? In a word, state interests must be greater than the federal interest and must be for a legitimate purpose.[4]

Perhaps another short-hand test, based upon Justice Holmes' analysis in *Standard Oil*, is whether the state can tax the activity at issue or traditionally regulates the conduct at issue. If the state can tax or otherwise regulate the activity under the federal constitution, then the state should be able to apply its antitrust laws to such activity or conduct. It should be emphasized that the critical concern is interstate commerce and interstate competition, not interstate firms. For example, the Supreme Court upheld a Maryland statute that barred ownership of retail gasoline stations by oil producers, regardless of the producer's domicile.[5]

The majority of state courts have held that state antitrust laws do not burden interstate commerce,[6] with exceptions where state laws were sought to be applied to what were deemed inherently interstate activities.[7]

B. Preemption Defenses

1. Preemption of state antitrust laws

The Supreme Court has upheld the enforcement of the state antitrust laws in state courts against claims that the state law was preempted by the federal antitrust laws, usually upon a finding of the absence of any congressional

[1] 21 Cong. Rec. Part 3: 2456, 2457, 51st Cong., 1st Sess. (1890).
[2] Rice v. Santa Fe Elevator Co., 331 U.S. 218, 230 (1946).
[3] 217 U.S. 413 (1910). Earlier, in National Cotton Oil Co. v. Texas, 197 U.S. 115 (1905), the Supreme Court upheld the nondiscriminatory application of the Texas antitrust law against a cotton trust.

[4] Brown-Forman Distillers v. New York State Liquor Auth., 476 U.S. 573 (1986) (citations omitted).
[5] Exxon Corp. v. Maryland, 437 U.S. 117, 127-29 (1978). *See also* United N.J. Bank v. Parell, 783 F.2d 360, 369 (3d Cir. 1986).
[6] Governor of Md. v. Exxon Corp., 370 A.2d 1102, 1116 (Md. 1977), *aff'd*, 437 U.S. 117 (1978); Opinion of the Justices, 117 N.H. 533, 376 A.2d 118 (1977); Elray v. Cathodic Protection, 507 S.W.2d 570 (Tex. App. 1974). *Accord* Younger v. Jenson, 161 Cal. Rptr. 905, 910, 605 P.2d 813 (1980) ("Neither the Sherman Act nor the Commerce Clause prevents . . . state laws from transactions that have interstate aspects," but significantly affect state interest); E.F.I. Inc. v. Marketers Int'l, 550 S.W.2d 401, 404 (Tex. Civ. App.), *cert. denied*, 435 U.S. 1008 (1978) (Texas antitrust laws applied notwithstanding their extraterritorial effects); Pounds Photo. Labs Inc. v. Noritsu Am. Corp., 1987-1 Trade Cas. (CCH) ¶67,599 (5th Cir. 1987).
[7] Partee v. San Diego Chargers, 180 Cal. Rptr. 416 (1982) (professional football); Baker v. Walter Read Theatres Inc., 37 Misc. 2d 172, 237 N.Y.S.2d 795 (S. Ct. 1962) (New York's antitrust act limited to conduct in New York); Young v. Seaway Pipeline Inc., 576 P.2d 1148, 1150 (Okla. 1977) (international pipeline industry practices are not the proper subject of state antitrust laws); State v. Milwaukee Braves, 31 Wis. 2d 699, 144 N.W.2d 1, 18 (1966) (professional baseball); Pillar Corp. v. Enercon Indus., 1986-1 Trade Cas. (CCH) ¶67,187 (Wis. Cir. Ct. 1986) (state monopolization claim limited to Wisconsin); HMC Mgmt. Corp. v. New Orleans Basketball Club, 375 So. 2d 700, 706-07 (La. App. 1979) (professional basketball except as to lease agreements); Lynch Display Corp. v. National Souvenir Center Inc., 640 S.W.2d 837, 840 (Tenn. Ct. App. 1982) (interstate lease agreement). *Contra* Younger v. Jenson, 161 Cal. Rptr. 905, 605 P.2d 813 (1980) (state antitrust investigation of interstate gas industry permitted); State *ex rel.* Pennsylvania Transformer Div. v. Electric City Supply Co., 74 N.M. 295, 393 P.2d 324 (1964) (only some allegations of intrastate commerce required to state a claim).

52 C.P.S. Copyright © 1988 by The Bureau of National Affairs, Inc., Washington, D.C. 20037 A – 1

This is the first page of a sample portfolio in the *Corporate Practice Series*, this one entitled "State Antitrust Law." The author's Detailed Analysis of the topic is followed by Worksheets (here, charts of state laws, attorneys' general guidelines, and sample court papers).

The service's weekly notification component provides news articles, analyses, and special reports on corporate law.

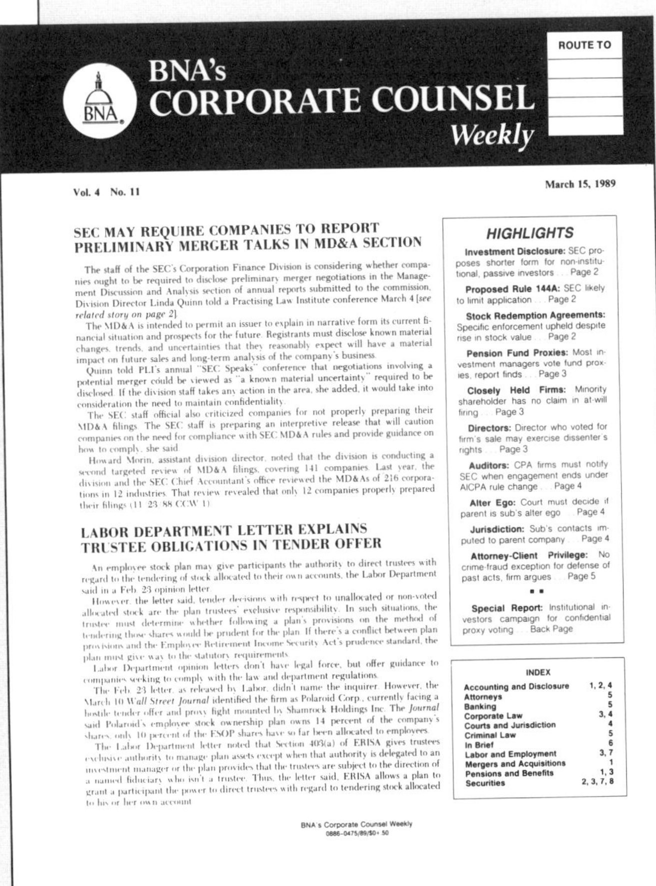

ROUTE TO

BNA's CORPORATE COUNSEL *Weekly*

Vol. 4 No. 11 **March 15, 1989**

SEC MAY REQUIRE COMPANIES TO REPORT PRELIMINARY MERGER TALKS IN MD&A SECTION

The staff of the SEC's Corporation Finance Division is considering whether companies ought to be required to disclose preliminary merger negotiations in the Management Discussion and Analysis section of annual reports submitted to the commission, Division Director Linda Quinn told a Practising Law Institute conference March 4 [*see related story on page 2*].

The MD&A is intended to permit an issuer to explain in narrative form its current financial situation and prospects for the future. Registrants must disclose known material changes, trends, and uncertainties that they reasonably expect will have a material impact on future sales and long-term analysis of the company's business.

Quinn told PLI's annual "SEC Speaks" conference that negotiations involving a potential merger could be viewed as "a known material uncertainty" required to be disclosed. If the division staff takes any action in the area, she added, it would take into consideration the need to maintain confidentiality.

The SEC staff official also criticized companies for not properly preparing their MD&A filings. The SEC staff is preparing an interpretive release that will caution companies on the need for compliance with SEC MD&A rules and provide guidance on how to comply, she said.

Howard Morin, assistant division director, noted that the division is conducting a second targeted review of MD&A filings, covering 141 companies. Last year, the division and the SEC Chief Accountant's office reviewed the MD&As of 216 corporations in 12 industries. That review revealed that only 12 companies properly prepared their filings (11/23/88 CCW 1).

LABOR DEPARTMENT LETTER EXPLAINS TRUSTEE OBLIGATIONS IN TENDER OFFER

An employee stock plan may give participants the authority to direct trustees with regard to the tendering of stock allocated to their own accounts, the Labor Department said in a Feb. 23 opinion letter.

However, the letter said, tender decisions with respect to unallocated or non-voted allocated stock are the plan trustees' exclusive responsibility. In such situations, the trustee must determine whether following a plan's provisions on the method of tendering those shares would be prudent for the plan. If there's a conflict between plan provisions and the Employee Retirement Income Security Act's prudence standard, the plan must give way to the statutory requirements.

Labor Department opinion letters don't have legal force, but offer guidance to companies seeking to comply with the law and department regulations.

The Feb. 23 letter, as released by Labor, didn't name the inquirer. However, the March 10 *Wall Street Journal* identified the firm as Polaroid Corp., currently facing a hostile tender offer and proxy fight mounted by Shamrock Holdings Inc. The *Journal* said Polaroid's employee stock ownership plan owns 14 percent of the company's shares; only 10 percent of the ESOP shares have so far been allocated to employees.

The Labor Department letter noted that Section 403(a) of ERISA gives trustees exclusive authority to manage plan assets except when that authority is delegated to an investment manager or the plan provides that the trustees are subject to the direction of a named fiduciary who isn't a trustee. Thus, the letter said, ERISA allows a plan to grant a participant the power to direct trustees with regard to tendering stock allocated to his or her own account.

HIGHLIGHTS

Investment Disclosure: SEC proposes shorter form for non-institutional, passive investors . . . Page 2

Proposed Rule 144A: SEC likely to limit application . . . Page 2

Stock Redemption Agreements: Specific enforcement upheld despite rise in stock value . . . Page 2

Pension Fund Proxies: Most investment managers vote fund proxies, report finds . . . Page 3

Closely Held Firms: Minority shareholder has no claim in at-will firing . . . Page 3

Directors: Director who voted for firm's sale may exercise dissenter's rights . . . Page 3

Auditors: CPA firms must notify SEC when engagement ends under AICPA rule change . . . Page 4

Alter Ego: Court must decide if parent is sub's alter ego . . . Page 4

Jurisdiction: Sub's contacts imputed to parent company . . . Page 4

Attorney-Client Privilege: No crime-fraud exception for defense of past acts, firm argues . . . Page 5

▪ ▪

Special Report: Institutional investors campaign for confidential proxy voting . . . Back Page

INDEX

Accounting and Disclosure	**1, 2, 4**
Attorneys	**5**
Banking	**5**
Corporate Law	**3, 4**
Courts and Jurisdiction	**4**
Criminal Law	**5**
In Brief	**6**
Labor and Employment	**3, 7**
Mergers and Acquisitions	**1**
Pensions and Benefits	**1, 3**
Securities	**2, 3, 7, 8**

BNA's Corporate Counsel Weekly
0886-0475/89/$0+.50

Other BNA Services

Daily Notification: Tax, Labor, Environment, and Business

Daily Tax Report. A daily notification service on developments in the tax field.

Daily Labor Report. Another daily notification service, this one provides across-the-board coverage of the labor field.

Daily Environment Report. Daily news and documents, plus periodic analyses, on environmental law, rules, and policies.

Daily Report for Executives. A comprehensive information source on regulatory, legislative, and judicial developments affecting U.S. businesses and industries.

Notification: Labor and Human Resources

Benefits Today. Reports recent events and trends involving employee benefits for those responsible for designing and managing employee benefit programs.

BNA's Employee Relations Weekly. Weekly reports on developments and trends affecting employment relations and other work-place issues.

Construction Labor Report. Weekly information service covering employment relations in the construction industry.

Government Employees Relations Report. Weekly notification of developments in federal, state, and municipal government employee relations.

Labor Relations Week. Weekly reports on the latest developments influencing labor-management relations in the private sector.

Reference and Notification: Labor

Affirmative Action Compliance Manual. A two-binder service containing the official text of the Office of Federal Contract Compliance Programs Manual and other documents, with monthly notification of related developments.

BNA Policy and Practice Series. A weekly multi-binder service designed for employee relations and human resources executives.

Collective Bargaining Negotiations & Contracts. Two looseleaf reference binders and a biweekly newsletter, all designed to supply labor contract negotiators—both union and management—with the factual data needed to prepare, negotiate, and administer contracts.

EEOC Compliance Manual. Two binders containing continually updated text of the EEOC Compliance Manual, as issued by the Equal Employment Opportunity Commission's Office of Compliance, and the monthly News and Developments, which notify subscribers of related developments.

Employment Guide. Reference and notification for business owners, office managers, and others with personnel responsibilities.

Payroll Administration Guide. Prompt updates on federal and state laws governing payroll administration.

Union Labor Report. Reference files for union officials, explaining labor laws, arbitration, and other labor issues; also includes a weekly newsletter and a quarterly newsletter for shop stewards.

Notification: Legal and Business

BNA's Eastern Europe Reporter. Biweekly reports on business opportunities opening up in Eastern and Central Europe and the republics of the former Soviet Union.

BNA's Medicare Report. Weekly coverage of legislation, regulations, court and administrative decisions, and health care reform policies affecting Medicare.

BNA's Workers' Compensation Report. Biweekly notification of court decisions and legislative and regulatory action affecting workers' compensation law.

Reference and Notification: Legal and Business

BNA/ACCA Compliance Manual: Prevention of Corporate Liability. A looseleaf reference binder, with monthly newsletter, instructing companies on how to establish and operate programs to comply with the U.S. Sentencing Guidelines and other laws and regulations governing their particular industries.

Reference and Notification: Environment and Safety

Air Pollution Control. A looseleaf, continually updated reference manual and a biweekly newsletter, both covering the control of air pollution.

BNA's Environmental Due Diligence Guide. Practical guidance on performing due diligence in real estate transactions, in order to protect against liability related to environmental hazards.

Chemical Regulation Reporter. Multi-binder reference file on federal chemical regulation, plus weekly notification service. A separate part of the service is the *Index to Government Regulation*, with tens of thousands of citations to the Code of Federal Regulations and to recent Federal Register announcements covering chemicals regulated by the federal government.

International Environment Reporter. Current Reports and Reference File on global developments affecting environmental protection and pollution control.

Job Safety and Health. Reference manual designed to explain job safety and health laws and compliance procedures to employers.

Right-To-Know Planning Guide. Biweekly newsletter and reference manual on emergency planning and community right-to-know laws.

Water Pollution Control. Reference and notification service providing guidance to industry on how to interpret and comply with water pollution control requirements.

BNA California

BNA California, based in Sacramento, produces California-oriented services in areas that BNA traditionally covers. Current BNA California subscription services include:
BNA California Safety & Health Report
BNA California-Environment Reporter
BNA California Employee Relations Report

BNA International Inc.

BNA's subsidiary in the United Kingdom serves the specialized information needs of lawyers and other professionals in corporations, organizations, and governments worldwide. Some BNA services are published in London to provide an international parallel to an existing U.S.-based service. An example is the weekly U.S. publication Patent, Trademark and Copyright Journal and its monthly version from London, World Intellectual Property Report. For more information on current titles, contact BNA International toll-free by telephone 1-800-727-3116 or by fax 1-800-473-9284.

Books

BNA Books publishes treatises and other reference books in the areas of labor and employment law, labor arbitration, intellectual property law, environmental law, and general legal practice. Many BNA Books titles are available in law school libraries. Some of the best known titles are listed below.

Environmental Law

CERCLA Law and Procedure
CERCLA Law and Procedure Compendium
Clean Air Law & Procedure
Endangered and Other Protected Species: Federal Law & Regulation
Hazardous Waste Liability
U.S. Environmental Laws

Intellectual Property

The Copyright Law
Drafting Patent License Agreements
Fair Use Privilege in Copyright Law
Intent to Use Trademark Practice
McCarthy's Desk Encyclopedia of Intellectual Property
Patents and the Federal Circuit
Patent, Trademark, and Copyright Laws
Patent, Trademark, and Copyright Regulation

Labor and Employment Law

The Developing Labor Law
Employee Benefits Law
Employment Discrimination Law
Employment Termination
Occupational Safety and Health Law

Labor Arbitration

How Arbitration Works
Practice and Procedure in Labor Arbitration

Legal Practice

Administrative Practice Manual
Supreme Court Practice

BNA Books also publishes a series of primers on various aspects of employment law that can provide students with a quick overview of labor relations, workers' compensation, ERISA, EEO, wage and hour regulation, occupational safety and health, and individual employment rights. For a free copy of a complete BNA Books catalog, call 1-800-372-1033.

Online Research

BNA Online. See the discussion on pages 14-16 of this book.

Document Research and Retrieval Services

BNA PLUS. The BNA PLUS Division gives lawyers and other BNA customers fast access to documents mentioned in the pages of BNA subscription services and other publications, including text of published and unpublished court opinions.

Custom Research

BNA PLUS. The BNA PLUS Division also provides comprehensive and confidential custom reports on various issues relating to BNA's publications, including labor relations, human resources, or environmental regulation.

Customer Support

BNA PLUS. Another important service provided by the BNA PLUS Division is a toll-free hotline to give BNA customers free assistance in locating previously published materials, verifying when specific new data will be published, and how to research efficiently using BNA services and indexes. The customer support hotline is 800-452-7773; 202-452-4323 in Washington, D.C.

Pike & Fischer

A subsidiary of The Bureau of National Affairs, Inc.

Established in 1939, Pike & Fischer is a respected publisher of looseleaf reference services, software, newsletters, special reports, and directories. It was acquired by BNA in 1984.

Pike & Fischer's services cover communications law, administrative law, shipping regulation, telecommunications, and fertilizer news and pricing. Several are available both in print and on disk.

Communications Law

Radio Regulation, Second Series. Weekly, comprehensive full text reporting of communications related laws, FCC rules, full text and digests of FCC and court decisions and proposed rules.

FCC Rules: Current Service. Weekly full text of all FCC rules, proposed rules, and FCC related statutes.

Broadcast Rules Service. Full text of FCC rules regulating radio and television stations. Includes proposed rules and FCC forms. Also available in PC software form.

Cable TV Rules Service. Full text of FCC rules regulating cable television operations. Includes proposed rules and FCC forms.

Common Carrier Rules Service. Full text of FCC rules that regulate telephone and telecommunications common carriers. Includes proposed rules.

Equipment Rules Service. Full text of FCC rules that specify FCC standards and requirements regarding the design of radio frequency devices, industrial, scientific, and medical equipment, and telephone related equipment. Includes proposed rules and FCC forms. Also available in PC software form.

Private Radio Rules Service. Full text of FCC rules that regulate industrial, public safety, special emergency, and land transportation and radiolocation communications. Includes proposed rules and FCC forms. Also available in PC software form.

Radio Common Carrier Rules Service. Full text of FCC rules that regulate cellular telephone, microwave, and paging communications. Includes proposed rules and FCC forms. Also available in PC software form.

Shipping Law

Shipping Regulation Reports. Comprehensive reporting of statutes, judicial and agency decisions, and administrative rule makings of U.S. regulation of ocean transportation.

Administrative Law

Administrative Law, Third Series. Comprehensive reporting of court and agency decisions on federal administrative practice, procedure, and access to judicial review. Full text and digested case reporting.

Methods of Research

Methods of Research

The same legal research methods used to find relevant information throughout an entire law library are used to uncover pertinent information contained in a reporter service, the only difference being that entry modes and all primary and secondary materials are available in one place—namely, in the reporter service itself.

Several research methods are common to all legal research, including that done with reporter services. For example, a topical or factual analysis of a problem sends the legal researcher to a topical or descriptive-word index. Sometimes the entries found in such an index will take the researcher directly to the volume and page number of the reporter service where the information the researcher wants was reported. This is the method most often used by BNA's notification services and those with reference files.

Other times, the topical index will direct the researcher to a classification system, in which numbers are assigned to specific subjects. When using services with such a classification system, the researcher can also go directly to the classification system's outline and find the appropriate subjects and numbers that way. Regardless of how they get it, once researchers are armed with a classification number, they can use it to find information throughout the service. This method of research is used in BNA's decisional or case services.

All services that report court decisions also have a table of cases. Researchers who know the name of a case can go directly to the table of cases in the relevant reporter service and from there to the service's account of the case or even to the case itself. In most BNA services, cases are listed under both the plaintiffs' and the defendants' names.

Most reporter services also have other types of indexes, lists, and finding aids unique to the type of information covered in the service.

Example: Traditional and Decisional Services

Labor Relations Reporter—By Subject

A business that your law firm represents on labor issues has decided to discharge a longtime employee who was recently convicted of possessing cocaine. The case is certain to go to arbitration, and you are assigned the tasks of writing a memorandum spelling out the general state of the law on the problem and of finding the most recent decisions on point.

First, you refer to the *Labor Relations Reporter's* Master Index Binder and inside there to Tab (A) where the General Index for the entire multi-binder service is kept. You look up the topic "Drug Possession," and find three entries under the subtopic "Discharge or discipline." The first two give you the classification number you're interested in (118.653) and tell you in what parts of the service you will find reported cases under that classification (here, both Labor Relations (LR) and Labor Arbitration (LA)). With that information you can find every case on the subject of discharge for drug possession ever reported in the *Labor Relations Reporter*. And you could have reached the same point by looking first under the major topic "Discharge" and then under its subtopic "Drug possession," if that sequence of topical words had occurred to you first.

DRU

A 252 MASTER INDEX BINDER

DRUG ABUSE—Contd.
Pipeline industry, control of drug use in natural gas, liquefied natural gas, hazardous liquid pipeline operations, RSPA final rule, text IERM 595:281
Rehabilitation, discharge or discipline LRX 510:232
Treatment programs, Illinois, act IERM 554:7

DRUG INDUSTRY

See
—PHARMACEUTICAL INDUSTRY

DRUG POSSESSION

Discharge or discipline
LR ▸ 118.653
LA ▸ 118.653
LRX 510:231
—Discrimination, LMRA LR ▸ 52.2708
—Wrongful IER ▸ 200.1511
Off-duty offenses, discharge or discipline LRX 510:231
Rehabilitation, discharge or discipline LRX 510:232

DRUG STORE INDUSTRY

See
—PHARMACY INDUSTRY

DRUG TESTS

Accuracy IERM 509:107
Administrative-search exception IERM 509:102
Arbitration decisions IERM 509:110
Aviation industry, anti-drug program, FAA final rule IERM 595:147
—Air carriers and commercial operators, testing (14 CFR 121.457) IERM 595:208
—Air taxi operators, testing (14 CFR 135.251) IERM 595:214
—Airmen, refusal to take test (14 CFR 65.23) IERM 595:206
—DOT procedures, Appendix I IERM 595:208
—Drug testing program, Appendix I IERM 595:208
—Employee assistance programs, Appendix I IERM 595:212
—Employees who must be tested, Appendix I IERM 595:209
—Employer's testing plan, Appendix I IERM 595:212
—Flight crewmembers, refusal to take test (14 CFR 63.12b) IERM 595:206
—Flight instructors (14 CFR 61.14) IERM 595:205
—Pilots (14 CFR 61.14) IERM 595:205
—Random testing, Appendix I IERM 595:209
—Reporting results, Appendix I IERM 595:213
—Review of test results, Appendix I IERM 595:210
—Substances for which testing must be conducted, Appendix I IERM 595:209
—Types of tests required, Appendix I IERM 595:209
California, San Francisco, act (Section 3300A.5) IERM 545:18
Coast Guard, chemical drug and alcohol programs for commercial vessel personnel, final rule, text IERM 595:231
—Employee assistance programs, Subpart D (46 CFR 16.401) IERM 595:264
—Mandatory chemical testing following serious marine incidents involving commercial vessels (46 CFR 4.06) IERM 595:256
—Random testing requirements (46 CFR 16.230) IERM 595:262
—Required chemical testing, Subpart B (46 CFR 16.201-16.260) IERM 595:260
—Standards for chemical testing for dangerous drugs, Subpart C (46 CFR 16.301-16.380) IERM 595:263
Commercial motor vehicle drivers, controlled substance testing, FHWA final rule, text IERM 595:403
—Applicability (49 CFR 391.83) IERM 595:435
—Drug use prohibitions (49 CFR 391.95) IERM 595:438
—Employee assistance program (49 CFR 391.119) IERM 595:440
—Random testing requirements (49 CFR 391.109) IERM 595:439
Connecticut, act IERM 547:12
Constitutionality IERM 509:101
Discharge or discipline LA ▸ 118.653
Drug-Free Workplace Act of 1988
—Governmentwide requirements for drug-free workplace (Grants), text IERM 595:829
—OMB questions and answers on act IERM 595:815
Drug-Free Workplace Act of 1988, interim final rules, text IERM 595:819
—Certification regarding a drug-free workplace (Section 52.223-5) IERM 595:823
—Contractor qualifications (Part 9) IERM 595:819
—Drug-free workplace (Section 52.223-6) IERM 595:824
—Environment, conservation, occupational safety, and drug-free workplace (Part 23) IERM 595:820
Drug-Free Workplace Act of 1988, text IERM 595:801
—Employee sanctions and remedies (Section 5154) IERM 595:804
—Federal contractors, requirements for (Section 5152) IERM 595:801
—Federal grant recipients, requirements for (Section 5153) IERM 595:803
Due process IERM 509:106
Executive Order 12564, federal workplace, text
LRX 4411
IERM 595:501
Federal guidelines IERM 509:108

FEPM = Fair Employment Practices Manual; FEP ▶ = Fair Employment Practice Outline;
IERM = Individual Employment Rights Manual; IER ▶ = Individual Employment Rights Outline;
LA ▶ = Labor Arbitration Outline; LR ▶ = Labor Relations Outline;

4-89 LRR GENERAL INDEX 152
1-55871-033-7/89/$0+.50

To start your research in the *Labor Relations Reporter*, look up your topic in the General Index in the Master Index Binder (for instance, Drug Possession, Discharge or discipline), and note the classification number (118.653) and any reference to the Labor Relations Expediter (page 510:231).

You can also find the classification number in the Expediter, which is organized alphabetically by topic. You will also find a brief summary of the law on the subject.

No. 660 DISCHARGE LRX 510:231

LA 567, *Bethlehem Steel Co.*, 24 LA 852, *J. H. Day Co.*, 22 LA 751.

The Internal Revenue Service's three-day suspensions of a revenue agent and two members of the union grievance committee—who forwarded an allegedly confidential taxpayer file to the union's chief counsel for use in investigating an unfavorable performance appraisal of the agent's audit work—were not for cause "such as would promote the efficiency of the service," an arbitrator held, even though he agreed that IRS employees were not supposed to reveal confidential information concerning taxpayers to the attorney. The arbitrator noted that the confidential nature of the particular file had been lost through extensive publicity of the case, that the IRS had permitted similar disclosure in the past, and that it had not notified the union of a change in its policy regarding confidential information. *Internal Revenue Service*, 67 LA 1261.

Another arbitrator overturned the discharge of a federal-agency employee who failed to request leave on a date on which she claimed she did not feel well and who had a history of non-cooperation and prior discipline, where the agency admitted that the employee's "whistleblowing" activities played a significant role in the discharge decision. *Air Force Logistics Command*, 84 LA 108.

§ 31. Drinking, possession or use of illegal drugs, and intoxication. (LA ▶ 118.653) Arbitrators do not question an employer's right to prohibit possession and consumption of alcohol or illegal drugs on the job or reporting to work under the influence of intoxicants, and generally uphold discipline and discharge when the rules are clear, fair, well publicized, and consistently enforced, and the testing procedures are sound. *Drackett, Inc.*, 89 LA 99, *Amoco Oil Co.*, 88 LA 1010, *Emhart Packaging Group*, 88 LA 51. But arbitrators often find discharge too severe in cases involving a first offense, *Kroger Company*, 88 LA 463, an employee with a good work record, *Morgan Adhesives Co.*, , 87 LA 1039, no impairment of the employee's job performance, *Union Oil Co. of Calif.*, 88 LA 91, or a testing program that is unfair or procedurally defective, *Transportation and Parking Authority*, 88 LA 492, *Bay Area Rapid Transit*, 88 LA 1.

Suspensions and discharges for alcohol or drug abuse are likely to be upheld, however, where the employee is a truck or valet driver, *Apcoa, Inc.*, 81 LA 449, operates public transportation, *Bi-State Development Agency*, 88 LA 854, is otherwise in personal contact with the public at the time of the offense, *Northwest Airlines*, 89 LA 621, *Orange County Transit District*, 89 LA 544, *Southern Bell Telephone & Telegraph Co.*, 28 LA 226, or works in a job with hazardous conditions. *Southern Calif. Edison Co.*, 90 LA 960, *Ashland Oil*, 89 LA 795.

Off-duty offenses — Arbitrators determine the propriety of discipline or discharge for off-duty, off-premises drug or alcohol-related offenses by the same standard applied to other off-duty misconduct, with the principal consideration being the impact upon the workplace. The discharge of an oil-refinery employee who was arrested in a drug raid at his home was upheld regardless of the outcome of criminal charges, where he admitted using the company phone to arrange an off-duty sale of a large quantity of cocaine. The "nature of the risk" from drug use by any employees in the "potentially hazardous work environment" cannot be ignored, even though the grievant may never have made any sales to co-workers in the past, the arbitrator explained. *Union Oil Co. of Calif.*, 89 LA 1.

Other cases in which discharges based on off-duty offenses were upheld involved a high-school home counselor, *Elyria Board of Education*, 86 LA 921, a campus police officer, *University of Missouri-Kansas City*, 82 LA 112, an employee arrested for possession of narcotics on the way home from work, where the preponderance of the evidence established that she violated the rule against on-duty

10-88
0148-7981/88/$0+.50

Next, look up the classification number in the appropriate Cumulative Digest and Index (CDI), and read the brief summaries of all the reported cases on point.

Final CDI 91 LA F-A287

▸ **118.6521** (Contd.)
ditions immediately, and to grieve any unsatisfactory response. (Nolan) 987

▸ **118.6523** Union steward who shouted and jabbed his finger at supervisor during argument was improperly suspended, where company did not give him required written warning, action was not contractually subject to immediate discharge, and employee handbook prohibiting abusive language toward supervisors does not override contract. (Strasshofer) 482

Discharge for alleged physical abuse of supervisor is reduced to disciplinary layoff, where grievant, who was upset at being removed from line, put his hand in supervisor's face, but touching, at most, was only with end of his finger, and supervisor had failed to give him written reprimand for previous insubordinate comments. (Brown) 550

Employee was discharged improperly for addressing profanity at supervisor, where supervisor admitted he initiated cursing tirade. (Nicholas) 905

▸ **118.653** Airline properly discharged flight attendant who was convicted of off-duty misdemeanor of drug possession, even though conviction record was expunged when he completed probation, where work rule allows discharge for serious misdemeanors, attendant did not use employee assistance program, and current grand jury and FAA investigations into drug use by airline employees create sufficient nexus between off-duty conduct and airline's business. (Ables) 6

Employee subject to last-chance conditional return-to-duty agreement in which he agreed to submit to random, comprehensive drug screening was properly discharged when he tested positive for cocaine and PCP after he reported to work in excited condition, threatening to kill himself and his wife, since being under influence of drugs on plant property is dischargeable offense; grievant did not offer evidence to support allegations of inadequate testing procedure or sample tampering, and negative test taken four-days later has no probative value. (Yarowsky) 363

Employer properly discharged admitted drug abuser who violated "last-chance" agreement's requirements that he remain drug free, where case histories purportedly proving disparate-treatment claim were not factually the same as grievant's and last-chance agreement did not provide for multiple rehabilitation opportunities. (Allen) 400

Coal-mine worker whose blood-alcohol level exceeded state intoxication standards in test administered three hours after he reported to work was properly discharged, since intoxicated employees in coal-mining environment present significant hazard to themselves and co-workers. (Cohen) 431

Just cause for discharge did not exist on basis of production manager's report that employee had brought three cans of beer onto company premises, even though employee did not deny presence of three beer cans in his cooler, where employee had good eight-year employment record, he claimed he had drunk beer off premises and cans were empty, and employer failed to prove they contained beer. (Gunderson) 512

Just cause did not exist to suspend electrician for reporting "under the influence" of alcohol, where alleged symptoms of alcohol abuse could have been caused by grievant's anger at being required to maintain certain tools, testimony that he had alcohol on breath was disputed, there is no evidence that his actions were impaired, and employer had never defined "under the influence." (Marcus) 539

Contractual progressive-discipline and double-jeopardy safeguards are inapplicable to discharge under 'last chance' agreement settling grievance arising from alcohol-abuse discharge; agreement is separate and distinct from contract and applies only to grievant's personal commitment to refrain from abuse of alcohol. (Howell) 544

Arbitrator lacks authority to modify discharge of longtime employee who violated 'last chance' agreement requiring him to refrain from alcohol abuse, even though he had satisfactory, five-year post-agreement record and voluntarily sought treatment upon relapse; parties executed agreement, which provided that "any repetition" would be "cause for immediate termination," without duress. *Id.*

Employer improperly denied full-shift pay to employee who was sent home, for being allegedly under influence of alcohol, without awaiting results of blood-alcohol test, even if employer has reserved right to relieve from duty employees who are under influence of alcohol, where test revealed that blood-alcohol level was not clinically significant. (Richard) 841

Probable cause did not exist for employer to conclude that employee was under influence of alcohol, despite claim that foremen smelled alcohol on employee's breath and employee had slipped on floor near mill; smell of alcohol is not by itself evidence that he was under influence, and unimpaired em-

The CDI gives you the page numbers of the cases on point. Now, you can turn to the full text of the decisions themselves in the appropriate binder. Simply repeat this process for the bound volumes.

91 LA 6 USAIR INC.

1. obtain immediate approval by the Office of Human Rights of its Affirmative Action Plan,

2. thereafter begin immediately to implement the plan with the objective of full implementation within six months. If the objective is not reached, advise the Union as to the reasons for the failure to complete the implementation and provide a detailed timetable for the Plan's ultimate implementation,

3. hold monthly meetings of the EEO Advisory Committee with the Union's Coordinator in attendance to assess progress towards Plan implementation,

4. send periodic progress reports on the implementation of the Affirmative Action Plan to the Union.

USAIR INC. —

Decision of Arbitrators

In re USAIR INC. and FLIGHT ATTENDANTS IN SERVICE OF USAIR INC., THE ASSOCIATION OF FLIGHT ATTENDANTS, May 16, 1988

System Board of Adjustment: Robert J. Ables, neutral referee; Ronald A. Holley and Lee R. Kafer Jr., company members; Bobbette Hake and Karen Lascoli, union members

DRUGS AND ALCOHOL

— Flight attendant — 'Possession' conviction — Discharge ▸118.634 ▸118.643 ▸118.653

Airline properly discharged flight attendant who was convicted of off-duty misdemeanor of drug possession, even though conviction record was expunged when he completed probation, where work rule allows discharge for serious misdemeanors, attendant did not use employee assistance program, and safety duties of flight attendants, public confidence in airline, and current grand jury and Federal Aviation Administration investigations into drug use by airline employees create sufficient nexus between off-duty conduct and airline's business.

Appearances: For the employer — D. Michael Underhill, attorney. For the union — Ben C. Elliott, Gary Gentile, attorneys.

OFF-DUTY CONDUCT

I. Issue

ABLES, Arbitrator: — At issue under a collective bargaining agreement is whether the employer, USAir, Inc., had just cause to discharge its employee and grievant, represented by his union, The Association of Flight Attendants, in circumstances where a Pennsylvania state court found the grievant guilty of possessing Percocet, a controlled substance, a misdemeanor, but because this was a first-time offense, imposed a modest sentence on the grievant later expunging the record of proceedings, after probation, and where, because there was no publicity about the arrest and, therefore, unknown to the employer, the grievant continued duties as a flight attendant for several months after his arrest, but where a national television broadcast and newspaper articles in Pittsburgh, Pennsylvania, a corporate hub for this airline, and elsewhere, featured reports, including grand jury proceedings, that USAir flight crews were on drugs.[1]

II. Arguments

The essential argument of the employer that the discharge was justified is that, apart from action by the state court, possession of a controlled substance, on or off duty, is a dischargeable offense under applicable company rules, particularly for the safety-sensitive job of flight attendant.

The essential argument of the union that the discharge was not justified, and therefore that the grievant should be reinstated with back pay and benefits, is that the grievant, a "very good" flight attendant for eight years without prior discipline was convicted only of a misdemeanor, which was effectively forgiven by the state and that because no publicity attended the grievant's arrest, trial and conviction, the company could not show the required nexus between outside private activity and adverse effect on company business. The union also argues disparate discipline because other flight attendants in like circumstances either were not disciplined or escaped discipline by turning themselves in for help under the company's employee assistance program.

---

[1] The parties stipulated that the grievant should not be identified by name or number in this opinion by this System Board of Adjustment but that the Board opinion and decision may be published.

The third entry under the subtopic "Discharge or discipline" is to the Labor Relations Expediter, which is the name given to two binders in the service designed to provide quick answers to day-to-day labor relations problems. The page in the Expediter to which you are referred is 510:231. If you go to the Expediter at this point in your research, you will find a brief overview of how courts and arbitrators have dealt with discharges for drug possession and you will be cited to several cases on point. You will also note that the classification number 118.653 is referred to. You could have bypassed the General Index and gone directly to the Expediter, which is organized in an alphabetical encyclopedic fashion. (You would have had to look, however, under the main topic "Discharge," there being no main entry "Drugs.") In doing so, you would by now be armed with the same information: namely, classification number 118.653, with which you can continue your research.

Now, you want to use that classification number to find cases addressing your problem, starting with the most recent. For that, you go back to the Master Index Binder (or simply stay there after you've used the General Index, and save the Expediter for later).

You go to the tab marked Cumulative Digest and Index LA. Cumulative Digest and Index, or CDI for short, is the name given to the research system used in this and other BNA decisional services. Behind this tab you will find one or more CDIs, each covering a volume of decisions that the Labor Arbitration part of the service has reported and that are currently stored and being cumulated in the looseleaf Labor Arbitration binder.

Reprinted in each CDI are the headnotes of all the decisions reported in the volume covered by that particular CDI. The headnotes are organized by classification number, so you look up 118.653 and you find the headnotes for several cases.

You read the headnotes and find one for a decision that looks particularly helpful. You note the volume and page number on which the full text of the decision is reported. Now, you can go to the decision itself by turning to the Labor Arbitration binder and finding the volume and page number you noted in the CDI.

After you've looked at the most recent decisions on your problem, you decide to find a few less recent ones. All you need is that same classification number, 118.653. Find the most recent bound CDI; usually, it will be a softbound volume. And proceed on just like you did above. The only difference is that now the decisions themselves will be found in hardbound volumes, and if you keep going back even further in time, the CDIs also will be in hard-bound volumes.

By Classification Outline

As seen in the preceding example, the key to unlocking *Labor Relations Reporter's* storehouse of decisional materials is the CDI classification system. The example shows how to determine the relevant CDI number through the General Index and through the Expediter. It is also possible to determine the number by going directly to the Outline of Classifications. Each of the five parts of the service has its own outline, which can be found in the Master Index Binder and in the bound CDIs. Each out-

These are sample pages from the Outline of Classifications for the Labor Arbitration part of the service. Each other part of the service has its own outline.

E-118 LA OUTLINE OF CLASSIFICATIONS

▶117.—Contd.

arbitration, see ▶94.166. For severance pay, see ▶123.13. See also ▶117.331 et seq., 120.04, and 122.]

▶118. Discharge, Discipline, and Work Rules
[For termination of employment for lack of work, see ▶117.101 et seq. For discharge under union-security clauses, see ▶8.54 and 8.633. For public employee cases, see also ▶100.55.]

.01 In general; what constitutes discharge or discipline; group discipline
[For quit versus discharge, see ▶118.07. For discharge, termination or retirement distinguished, see ▶117.105. See also ▶118.6603.]

.02 Management rights; contract limitations; demotion, denial of benefits, etc., as penalty; probationary employees
[For arbitrability, see ▶94.117. For deductions from or offsets against wages, see ▶114.16. For non-disciplinary demotion, see ▶119.801 et seq. For union representation at meetings and interviews, see ▶93.27.]

.03 Modification of disciplinary penalty; authority of arbitrator
[See ▶94.551 and 94.559 for cases prior to LA Vol. 21. See also ▶94.117.]

.07 Quit or discharge; constructive discharge
[For general definition of a quit, for retraction of resignation, and for rehiring after quit, see ▶117.14. See also ▶118.654.]

.08 Indefinite suspension

.25 Establishment, revision, and posting of work rules; reasonableness of rules
[See also ▶118.6561 et seq. and 124.70.]

.27 Production standards, establishment
[For discipline for failure to meet production standards, see ▶118.651.]

Procedure in discipline cases; timeliness of disciplinary action; progressive discipline
[See also ▶118.3133, 118.41, and 118.6604.]

.301 —In general

.303 —Reprimands and warnings; steps in advance of discharge, etc.

.305 —Notice of disciplinary action; consultation or hearing

Evidence before arbitrator

.311 —In general; circumstances surrounding complained-of misconduct
[See also ▶94.605.]

▶118.—Contd.

—Admissibility of evidence

.3131 ——In general

.3133 ——Prior work record of employee
[See also ▶118.301 et seq.]

.3135 ——Lie detector tests

.315 —Burden of proof; presumptions; degree of proof required; weight of evidence
[See also ▶94.605.]

.41 Successive penalties; double punishment for same offense
[See also ▶118.301 et seq. and 118.6604.]

Reason for discharge or other discipline

.632 —In general

.634 —Off-duty or off-premises misconduct
[See also ▶118.6363, 118.643, and 118.6523.]

—Absence from work; absenteeism
[For early quitting, see ▶118.654.]

.6361 ——In general

.6363 ——Confinement in jail or other emergency
[See also ▶118.634 and 118.643.]

.6366 ——Sickness or disability
[See also ▶116.25 and 118.655.]

.6367 ——Tardiness

.637 —Accident record; traffic violations
[See also ▶118.651.]

.640 —Assault; fighting; troublemaking; name calling; profanity; obscene language or other misconduct
[For picket-line disturbances or other altercations incidental to strikes, see ▶118.6604. For fighting with supervisors and use of abusive language to supervisors, see ▶118.6523. See also ▶118.645.]

.641 —Attachment or garnishment; bankruptcy or insolvency of employee
[See ▶118.632 for cases prior to LA Vol. 21. For management's right to establish work rules on garnishment of wages and reasonableness of such rules, see ▶118.25.]

.643 —Criminal prosecution or conviction; sabotage; damage to property
[See also ▶118.651, 118.634 and 118.6363. For use of drugs or narcotics, see ▶118.653.]

.645 —Horseplay
[See also ▶118.640.]

.646 —Discourtesy to or complaints by patrons or customers
[See ▶118.632 for cases prior to LA Vol. 21.]

—Dishonesty, theft, or disloyalty

.6481 ——In general

By referring to the outline, you can see where your topic fits into the rest of the indexing scheme, and you can find the classification numbers for related topics. Frequent users of the service soon become familiar with the outlines and can often bypass the General Index.

LA OUTLINE OF CLASSIFICATIONS E-119

▶118.—Contd.

.6482 ——Disloyalty to employer; conflict of interest; aid to competitors; moonlighting
[See also ▶124.45 and 124.50.]

.6484 ——Falsification of employment application or work records

.6488 ——Theft

—Disloyalty to Government

.6491 ——In general

.6495 ——Refusal to testify before Congressional committees or state commissions

.6497 ——Security clearance

.650 —Gambling

.651 —Incompetence, negligence, or low production
[Includes unsatisfactory performance. For incompetence resulting from physical disability, see ▶118.655. For accident record as reason for discharge or discipline, see ▶118.637. For production standards, see ▶118.27. See also ▶118.643.]

—Insubordination
[For refusal to accept work assignment or overtime or holiday work, see ▶118.658. See also ▶93.40.]

.6521 ——In general
[See also ▶118.657.]

.6523 ——Assault on, offensive language, or other misconduct toward management personnel

.6527 ——Union representatives
[See also ▶118.6609 and 118.664.]

.653 —Intoxication; possession or use of intoxicants; drugs or narcotics

.654 —Loafing, leaving post, early quitting, sleeping on duty
[See also ▶118.07 and 118.6361 et seq. For slowdowns, see ▶118.6607.]

.655 —Physical or mental disability; failure to submit to physical examination or give doctor's certificate
[See also ▶116.43, 117.1133, 117.123, 118.6366, and 124.70.]

—Work rules
[See also ▶118.25.]

.6561 ——In general
[For use of drugs or narcotics, see ▶118.653.]

.6563 ——Eating and coffee breaks

.6564 ——Personal appearance

.6565 ——Time cards

.6567 ——Safety rules
[See also ▶124.70.]

.657 —Pressure from union or fellow employees
[See also ▶118.6521.]

.658 —Refusal to accept job assignment, overtime, or holiday work

—Strikes, picketing, and slowdowns
[See also ▶93.40.]

▶118.—Contd.

.6601 ——In general
[See ▶118.6600 for cases prior to LA Vol. 51.]

.6603 ——Instigating, inciting, or participating in strike; selective or group discipline
[For union representatives, see ▶118.6609.]

.6604 ——Misconduct during strike; picketing; progressive discipline
[For progressive discipline, see also ▶118.301 et seq.]

.6605 ——Refusal to cross picket lines
[For crossing picket lines, see ▶81.06.]

.6607 ——Slowdowns; partial strikes
[See also ▶80.552 and 118.654.]

.6608 ——Strike settlement agreements
[See also ▶80.47.]

.6609 ——Union representatives
[See also ▶118.6603 and 118.664.]

.6611 ——Unsafe working conditions, claim of

.664 —Union activities and union business; protection of employees and union representatives
[For insubordination, see ▶118.6527. For leaving post, see ▶118.654. For strikes, picketing, and slowdowns, see ▶118.6609. See also ▶24.365, 93.241, and 118.67.]

.67 Equality of treatment of employees; discrimination
[For discipline for instigating or participating in work stoppage, see ▶118.6603 and 118.6609. See also ▶106.25, 107.30, and 118.664. For discrimination due to union activity, see ▶4.01 et seq.]

.70 Management's duty to enforce discipline

Reinstatement, back pay, or other remedy after proper discharge or discipline
[See ▶117.15 for cases prior to LA Vol. 21. See also ▶94.62, 114.75, and 118.801 et seq.]

.751 —In general
[See ▶118.75 for cases prior to LA Vol. 51.]

.752 —Conditions to reinstatement; violation

Reinstatement, back pay, or other remedy for wrongful discharge or discipline
[See also ▶94.62 and 114.75.]

.801 —In general; conditions to reinstatement

.802 —Court jurisdiction and procedure in general; right to sue

.803 —Duty to exhaust contract or administrative remedies before suit; election of remedies

line organizes the topics covered in the service in a logical sequence. By scanning through the outline for either the Labor Arbitration or the Labor Relations part of the service, you could have discovered the number you needed, 118.653, which stands for Discharge or Discipline for Possession or Use of Intoxicants. Frequent users of *Labor Relations Reporter* or of other decisional services become familiar with the applicable outlines and can often turn directly to the CDIs and the numbers they want.

Example: Notification Services

The United States Law Week—By Subject and Case Name

You clerk for a state supreme court justice in a state that has adopted a new abortion law requiring that parents of a minor be notified before an abortion is performed on her. The constitutionality of the law has been challenged, and you are asked to find out how similar challenges have fared elsewhere and also whether the U.S. Supreme Court has had anything to say lately on the subject of abortion or is likely to in the near future. You turn to *The United States Law Week*.

Law Week is primarily a notification service, designed to be used weekly to keep abreast of significant legal developments in all fields. All notification services, however, have a secondary, reference value, *Law Week* more so than most. Each volume of *Law Week* is divided into two separate binders: one for General Law, which includes reports on decisions from state and federal courts other than the U.S. Supreme Court, and one for the Supreme Court.

You turn first to the General Law binder of the current *Law Week* volume in order to find out if there have been any recent challenges to statutes similar to your state's. Behind the last tab in the binder is the index, which is very similar to ones found in other BNA notification services.

You quickly find the main topic heading "Abortion" on the front page, and you find two entries under the subtopic "Notice to parents." The number at the end of each entry is the page number where a more complete account—a headnote and a summary—of the case can be found. Any 2000 series page number refers to *Law Week's* Section 2, which you will find in the same binder as the index, behind the tab marked "New Court Decisions."

After you've read the accounts of these cases in *Law Week*, you might decide you need the full text. One easy way of finding it is to refer to the Table of Cases, which is toward the back of the same index you've been using. There you look up the names of the cases you looked at in Section 2 and discover that citations to the West Reporters are given. Not all cases in the Table of Cases have West cites; many have not yet been published by West, and some never will be. But it's always worth giving a quick look at the Table of Cases to see if it contains the parallel cite to the cases in which you are interested.

All BNA reporter services that report court decisions have a Table of Cases. *Law Week's*, like all the others, can be used directly to find information contained in the service, if you already know the name of the case in which you are interested. For instance, in this example, if you already knew there was a recent abortion case named *Hodgson* that arose out of Minnesota, you could find the case *Hodgson v. Minnesota* by looking in *Law Week's* Table of Cases

The United States
LAW WEEK

March 14, 1989 — Volume 57, No. 35

TOPICAL INDEX — SUMMARY
GENERAL LAW SECTIONS

Covering Section 2 of
Volume 57, Nos. 1-33

July 5, 1988—February 28, 1989

FILE with Vol. 57, General Law Sections binder behind Index tab.
DISCARD prior Topical Index for Vol. 57.

TABLE OF DECISIONS AND ORDERS

See Table at end of Index

A

ABORTION
Notice to parents
—24-Hour notice to one parent by person who seeks to perform abortion on unmarried minor or, alternatively, judicial bypass procedure involving complex pleading requirements and clear and convincing evidence of sufficient maturity, state statute requiring is unconstitutional (CA 8) 2106
—48-Hour notice to both parents by minor child before obtaining abortion, with judicial bypass option, state statute requiring is constitutional (CA 8) 2105
Physician's negligent failure to give pregnancy test before advising woman she was not pregnant, and prescription of drugs that could cause congenital defects in child, precipitating abortion, recovery for physical and emotional injuries allowed (NY CtApp) 2287
Picketing and shouting in front of abortion clinic, injunction creating "free zone" not violative of First Amendment rights (CA 9) 2239
Title X regulations prohibiting counseling on abortion as method of family planning, and requiring separation of Title X projects from abortion clinics, reasonably interpret statute and are constitutional (DC SNY) 2033

ACCOUNTANTS
Computer software firm's accountant was "needlessly harassed" by SEC in injunctive action charging book-cooking, attorney's fees and expenses awarded under EAJA (DC Minn) 2374
Ethics code, AICPA members may proceed with suit to block implementation of major revisions requiring quality assurance reviews (NY SupCtAppDiv) 2449
Malpractice limitations statute begins to run when IRS issues statutory notice of deficiency or taxpayer indicates agreement with IRS' proposed tax changes, not when taxpayer receives IRS notice (Wyo SupCt) 2453
Promoter who engaged accounting firm to furnish tax and other services on future corporation's behalf is personally liable for accounting firm's fees (Colo CtApp) 2026
State statute limiting terms non-certified public accountants may use in describing themselves and preparing documents for clients survives First Amendment scrutiny (CA 4) 2281
Tax information submitted to accountant for use in preparation of returns is not within scope of Illinois statutory accountant's privilege (Ill SupCt) 2265

ADDRESSES, ARTICLES, STATEMENTS
See BOOKS, CONFERENCES AND MEETINGS, SPEAKERS AND AUTHORS

ADMINISTRATIVE LAW
(Limited to items relating to procedure before agencies, etc.; see also specific subject headings)
Administrative law judges corps, discussion at ABA annual meeting 2096
Agency subpoenas
—ABA annual meeting, discussion 2097
—Defense Contract Audit Agency's statutory subpoena power extends to objective factual materials useful in verifying actual costs, including general and administrative overhead costs, charged by companies performing cost-type contracts for government (CA 4) 2369
—"First-filed" rule, dismissal of EEOC suit declined because of employer's earlier-filed suit challenging subpoena in another federal court, filed in part to evade unfavorable local precedent, not abuse of discretion (CA 3) 2019
Enforcement
—EPA administrative order under RCRA, direct court assistance allowed where company against whom order issued did not make good faith attempt to comply (DC WWash) 2043
—Subpoena enforcement, "first-filed" rule, dismissal of EEOC suit declined because of employer's earlier-filed suit challenging subpoena in another federal court, filed in part to evade unfavorable local precedent, not abuse of discretion (CA 3) 2019
Freedom of information
—See FREEDOM OF INFORMATION
Judicial review
—Advisory opinions issued by FEC pursuant to FECA are not sufficiently final or binding to be judicially reviewable (CA 2) 2310
—Arbitrary and capricious, not de novo, standard of review applies to FSLIC decisions as insurer (CA 3) 2045
—Comptroller of currency's ruling construing Bank Holding Company Act to permit national bank to acquire insurance subsidiary is without precendential effect and inappropriate for judicial review, Federal Reserve Board has initial jurisdiction over BHCA issues (CA DC) 2405
—EPA assumption of permit-issuing authority over discharger because of disagreement with state over permit requirements, but determination of whether to issue or to deny not yet made, judicial review not available (CA 4) 2020
—EPA compliance order issued for violation of hazardous air pollutant standard not "final action" reviewable under Clean Water Act Sec. 307(b)(1) ... (CA 2) 2005
—Exhaustion of administrative remedies required before seeking district court injunction against federal agency debarment action claiming preclusion by previous related debarment imposed by different agency (CA 3) 2275
—Federal Employees Compensation Act proceedings, administrative denial of petition for EAJA attorney's fees is not judicially reviewable (CA 6) 2316
—ITC advisory opinions not "final determinations," appellate jurisdiction declined, but modified exclusion order resulting from advisory opinion reviewed (CA FC) 2083
—Medicaid claims, unavailability of judicial review for denial of federal Medicare claims precludes collateral estoppel of judicial review of denial of similar claims under state Medicaid program (Conn SupCt) 2065
—NRC regulations lack judicially meaningful standard of review, thus NRC decisions not to take requested enforcement actions are not subject to judicial review (CA 1) 2077
—Nuclear power plant license, NRC denial of petition to review is discretionary agency enforcement decision, precluding judicial review (CA 7) 2490
—Petition for reconsideration renders otherwise final order non-final, thus precluding concurrent judicial review (CA 3) 2293
—Toxic Substances Control Act provision permitting de novo review of EPA's denial of citizen petition to initiate rulemaking on testing does not violate separation of powers doctrine (DC EIll) 2444
Licensing
—Presumption by NRC that state and local governments that have refused to participate in nuclear emergency planning will, in actual emergency, comply with utility's plan is not violative of Administrative Procedure Act or Atomic Energy Act (CA 1) 2175
Procedure
—Attorney's fees, Handicapped Children's Protection Act
——Parents or guardians successful at administrative level may recover (CA 6) 2141
——Separate suit solely to recover attorney's fees may be maintained by prevailing parties at administrative level (CA 5) 2356
—Exclusion of employee's representative from OSHA proceedings for "exploiting" union's status violates First Amendment free speech rights, absent showing of actual interference (CA 1) 2274
—Hearing denial to citizens contesting bank merger on Community Reinvestment Act grounds upheld, review properly confined to OCC administrative record (CA 11) 2262
—Notice and hearing requirements of Sec. 111 of 1974 Act, rather than those of Sec. 104(d), are required when HUD proposes to reduce, terminate, or limit city's entitlement to community development block grants because of alleged past non-compliance (CA DC) 2325
Rulemaking
—Toxic Substances Control Act provision permitting de novo review of EPA's denial of citizen petition to initiate rulemaking on testing does not violate separation of powers doctrine (DC EIll) 2444
—Waste disposal, tentative method established by DOE for allocating costs of nuclear waste repositories between government and commercial generators, interpretive rule exempt from APA rulemaking requirements (CA DC) 2043

ADMIRALTY
See SHIPPING AND LONGSHORING

ADOPTION
See FAMILY LAW

Note: The Supreme Court Index covering sections 3 and 4 of LAW WEEK is issued separately.

0148-8139/89/$0+.50

Law Week's index uses a purely topical approach. Each entry provides a brief description of the case, the name of the court, and the page number where a full account of the case can be found.

Pages referred to in the General Law index are found in *Law Week's* Section 2.

8–23–88 — *The United States* **LAW WEEK** — **57 LW 2105**

tice of the allegations and to permit conciliation by the EEOC. In contrast, the FLSA has no prelitigation charge-filing requirement, and conciliation is not an objective of FLSA procedures. The strong parallelism between the charge-filing requirements of the ADEA and Title VII cannot be ignored. We conclude, therefore, that Congress did not intend to require that every individual who files a suit under the ADEA also must have filed an individual charge.

However, we also believe that the charge-filing requirements under the ADEA cannot be interpreted without any reference to the FLSA-based litigation process that Congress has mandated. In opting for the FLSA scheme, Congress also chose the "opt-in" provision of the FLSA, 29 USC 216(b), under which all plaintiffs in an ADEA representative action must affirmatively opt-in to the suit. Thus, there are no anonymous plaintiffs under the ADEA. In light of this litigation procedure, we believe it is necessary that the defendant at least be apprised during the conciliation process of the possibility of a subsequent lawsuit with many plaintiffs. We agree with *Kloos v. Carter-Day Co.*, 799 F2d 397 (CA 8 1986) that "[t]o be faithful to the purposes of the filing requirement, an administrative charge must allege class-wide age discrimination or claim to represent a class in order to serve as the basis for an ADEA class action under Section 216(b)." This notification is necessary in order to satisfy Congress' express desire that the defendant understand, during the conciliation stage, the magnitude of his potential liability.

Here at least 27 charges, 23 of which were timely, contained plain allegations of class-based discrimination. The employer certainly knew that it faced a class-wide ADEA suit. Thus, all purposes of ADEA's charge-filing requirement have been met.

The employer urges that the district court erred when it allowed the plaintiffs to amend their complaint into a representative action because the ADEA's three-year statute of limitations had expired. This contention is without merit for two reasons. First, it was not necessary for the plaintiffs to amend their complaint to plead a representative action. Every court of appeals that has addressed the issue has held, under Title VII, that plaintiffs who have not timely filed a charge can rely on a timely charge of another plaintiff in a class action or in a multiple plaintiff joint action. Second, Fed.R.Civ.P. 15(c) allows the date of an amended pleading to relate back to the date of the original pleading if the claim asserted in the amended pleading arose out of the same conduct, transaction, or occurrence set forth in the original pleading.—Ripple, J.

Health Care

ABORTIONS—

Minnesota statute that requires minor to notify both parents at least 48 hours before obtaining abortion, or to submit to judicial bypass procedure in which court may authorize abortion without parental notice if it determines that minor is mature and capable of giving informed consent or that notification would not be in her best interests, is constitutional.

(*Hodgson v. Minnesota*, CA 8 (en banc), No. 86-5423, 8/8/88; see 56 LW 2138)

In 1981, Minnesota enacted a statute that provides that no abortion may be performed upon an unemancipated minor until at least 48 hours after written notice to her parent. Parent is defined as "both parents of the pregnant woman if they are both living, one parent of the pregnant woman if only one is living or if the second one cannot be located through reasonably diligent effort . . . ." The statute provides that if the notification provision is restrained by judicial order, an alternative court bypass procedure goes into effect. Under the court bypass, a judge, after an expedited confidential hearing, may authorize an abortion without parental notice after determining "that the pregnant woman is mature and capable of giving informed consent," or that the performance of an abortion without notification would be for "best interests."

Enforcement of the statute's "pure notice" provision was temporarily restrained, thus activating the bypass provision. After a trial on the merits, the district court held that the notification requirement without judicial bypass was unconstitutional. The court then considered in isolation the two-parent notification and the 48 hour waiting period requirement and found both to be constitutionally wanting.

Although states have a significant interest in certain abortion regulations aimed at protecting children, that interest must give way to the constitutional right of a mature minor or of an immature minor whose best interests are contrary to parental involvement to obtain an abortion without consulting or notifying her parents. *Akron v. Akron Center for Reproductive Health*, 462 U.S. 416, 51 LW 4767 (1983). Thus, a state choosing to encourage parental involvement must provide an alternative procedure through which a minor may demonstrate that she is mature enough to make her own decision or that the abortion is in her best interests.

Careful study of *Bellotti v. Baird*, 443 U.S. 622 (1979) (*Bellotti II*), *Planned Parenthood v. Ashcroft*, 462 U.S. 476, 51 LW 4783 (1983), and *H.L. v. Matheson*, 450 U.S. 398 (1981), reveals the significant state interests that justify Minnesota's notice/bypass statute. In *Bellotti II*, a plurality of the court identified the significant state and parental interests at stake when a minor faces the decision of whether to have an abortion. The special importance and consequences of the abortion decision for the minor are recognized as a sufficient justification for reasonable state efforts to ensure that the decision be wisely made.

In addition, the state has an interest in the family itself. Parents have a traditional and substantial interest in, as well as a responsibility for, the rearing and welfare of their children.

Finally, the Supreme Court has recognized the significant state interest in providing an opportunity for parents to supply essential medical and other information to a physician.

Because of these interests, a plurality in *Bellotti II* concluded that a parental consent statute, when an alternative bypass mechanism is in place, does not unconstitutionally burden a minor's abortion right.

After affirming the constitutionality of the statute as a whole, the district court considered in isolation the two-parent notice requirement. The court concluded that the notice requirement actively interferes with parent-child communication and thus failed to further the state's interest in protecting pregnant minors and promoting family communication. This conclusion was based primarily on the court's factual findings regarding the burden imposed on minors of family units that have either broken apart or never been formed.

A plurality in *Bellotti II* indicated that the requirement of obtaining both parents' consent does not unconstitutionally burden a minor's abortion right when there is an alternative judicial bypass in place. Unlike the statute in *Bellotti II*, which required consent, the statute here only requires notice. A notification requirement is substantially less burdensome than a consent requirement.

While the district court found that the non-custodial parent often has little communication with a child, this does not mandate completely casting aside the principles enunciated by the Supreme Court as to the parental role, which apply to non-custodial parents as well as custodial parents. By providing for judicial bypass, the statute safeguards those minors for whom parental involvement may not be in their best interests.

The district court enjoined the entire statute because of the impact of the two-parent notice requirement primarily on one group of pregnant minors, without considering the effect of the bypass or the parental and family interests that have been recognized by the Supreme Court. Considering the statute as a whole and as applied to all pregnant minors, the two-parent notice re-

0148-8139/88/$0+.50

Many cases listed in the Table of Cases provide a parallel citation to the West reporter system. Cases are listed under both the plaintiff's name and the defendant's.

The United States LAW WEEK—GENERAL INDEX 37

Volume 57, Nos. 1-33, July 5, 1988—February 28, 1989

Fraternal Order of Police, Lodge 121 v. Hobart (CA 7) 2407
Frazier v. Conrail (CA DC, 851 F.2d 1447) 2146
FRB; Credit Union National Assn. v. (DC DC) 2130
FRB; National Assn. of Casualty and Surety Agents v. (CA DC) 2166
FRB; Northeast Bancorp Inc. v. (CA DC) 2011
FRB of New York; Greater Buffalo Press Inc. v. (CA 2) 2439
Freede v. IRS, Comr. of (CA 10) 2289
Freedonia Group Inc.; Business Trends Analysis Inc. v. (DC SNY) 2482
Freeman; California v. (Calif SupCt) 2162
Freitas; U.S. v. (CA 9, 856 F.2d 1425) 2262
Friedman v. Ganassi (CA 3, 853 F.2d 207) 2109
Frito-Lay Inc.; Teamsters, Local 287 v. (CA 9) 2056
Frontier Savings and Loan Assn. v. IRS, Comr. of (CA 7, 854 F.2d 1001) 2148
Frumenti Development Corp.; FSLIC v. (CA 9) 2200
FSLIC v. Capozzi (CA 8, 855 F.2d 1319) 2178
FSLIC v. Frumenti Development Corp. (CA 9, 857 F.2d 665) 2200
FSLIC v. Israel (DC CCalif, 686 F.Supp. 819) 2025
FSLIC v. Roy (DC Md) 2099
FSLIC; York Bank and Trust Co. v. (CA 3) 2045
FTC v. AMREP Corp. (DC SNY) 2344
FTC v. Elders Grain Inc. (CA 7) 2469
FTC v. Illinois Cereal Mills Inc. (DC NIll, 691 F.Supp. 1131) 2070
FTC v. Security Rare Coin & Bullion Corp. (DC Minn) 2068
FTC; Superior Court Trial Lawyers Assn. v. (CA DC) 2133
FTC v. World Travel Vacation Brokers Inc. (CA 7) 2360
Fuchs v. Rural Electric Convenience Cooperative Inc. (CA 7, 858 F.2d 1210) 2210
Fulflex; Abenante v. (DC RI) 2420
G. Heileman Brewing Co. v. Joseph Oat Corp. (CA 7, 848 F.2d 1415) 2003
G. W. Galloway Co. v. NLRB (CA DC, 856 F.2d 275) 2173
Gainey v. Olivo (Ga SupCt) 2291
Gallagher v. Lambert (NY AppDiv, 532 N.Y.S.2d 255) 2211
Gallego; Michigan v. (Mich SupCt) 2026
Gallo; U.S. v. (Appeal of Miron) (CA 2, 859 F.2d 1078) 2279
Galvin v. OSHA (CA DC) 2359
Ganassi; Friedman v. (CA 3) 2109
Gardner; Baker v. (Ariz SupCt) 2399
Gardner v. Honda Motor Co. (NY AppDiv) 2451
Gardner v. Telegraph Employees, Local 9 (CA 9, 850 F.2d 518) 2056
Garlow; Mills v. (Wyo SupCt) 2453
Garnett v. Renton School District No. 403 (CA 9) 2430
Gaste v. Kaiserman (CA 2) 2390
Gates v. Zant (CA 11) 2450
Gaubert v. FHLBB (CA DC) 2361
Gay and Lesbian Students Assn. v. Gohn (CA 8, 850 F.2d 361) 2007
Gearhart, Ind.; McGonigal v. (CA 5) 2148
General Accident Insurance Co. of America v. Bank of New England-West N.A. (Mass SupJudCt) 2496
General Drivers, Warehousemen and Helpers, Local Union 89, see Teamsters, Local 89
General Dynamics Corp. v. Horrigan (CA 1, 848 F.2d 321) 2009
General Electric Co.; Cincinnati Gas and Electric Co. v. (CA 6) 2123
General Metal Works Inc.; Wedding & Associates Inc. v. (DC SOhio) 2419
General Motors Corp., see GMC
Georgetown University Hospital v. HHS (CA DC) 2312
Getty Petroleum Corp. v. Bartco Petroleum Corp. (CA 2, 858 F.2d 103) 2209
Giardina v. HHS (NJ SupCt) 2127
Giardono v. Jones (CA 7) 2490
Giarratano v. Murray (CA 4, 847 F.2d 1118) 2011
Gibbs; Pennsylvania v. (Pa SupCt) 2496
Gilchrist; Cinema Blue of Charlotte Inc. v. (DC WNC) 2482
Gladstone v. Hillel (Calif CtApp, 250 Cal.Rptr. 372) 2146
Glendening v. Florida (Fla SupCt) 2391
Glosser Brothers Inc., In re (Pa SuperCt) 2496
Glover v. Eastern Nebraska Community Office of Retardation (CA 8) 2470
GMC v. Abrams (DC SNY) 2464
GMC; Arnold Pontiac-GMC Inc. v. (DC WPa) 2357
GMC; Skelton v. (CA 7) 2267
GMC; Waterson v. (NJ SupCt) 2090
GMC; Wood v. (CA 1) 2398
Godchaux v. Conveying Techniques Inc. (CA 5, 846 F.2d 306) 2027
Godway; Ross v. (NH SupCt) 2467
Gohn; Gay and Lesbian Students Assn. v. (CA 8) 2007
Gold Bond Building Products; Grohs v. (CA 7) 2279
Golden State Transit Corp. v. Los Angeles (CA 9, 857 F.2d 631) 2263
Gollust; Mendell v. (DC SNY) 2391
Gommerman; Dumas v. (CA 9) 2456
Goodyear Tire & Rubber Co.; C. R. A. Realty Corp. v. (DC SNY) 2476
Gould v. Control Laser (CA FC) 2483
Gowen v. HHS (CA 8, 855 F.2d 613) 2160
Grabrian; Destefano v. (Colo SupCt) 2291
Grace Community Church of the Valley; Nally v. (Calif SupCt) 2341
Grand Jury Investigation (Oreski), In re (CA 3) 2466
Grand Jury Proceedings, In re (CA 6, 851 F.2d 860) 2073
Grand Jury Subpoenas for Locals 17, 135, 257, and 608, Carpenters, In re (NY CtApp, 528 N.W.2d 1195) 2047
Grand Metropolitan PLC v. Pillsbury Co. (Del ChanCt) 2376
Granite Rock Co.; Teamsters, Local 216 v. (CA 9) 2100
Grappone Inc. v. Subaru of New England Inc. (CA 1, 858 F.2d 792) 2278
Gray v. Romeo (DC RI, 697 F.Supp. 580) 2256
Greater Buffalo Press Inc. v. FRB of New York (CA 2) 2439
Greater Lowell Bd. of Realtors; Wells Real Estate Inc. v. (CA 1) 2041
Green v. IRS, Comr. of (CA 6, 855 F.2d 289) 2179
Greenhow v. HHS (CA 9) 2363
Gregori v. Bank of America (Calif CtApp) 2481
Greiner Engineering Inc.; STV Engineers Inc. v. (CA 3) 2307
Grice v. Hungerford (Va SupCt) 2360
Grider v. Texas Oil & Gas Corp. (CA 10) 2412
Griffin v. Jackson (Colo CtApp, 759 P.2d 839) 2148
Griffis v. Gulf Coast Pre-Stress Co. (CA 5, 850 F.2d 1090) 2109
Grimaldi; Rogers v. (DC SNY) 2196
Grimsley v. First Alabama Bank (DC SAla) 2420
Grinnell Mutual Reinsurance Co. v. Wasmuth (Minn CtApp) 2435
Grohs v. Gold Bond Building Products (CA 7, 859 F.2d 1283) 2279
Grubka v. Treasury Dept. (CA FC, 858 F.2d 1570) 2303
Gruenemeier v. Seven-Up Co. (Neb SupCt, 426 N.W.2d 510) 2084
Grumman Corp.; North Coast Air Services Ltd. v. (Wash SupCt) 2100
Gubiensio-Ortiz v. Kanahele (CA 9, 857 F.2d 1245) 2136
Guidry v. Sheet Metal Workers National Pension Fund (CA 10, 856 F.2d 1457) 2140
Guillermo v. Brennan (DC EIll, 691 F.Supp. 1151) 2116
Guinn v. Church of Christ of Collinsville, Okla. (Okla SupCt) 2462
Gulf Coast Pre-Stress Co.; Griffis v. (CA 5) 2109
Gumbinner; Marx v. (CA 11) 2236
H. C. Elliott Inc. v. Carpenters Pension Trust Fund for Northern California (CA 9) 2300
Haagen-Dazs Co. v. Double Rainbow Gourmet Ice Creams Inc. (DC NCalif, 691 F.Supp. 1262) 2099
Haeffele v. Hercules Inc. (DC Del) 2467
Haile v. New York State Higher Education Services Corp. (DC WNY, 90 B.R. 51) 2151
Halifax Hospital Medical Center; Bolt v. (CA 11) 2101
Hamblen v. Florida (Fla SupCt, 527 So.2d 800) 2026
Hamman v. Maricopa County (Ariz SupCt) 2448
Hammond, In re (CA 2) 2222
Hancock v. Egger (CA 6, 848 F.2d 87) 2011
Hand; U.S. v. (CA 3) 2395
Hanify v. Hanify (Mass SupJudCt, 526 N.E.2d 1056) 2163
Harbor House Restaurant; Ethridge v. (CA 9) 2337
Hardy v. Johns-Manville Sales Corp. (CA 5, 851 F.2d 742) 2148
Hardy; U.S. v. (CA 11, 861 F.2d 1281) 2279
Harman v. LyphoMed Inc. (DC NIll) 2304
Harmon; Cruzan v. (Mo SupCt) 2324
Harmon v. DOJ (DC DC, 690 F.Supp. 65) 2093
Harnischfeger Corp.; Sartori v. (Minn SupCt) 2376
Harris v. Harris (NC CtApp) 2359
Harris; Humboldt, County of v. (Calif CtApp) 2435
Harris; Luckey v. (CA 11) 2391
Harris v. Melnick (Md CtApp) 2483
Harris; National Commercial Banking Corp. of Australia Ltd. v. (Ill SupCt) 2377
Harris Hospital; Diggs v. (CA 5) 2042
Harris, In re (DC NJ) 2456
Harry Brandt Booking Office Inc.; Auwood v. (CA 2) 2041
Hartford; U.S. v. (CA 4) 2449
Hartford Accident and Indemnity Co.; Intel Corp. v. (DC NCalif) 2011, 2146
Hartford Insurance Co. of Illinois; FDIC v. (DC NIll) 2145
Hartigan (Illinois ex rel.) v. Panhandle Eastern Pipe Line Co. (CA 7) 2057
Hartman; Rawles v. (Ill AppCt) 2211
Harvey; Antolik v. (Hawaii IntermCtApp) 2211
Hase v. New York State Civil Service Dept. (NY SupCt) 2340
Havens; Aaron v. (Mo SupCt) 2273
Hawkins v. Texas (Texas CtCrimApp, 758 S.W.2d 255) 2262
Hazardous Waste Treatment Council v. EPA (CA DC, 861 F.2d 270) 2263
Health and Human Services Dept., see HHS
Health Care Equalization Committee of the Iowa Chiropractic Society v. Iowa Medical Society (CA 8, 851 F.2d 1020) 2041
Healy; Beer Institute v. (CA 2) 2010
Healy v. New York Life Insurance Co. (CA 3) 2358
Heffernan; Levine v. (CA 7) 2361
Heim; Roberts v. (DC NCalif) 2449
Helmsley; Beauford v. (CA 2) 2429
Heltzel; Indiana v. (Ind CtApp) 2483
Hempel Financial Corp.; Firstmark Capital Corp. v. (CA 9) 2262
Hendricks Music Co. v. Steinway Inc. (DC NIll, 689 F.Supp. 1501) 2066
Henry Holt and Co.; New Era Publications International ApS v. (DC SNY) 2178
Henslee v. Madison Guaranty Savings and Loan Assn. (Ark SupCt) 2434
Hercules Inc.; Haeffele v. (DC Del) 2467
Hermann Hospital v. MEBA Medical & Benefits Plan (CA 5, 845 F.2d 1286) 2068
Hermes v. Pfizer Inc. (CA 5, 848 F.2d 66) 2115
Herrell v. Herrell (Wis SupCt, 424 N.W.2d 403) 2043
Herron v. Jupiter Transportation Co. (CA 6, 858 F.2d 332) 2278
Hessel v. Hessel (Mich CtApp, 424 N.W.2d 59) 2027
HHS; Adamson v. (CA 10) 2144
HHS; Charlotte Memorial Hospital v. (CA 4) 2188
HHS; Condon v. (CA 2) 2078
HHS; Duggan v. (DC DC) 2087
HHS v. FLRA (CA 7, 858 F.2d 1278) 2260
HHS; Georgetown University Hospital v. (CA DC) 2312
HHS; Giardina v. (NJ SupCt) 2127
HHS; Gowen v. (CA 8) 2160
HHS; Greenhow v. (CA 9) 2363
HHS; New York v. (DC SNY) 2033
HHS; Paxton v. (CA 9) 2175
HHS; Rodriguez v. (CA 1) 2159
HHS; Rodriquez v. (CA 6) 2432
HHS; Smith v. (CA 2) 2465
HHS; Straw v. (CA 9) 2492
HHS; Varney v. (CA 9) 2276
HHS; Wayside Farm Inc. v. (CA 6) 2384
HHS; Wells v. (CA 2) 2126
HHS; West Allis Memorial Hospital Inc. v. (CA 7) 2076
HHS; Zebley v. (CA 3) 2110
Hibernia National Bank; Cullom v. (CA 5) 2328
Hicks v. Enlow (Ky SupCt) 2483
Higgins v. E. I. duPont de Nemours & Co. (CA 4) 2420
Higgins v. SEC (CA 2) 2452
Highland Hospital v. NLRB (CA 2) 2359
Hill v. Equitable Trust Co. (CA 3) 2116
Hill; U.S. v. (DC Kan) 2418
Hillel; Gladstone v. (Calif CtApp) 2146
Hilliker v. Hilliker (Alaska SupCt) 2279
Hilling; U.S. v. (CA 9) 2417
Hills; New York v. (NY AppDiv) 2195
Hillsboro, City of v. Purcell (Ore SupCt, 751 P.2d 510) 2199
Hilton-Davis; King v. (CA 3) 2248
Himmel, In re (Ill SupCt) 2246
Himmelfarb; Danner v. (CA 9) 2264
Hlinka v. Bethlehem Steel Corp. (CA 3) 2392
Hobart; Fraternal Order of Police Hobart Lodge 121 Inc. v. (CA 7) 2407
Hodel, Secretary of Interior Dept., see DOI
Hodgson v. Minnesota (CA 8, 853 F.2d 1452) 2105
Hoffman v. Connecticut (In re Willington Convalescent Home Inc.) (CA 2, 850 F.2d 50) 2001
Hoke Co. v. TVA (CA 6, 854 F.2d 820) 2147
Holder v. Polanski (NJ SupCt, 544 A.2d 852) 2163
Hollar v. Virgin Islands (CA 3, 857 F.2d 163) 2246
Hollingsworth; First National Bank and Trust Co. v. (DC WArk) 2484
Holly Farms Corp. Shareholders Litigation, In re (Del ChanCt) 2403
Holmquist; Dahlin v. (Mont SupCt) 2391
Holy Spirit Assn. for the Unification of World Christianity; Molko v. (Calif SupCt) 2276
Home Group Inc. v. IRS (TC) 2130
Honda Motor Co.; Gardner v. (NY AppDiv) 2451
Hopper v. Euclid Manor Nursing Home Inc. (CA 6) 2487
Horning; Arizona v. (Ariz CtApp) 2318
Horrigan; General Dynamics Corp. v. (CA 1) 2009
Houghton; Keystone Insurance Co. v. (CA 3) 2370
Housing and Urban Development Dept., see HUD
Howard Gault Co. v. Texas Rural Legal Aid Inc. (CA 5, 848 F.2d 544) 2035
Huber v. Niagara Machine and Tool Works (Minn SupCt, 430 N.W.2d 465) 2280
Hubert; Strength v. (CA 11) 2178
HUD; Electrical Workers, Local 5 v. (CA 3) 2116
HUD; Kansas City, Mo. v. (CA DC) 2325
HUD; Orrego v. (DC NIll) 2366
Hudgins; Mitchum v. (Ala SupCt) 2374
Hudson; Jordan v. (DC EVa) 2114

Refer to the back page of recent *Law Week* Section 1's to locate items not yet covered in the index. The front page of each index will indicate the dates and issue numbers that the index covers.

bly delegate to hospitals the authority to determine who may perform abortions. (Page 2570)

Justices Hear Work For Hire Dispute Involving Statue For Homeless Group

A dispute over exactly who owns the copyright on a statue depicting a homeless family came before the U.S. Supreme Court on March 29, with the legal stake being what interpretation the justices will put on the work for hire doctrine. The statue in question was produced by an artist, who now claims the copyright, at the request of a homeless advocacy group. (*Community for Creative Non-Violence v. Reid*, argued 3/29/89)

The meaning of the work for hire doctrine has split federal courts in the last few years, mainly as a result of the 1976 Copyright Act's definition of the term "work made for hire." The definition, contained in Section 101 of the act, says that a work made for hire is one "prepared by an employee within the scope of his or her employment" or a "work specially ordered or commissioned" that fits one of nine categories spelled out in the act, "if the parties expressly agree in a written instrument . . . that the work shall be considered a work made for hire."

Counsel for the homeless advocacy group that asserts ownership of the copyright maintained that the dispute should be settled by looking to principles of the law of agency. But Justice O'Connor remarked that the principles established by this case may have far reaching consequences beyond the controversy facing these parties, affecting the rights to both software and written works.

The artist's lawyer told the court that, by any standard, the artist was an independent contractor. Justice White asked why, if the Copyright Act allows parties to contract work for hire arrangements, any further clarification of the issue is needed. The lawyer responded that oral contracts are common and that clarification is needed so that commissioning parties in such situations do not "come in through the backdoor" when the work is completed and "hijack" the artist's copyright. The Copyright Office appeared as an amicus curiae on behalf of the artist. (Page 3664)

TOPICAL SUMMARY

The following sections appear in this issue: Section 1, Summary and Analysis; Section 2, New Court Decisions and Agency Rulings; Section 3, Supreme Court Proceedings; and Supreme Court Topical Index.

Court Decisions

ANTITRUST, Standing—Consolidated Gold Fields PLC v. Minorco S.A., CA 2 2565
BANKING AND FINANCE, Credit Reports—MSA Tubular Products Inc. v. First Bank and Trust Co., CA 10 2565
COURTS AND PROCEDURE, Settlement—G. Heileman Brewing Co. v. Joseph Oat Corp., CA 7 2566
CRIMINAL LAW AND PROCEDURE, Search and Seizure—U.S. v. Hoyos, CA 9 2567
EMPLOYMENT DISCRIMINATION, Age Discrimination—Equal Employment Opportunity Commission v. Cherokee Nation, CA 10 ... 2568
ENVIRONMENT AND CONSERVATION, Air—Environmental Defense Fund v. Thomas, CA 2 2568
ENVIRONMENT AND CONSERVATION, Environmental Impact—Stop H-3 Association v. Dole, CA 9 2569
HEALTH CARE, Abortions—Women's Health Care of West County Inc. v. Webster, CA 8 2570
LABOR, Pre-emption—Washington v. Union Carbide Corp., CA 4 2571
MASS MEDIA, Licenses—Shurberg Broadcasting of Hartford Inc. v. Federal Communications Commission, CA DC 2571
MINES AND MINERALS, Mine Safety and Health—Western Fuels-Utah Inc. v. Federal Mine Safety & Health Review Commission, CA DC 2573
PENSIONS AND BENEFITS, Withdrawal Liability—Joyce v. Clyde Sandoz Masonry, CA DC 2573
PRODUCT SAFETY AND LIABILITY, Pre-emption—Callan v. G.D. Searle & Co., DC Md 2574
SOCIAL SECURITY, Child Welfare—Stroop v. Bowen, CA 4 2575
TAXATION, Corporate Income Tax—National Can Corp. v. Commissioner of Revenue, Minn SupCt 2575
UNITED STATES, Federal Tort Claims Act—Dube v. Pittsburgh Corning, CA 1 2576

Agency Rulings

MASS MEDIA, Licenses—Final Rule, Federal Communications Commission 2577
News In Brief 2577

The United States Law Week (ISSN 0148-8139) is published weekly on Tuesday except first Tuesday in September and last Tuesday in December for $544.00 per year and $516.00 per year thereafter, by The Bureau of National Affairs, Inc., 1231 25th Street, N.W., Washington, D.C. 20037. Second-Class postage paid at Washington, D.C. and additional mailing offices. POSTMASTER: Send address changes to The United States Law Week, The Bureau of National Affairs, Inc., P.O. Box 40949, Washington, D.C. 20016-0949.

57 LW 1156 0148-8139/89/$0+.50 **April 11, 1989**

The United States
LAW WEEK
April 11, 1989 Volume 57, No. 39
SUPREME COURT INDEX—1988-1989 TERM
TOPICAL INDEX—SUMMARY
Volume 57, Nos. 1-37
July 5, 1988 - March 28, 1989
FILE with Vol. 57, Supreme Court Sections binder, behind Index tab. DISCARD prior Topical Index for Vol. 57.
EXPLANATORY NOTE
SUPPLEMENTAL ITEMS
(References are to Law Week pages)
A
ABORTION
ACCOUNTANTS
ADMINISTRATIVE LAW
Copyright © 1989 by The Bureau of National Affairs, Inc., Washington, D.C.

Cases in the Supreme Court are covered in a separate index. First, use the Topical Index and note the Supreme Court docket numbers for the cases that interest you.

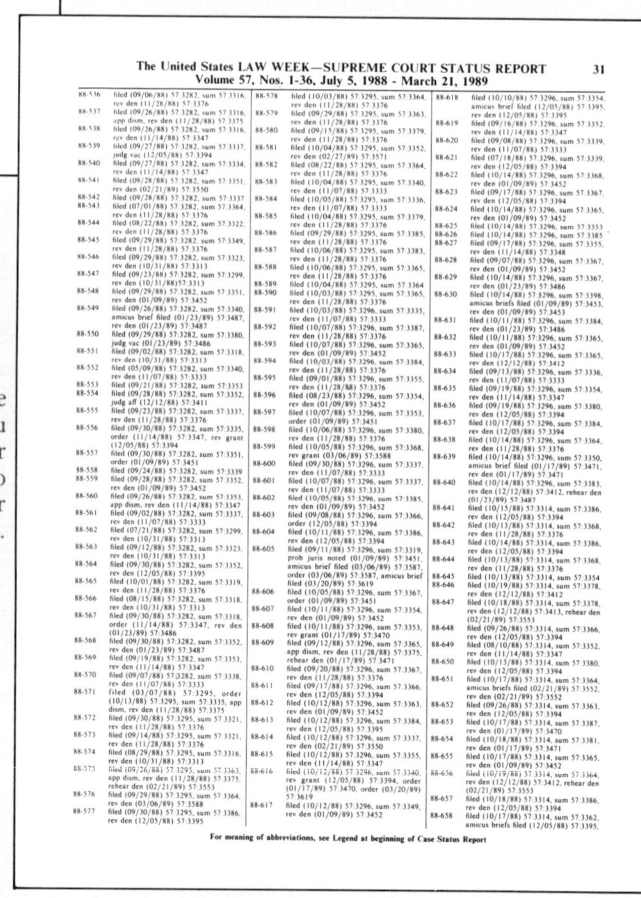
The United States LAW WEEK—SUPREME COURT STATUS REPORT 31
Volume 57, Nos. 1-36, July 5, 1988 - March 21, 1989
For meaning of abbreviations, see Legend at beginning of Case Status Report

Then, find the numbers in the Case Status Report, which will tell you whether the court has granted or denied review and refer you to pages in *Law Week's* Section 3 for more complete information.

under either "Hodgson" or "Minnesota." Most Tables of Cases in BNA services list cases under both parties' names.

This index, which contains both the Topical Index and the Table of Cases, is reissued periodically throughout the year, culminating in a final index at the close of the annual volume. Unavoidably, at various points throughout the year, the interim indexes will not cover every issue of the service that has been released. In order to find cases reported since the latest index was issued, the best place to look is the Topical Summary that appears on the back page of each week's Section 1. (Many other BNA services put their Topical Summary on the second page of each issue.)

First note the dates or issue numbers covered by the index you've been using; then look behind the tab Summary and Analysis to find the Section 1's for the issues not covered by the index. In this example, you find that an abortion case has indeed been reported since the index was released and that it appears on page 2570.

You can also take your research back in time, by referring to previous volumes of *Law Week*. These, too, are stored in binders and cover annual periods. Each annual volume has its own index, which refers only to material contained in that volume. Many BNA notification services are maintained over the years and indexed in the same manner.

Now, it's time to find out what the Supreme Court is up to. For this, you switch binders and go to the one marked Supreme Court. In this binder, you will find *Law Week's* Section 3, which records virtually every case brought to the Supreme Court and faithfully follows their progress through the court, and Section 4, which contains full text, with headnotes, of every Supreme Court opinion handed down after oral argument.

Behind the index tab in this binder, you will find two separate indexes. You use the first one, the Topical Index, first and find several entries under "Abortion" for "Notice to parents of minor." You also notice several entries for "Roe v. Wade," which indicate that the underpinnings of the Supreme Court's landmark abortion case are being challenged. At the end of each one of these entries is a number; this is the docket number given the case by the Supreme Court.

To find out more about the cases you're interested in, you turn to the second index behind the tab, the one designated Table of Cases and Case Status Report. In the Case Status Report, you look up the docket numbers of the cases and find that, although the Supreme Court has refused to review most of them, it has accepted jurisdiction over No. 88-605. You note that a summary of the case—describing the decision in the court below and the questions presented to the Supreme Court for review—appears in Volume 57 on page 3319.

As the case proceeds through the court, *Law Week* will report on the oral argument with particular attention to the give-and-take between the justices and the lawyers in the case, and, of course, will report the court's opinion in full text.

In Section 3, you can read summaries of the cases you're interested in.

11-1-88 *The United States* **LAW WEEK** 57 LW 3319

Questions presented: (1) May EEOC, in investigation conducted under Title VII of 1964 Civil Rights Act, compel disclosure of confidential academic peer review tenure materials that are protected by First Amendment without affording any consideration to First Amendment interests at stake? (2) Is "first-filed" rule of federal comity, which counsels stay or dismissal of action that is duplicative of previously-filed action in another federal court, violated when court retains jurisdiction over second-filed action on ground that it disapproves of first plaintiff's choice of forum, even though that choice has been upheld by first court?

Petition for certiorari filed 9/19/88, by Steven B. Feirson, Alan D. Berkowitz, Nancy J. Bregstein, Dechert Price & Rhoads, Shelley Z. Green and Neil J. Hamburg, all of Philadelphia, Pa.

88-520 ROBINSON v. ADAMS

Race—Title VII—42 USC 1981—Disparate treatment.

Ruling below (CA 9, 847 F2d 1315):

Under Title VII of 1964 Civil Rights Act or 42 USC 1981, plaintiff cannot establish prima facie case of intentional race discrimination without showing by direct or indirect evidence that decision-maker knew plaintiff's race; job applications stated that demographic information block would not be used in hiring process, and plaintiff presented no evidence to rebut application screeners' affidavits declaring they were unaware of his race, and thus there was no genuine issue whether screeners were aware of plaintiff's race; showing that black males are statistically underrepresented in county's work force cannot, standing alone, show racially discriminatory impact on blacks as whole; plaintiff failed to identify specific employment practices or selection criteria or to show causal relationship between identified practices and impact, and thus failed to establish prima facie case of disparate impact of employer's practices on black males.

Questions presented: (1) In Title VII disparate impact case challenging discrimination against black men, is employer with no black male employees entitled to summary judgment based on fact that it has some black female employees? (2) In order to withstand motion for summary judgment, is plaintiff in Title VII disparate impact case required (a) to establish adverse impact, (b) to identify specific employment practices or selection criteria, and (c) to show causal relationship between identified practices and adverse impact? (3) Is summary judgment appropriate in disparate treatment case under Title VII and 42 USC 1981 where record contains conflicting evidence as to employer's knowledge of plaintiff's race?

Petition for certiorari filed 9/23/88, by Patrick O. Patterson Jr., and Bill Lann Lee, both of Los Angeles, Calif., and Julius L. Chambers, Charles Stephen Ralston, Ronald L. Ellis, and Judith Reed, all of New York, N.Y.

Environment and Conservation

88-428 VERITY v. CENTER FOR ENVIRONMENTAL EDUCATION

Marine Mammal Protection Act—Permits—Commercial fishing.

Ruling below (*Kokechik Fishermen's Association v. Secretary of Commerce*, CA DC, 839 F2d 795):

Provision of 1972 Marine Mammal Protection Act that authorizes secretary of commerce to issue permit allowing commercial fishing operations to avoid act's ban on taking of marine mammals and to take some marine mammals incidental to fishing operations does not permit secretary to issue permit for incidental taking of non-depleted species of marine mammal when fishing activity authorized by permit will allow incidental taking of another protected marine mammal species.

Question presented: Does 1972 Marine Mammal Protection Act, which authorizes secretary of commerce to issue permits in specified circumstances for taking of marine mammals incidental to commercial fishing, prohibit secretary from issuing permit for incidental taking of non-depleted species of marine mammal when same fishing activity will result in incidental taking of another species for which permit cannot lawfully be issued under act?

Petition for certiorari filed 9/8/88, by Charles Fried, Sol. Gen., Roger J. Marzulla, Asst. Atty. Gen., Lawrence G. Wallace, Dpty. Sol. Gen., Richard J. Lazarus, Asst. to the Sol. Gen., and Anne S. Almy, Dept. of Justice atty.

Health Care

88-565 COWHERD v. DOE

Mental health commitments—Consent—Guardians—Judicial review.

Ruling below (*Doe v. Austin*, CA 6, 848 F2d 1386, 57 LW 2005):

Prior judicial hearing is not required by Due Process Clause for involuntary commitment of mentally retarded adults, but Kentucky cannot, consistent with Equal Protection Clause, deny mentally retarded persons either pre-commitment judicial hearing or subsequent periodic judicial review that it provides for mentally ill persons.

Questions presented: (1) Do admissions procedures of state residential treatment center for mentally retarded that permit guardian to provide substituted consent of his adult ward for admission to facility on voluntary basis violate Due Process or Equal Protection Clauses? (2) Does Due Process Clause require periodic judicial review of continued placement of adult mentally retarded persons in state residential treatment center when such persons were voluntarily admitted to facility upon application of their guardians?

Petition for certiorari filed 10/1/88, by Ryan M. Halloran, Stanley A. Stratford, and William K. Moore, all of Frankfort, Ky.

88-605 WEBSTER v. REPRODUCTIVE HEALTH SERVICES

Abortions—Preamble to statute—Standing—Viability—Medical testing—Counseling—State employees—State assistance for abortions—Trimesters.

Ruling below (CA 8, 851 F2d 1071):

Provision of Missouri abortion statute that requires doctors to determine whether fetus is viable before performing abortion on any woman whom doctor has reason to believe is 20 or more weeks pregnant, and that requires doctor to perform certain tests to determine viability, is unconstitutional; class of plaintiffs consisting of health care professionals, facilities offering abortion counseling and services, and pregnant women seeking abortion services or pregnancy counseling has standing to challenge constitutionality of provisions of Missouri's abortion statute that provide that life of each human being begins at conception and that unborn children have protectable interests in life, health, and well being; provisions declaring that human life begins at conception and that unborn children have protectable interests in life, health, and well-being are not "abortion-neutral" and thus are unconstitutional; Missouri abortion statute's prohibition on use of public funds, facilities, or employees to "encourage or counsel" woman to have abortion is void for vagueness and violative of right to privacy; statute's provision prohibiting use of public employees, facilities, and funds to "perform or assist" abortions is unconstitutional.

Questions presented: (1) Do physicians or other medical personnel have standing to contest constitutionality of state legislative preamble in abortion statute? (2) Are legislative findings in preamble to state abortion bill that "the life of each human being begins at conception" and that "unborn children have protectable interests in life, health, and well being" facially unconstitutional? (3) Where statute requiring determination of fetal viability when physician "has reason to believe" that fetus is "of 20 or more weeks gestational age" has been held to be constitutional, is it facially unconstitutional to require that, in making this determination, physician shall cause to be performed such "medical examination and tests as are necessary to make finding of gestational age, weight, and lung maturity of unborn child . . ."? (4) Is state statute facially unconstitutional that makes it "unlawful for any public funds to be expended . . . for the purpose of encouraging or counseling a woman to have an abortion not necessary to save her life."? (5) Is state statute facially unconstitutional that makes it "unlawful for any public employee within scope of his employment to perform or assist an abortion, not necessary to save the life of the mother"? (6) Is state statute facially unconstitutional that makes it "unlawful for any public facility to be used for the purpose of performing or assisting an abortion not necessary to save the life of the mother"? (7) Should *Roe v. Wade*, 410 U.S. 113 (1973), trimester approach for selecting test by which state regulation of abortion services is reviewed be reconsidered and discarded in favor of rational basis test?

Appeal filed 9/11/88, by William L. Webster, Mo. Atty. Gen., and Michael L. Boicourt and Jerry L. Short, Asst. Attys. Gen.

Indians

88-459 ANDERSON v. U.S.

Federal income tax—Rent from tribal lands—Distribution to members of tribe.

Ruling below (CA 9, 56 LW 2647):

Indian tribe's distribution of accumulated rents from unallotted tribal trust lands, which are not exempt from taxation by either statute or treaty, are taxable income to tribal members who receive payments.

Questions presented: (1) Is Indian tribe subject to income tax on income it derives from rental of tribal trust land? (2) Does tax-exempt character of income derived from tribal trust lands change upon its distribution to tribal members who are beneficiaries of trust?

Petition for certiorari filed 9/12/88, by Peter J. Sferrazza, of Reno, Nev.

88-492 SHOSHONE TRIBE v. WYOMING

Reservation lands—Water rights—Treaties.

Ruling below (Wyoming v. Owl Creek Irrigation District Members (In re: The General Adjudication of All Rights to Use Water in the Big Horn River System), Wyo SupCt, 753 P2d 76):

Congress intended through 1868 treaty establishing Wind River Indian Reservation to reserve water for use of Indians, and nothing in Act of March 3, 1905, 33 Stat. 1016, expressly abrogated that intent; measure of tribes' reserved water right is water necessary to irrigate acreage on reservation that may practicably be irrigated, but does not include groundwater, which is owned by state; tribes did not seek permission to export reserved water, and United States concedes that no federal law permits sale of reserved water to

0148-8139/88/$0+.50

And you can follow their progress through the Supreme Court: the decision to grant or deny review, the scheduling of oral argument, and often the argument itself. The full text of all opinions issued by the court are reported either in this section or in Section 4.

The United States **LAW WEEK** — **Supreme Court Proceedings**

January 10, 1989 • THE BUREAU OF NATIONAL AFFAIRS, INC., WASHINGTON, D.C. • Volume 57, No. 26

SUMMARY OF ORDERS

At its Jan. 9, 1989, session, the Supreme Court granted review in nine cases on the Appellate Docket and summarily disposed of six others. By other orders, the Court denied review in 107 Appellate Docket cases. Review was also granted in two cases and denied in 125 others in the 5000 series, which is sometimes called the in forma pauperis docket. The 5000-series cases in which the Court granted review were *Gomez v. U.S.*, No. 88-5014, and *Chavez-Testina v. U.S.*, No. 88-5158. These cases were consolidated. A summary of these two cases will appear in an upcoming issue of Law Week. The Court acted summarily in four 5000-series cases.

Grant of review, as used in the following summary of orders, is evidenced in appeal cases by the Court's action noting probable jurisdiction or postponing the question of jurisdiction to the hearing on the merits; in certiorari cases, by the granting of certiorari. In all cases where review is granted, oral argument will ordinarily follow.

Disposal by summary action is evidenced in appeal cases by a per curiam order affirming, reversing, or vacating the judgment below or dismissing the appeal; in certiorari cases, by a per curiam order granting the petition for certiorari and simultaneously affirming, reversing, or vacating the judgment below.

Denial of review relates principally to certiorari cases and is normally evidenced by denial of certiorari.

The summary below lists the cases on the Appellate Docket in which the Court granted review, took summary action, or denied review. For each case, there is given (1) its number and title; (2) a citation to the lower court's opinion or order; (3) the ruling of the court below; and (4) the principal questions presented if the case has been granted review.

Other orders appear only in the journal of proceedings elsewhere in this issue of Law Week.

Review Granted

BANKRUPTCY

88-412 HOFFMAN v. CONNECTICUT DEPARTMENT OF INCOME MAINTENANCE

Ruling below (*Hoffman v. Connecticut (In re Willington Convalescent Home)*, CA 2, 57 LW 2001):

Bankruptcy trustee's suit, commenced in federal court, to recover damages against state is barred by Eleventh Amendment; Congress, by enacting 11 USC 106(c), which "binds" governmental units by bankruptcy court "determination[s]" did not make its intention unmistakably clear that states are subject to adversarial proceedings in bankruptcy that involve payment of funds to bankrupt estate.

Questions presented: (1) Does 11 USC 106(c) authorize bankruptcy trustee to recover money judgment against state which has not voluntarily waived sovereign immunity? (2) Did Congress, in enacting 11 USC 106(c) and 28 USC 157(a) and 1334(b), abrogate state's Eleventh Amendment immunity to suit in federal court by trustee in bankruptcy?

COURTS AND PROCEDURE

88-774 NEWMAN-GREEN INC v. ALFONZO-LARRAIN

Ruling below (CA 7 (en banc), 854 F2d 916, 57 LW 2162):

Court of appeals, upon discovery that district court lacked jurisdiction over diversity action based solely on state law, is without authority to dismiss non-diverse party in order to correct jurisdictional defect.

Questions presented: (1) Do courts of appeals have power to cure defect in subject-matter jurisdiction, first noticed on appeal, by permitting plaintiff to dismiss non-essential non-diverse defendant? (2) Is such curative action at appellate level authorized by either 28 USC 1653 or by Fed.R.Civ.P. 21 or by combination of both? (3) If not, is power to permit such curative action implied or inherent in appellate jurisdiction conferred by 28 USC 1291 and 1292?

CRIMINAL LAW AND PROCEDURE

88-333 ALABAMA v. SMITH

Ruling below (Ala SupCt, 6/24/88):

Life sentence imposed at end of trial by same judge who had previously sentenced defendant to 30 years under plea bargain, conviction on which was successfully appealed on basis of judge's failure to inform defendant of potential sentences prior to entry of plea, was clearly result of judge's subjective observations of defendant during trial rather than of any objective evidence of events subsequent to defendant's first conviction; accordingly, judge violated due process rule of *North Carolina v. Pearce*, 395 U.S. 711 (1969), that sentence may be enhanced on remand only if warranted by events occurring subsequent to the original sentence; defendant's sentence is therefore reversed.

Questions presented: (1) Does *North Carolina v. Pearce* apply where defendant's guilty plea is withdrawn and, after trial, he receives greater sentence than he would have received under withdrawn plea bargain? (2) Does decision below misapply federal constitutional law by presuming judicial vindictiveness merely because defendant received greater sentence after trial than he would have had he pleaded guilty?

88-420 JONES v. THOMAS

Ruling below (*Thomas v. Morris*, CA 8, 844 F2d 1337):

Governor's commutation of habeas corpus petitioner's 15-year sentence for attempted armed robbery means that petitioner has fully satisfied that sentence; consequently, Double Jeopardy Clause prevented state court, which held that state legislature did not intend to authorize separate punishments for felony murder and underlying felony, from leaving petitioner's life sentence for felony murder standing when, after governor's commutation, it vacated attempted robbery conviction; instead, petitioner is entitled to be released.

Question presented: May federal appeals court overturn remedy granted by state court for double jeopardy violation as being contrary to its understanding of state law?

HEALTH CARE

88-605 WEBSTER v. REPRODUCTIVE HEALTH SERVICES

Ruling below (CA 8, 851 F2d 1071):

Provision of Missouri abortion statute that requires doctors to determine whether fetus is viable before performing abortion on any woman whom doctor has reason to believe is 20 or more weeks pregnant, and that requires doctor to perform certain tests to determine viability, is unconstitutional; class of plaintiffs consisting of health care professionals, facilities offering abortion counseling and services, and pregnant women seeking abortion services or pregnancy counseling has standing to challenge constitutionality of provisions of Missouri's abortion statute that provide that life of each human being begins at conception and that unborn children have protectable interests in life, health, and well being; provisions declaring that human life begins at conception and that unborn children have protectable interests in life, health, and well-being are not "abortion-neutral" and thus are unconstitutional; Missouri abortion statute's prohibition on use of public funds, facilities, or employees to "encourage or counsel" woman to have abortion is void for vagueness and violative of right to privacy; statute's provision prohibiting use of public employees, facilities, and funds to "perform or assist" abortions is unconstitutional.

Questions presented: (1) Do physicians or other medical personnel have standing to contest constitutionality of state legislative preamble in

Inside Section 3

	Page
Journal of Proceedings	3450
In-Chambers Opinion	3454
Cases Docketed	3454
Hearings Scheduled	3463

Section 3 — *Contents Copyright © 1989 by The Bureau of National Affairs, Inc.* 0148-8139/89/$0+.50 — 57 LW 3441

BNA Customer Relations
by phone: 1-800-372-1033
by fax: 1-800-253-0332

BNA Customer Relations representatives handle inquiries concerning all BNA subscription services, BNA Software products, and BNA Books.

The Customer Relations telephone lines are answered from 8:30 a.m. to 8:00 p.m. Eastern Time; fax inquiries may be made at any time.

For written queries, contact BNA Customer Relations at 9435 Key West Avenue, Rockville MD 20850.

STUDENT PRICES ON BNA SUBSCRIPTION SERVICES

All BNA subscription services are available to students who are enrolled in bona fide educational institutions, or to groups of individuals taking special courses on subjects that utilize student materials for the duration of the course.

The prices quoted apply to delivery of weekly and biweekly issues in bulk to one address with billing to one address, often the school's law library. A minimum of five copies per publication title is needed to qualify for a bulk order.

Notification Services

Students may subscribe to notification services or the notification portion of reference services for $25.00 per academic year or $30.00 for the full calendar year. For student subscriptions, BNA defines the academic year as September 1 through June 30 of the following year; a full student year is September 1 through August 31 of the following year.

The notification services discussed in this book—and others published by BNA—are available under this special student bulk rate. BNA notification services include the following, which are listed in alphabetical order:

- ABA/BNA Lawyers' Manual on Professional Conduct (Current Reports only)
- Antitrust & Trade Regulation Report
- BNA Civil Trial Manual (Civil Litigation Reporter only)
- BNA Criminal Practice Manual (Current Reports only)
- BNA Pension Reporter (Current Reports only)
- BNA's Americans with Disabilities Act Manual (newsletter only)
- BNA's Banking Report
- BNA's Bankruptcy Law Reporter
- BNA's Health Law Reporter
- BNA's Patent, Trademark and Copyright Journal
- Corporate Practice Series (BNA's Corporate Counsel Weekly only)
- Criminal Law Reporter
- Environment Reporter (Current Developments only)
- Family Law Reporter (Current Reports only)
- Federal Contracts Report
- International Trade Reporter (Current Reports only)
- Labor Relations Reporter (weekly notification only)
- Occupational Safety & Health Reporter (Current Reports only)
- Product Safety & Liability Reporter (Current Reports only)
- Securities Regulation & Law Report
- Toxics Law Reporter
- United States Law Week

Portfolios

Portfolios will not be supplemented and must be billed and mailed to the university address. Orders are accepted based on current inventory.

Corporate Practice Series Portfolios: $15 each.
Tax Management Portfolios: $15 each.

Other BNA Subscription Products

Students may purchase BNA special topical reports and special supplements published in conjunction with a BNA service, such as text of new legislation, for $3.00 per copy.

For additional information on student pricing and the most recent list of BNA subscription services, please contact BNA Customer Relations toll-free by telephone 1-800-372-1033 or by fax 1-800-253-0332.

For additional information on BNA programs for the academic community, contact BNA's Office of Academic Relations, 1231 25th Street N.W., Washington DC 20037; telephone 202-452-4169.